About the Author

Ann-Christin Sjölander Holland is a prizewinning Swedish journalist, now working for *Kommunalarbetaren*, the biggest trade union magazine in Sweden. During the last fifteen years, she has specialised in writing articles about how privatisation affects employees and the different ways in which commercial companies now operate within the public sector. In researching this book, she interviewed key individuals from multinational corporations and from research and grassroots organisations around the world, travelling extensively in Latin America and Europe.

The Water Business

Corporations versus People

_____

Ann-Christin Sjölander Holland

University Press
Dhaka

White Lotus
Bangkok

Fernwood Publishing
Nova Scotia

Books for Change
Bangalore

World Book Publishing
Beirut

SIRD
Kuala Lumpur

David Philip
Cape Town

ZED BOOKS
London & New York

To Mattias

The Water Business was first published in 2005 by

In Bangladesh: The University Press Ltd,
Red Crescent Building, 114 Motijheel C/A, PO Box 2611, Dhaka 1000

In Burma, Cambodia, Laos, Thailand and Vietnam:
White Lotus Co. Ltd, GPO Box 1141, Bangkok 10501, Thailand

In Canada: Fernwood Publishing Ltd,
8422 St Margaret's Bay Road (Hwy 3) Site 2A, Box 5,
Black Point, Nova Scotia, BOJ 1BO

In India: Books for Change,
139 Richmond Road, Bangalore 560 025

**In Lebanon, Bahrain, Egypt, Jordan, Kuwait, Qatar, Saudi Arabia
and United Arab Emirates:** World Book Publishing, 282 Emile Eddeh Street,
Ben Salem bldg, PO Box 3176, Beirut, Lebanon www.wbpbooks.com

In Malaysia: Strategic Information Research Development (SIRD),
No. 11/4E, Petaling Jaya, 46200 Selangor

In Southern Africa: David Philip (an imprint of New Africa Books),
99 Garfield Road, Claremont 7700, South Africa

In the rest of the world: Zed Books Ltd, 7 Cynthia Street, London N1 9JF, UK,
and Room 400, 175 Fifth Avenue, New York, NY 10010, USA

www.zedbooks.co.uk

Copyright © Ann-Christin Sjölander Holland 2005

The right of Ann-Christin Sjölander Holland to be identified as the author
of this work has been asserted by her in accordance with the Copyright, Designs
and Patents Act, 1988

Designed and typeset in Monotype Bembo by Illuminati, Grosmont
Cover designed by Andrew Corbett
Printed and bound in the EU by Cox & Wyman, Reading

Distributed in the USA exclusively by Palgrave Macmillan, a division of
St Martin's Press, LLC, 175 Fifth Avenue, New York, NY 10010

A catalogue record for this book is available from the British Library
Library of Congress Cataloging-in-Publication Data available
Canadian CIP data is available from the National Library of Canada

ISBN 1 55266 166 0 Pb (Canada)
ISBN 81 8291 010 2 Pb (India)
ISBN 9 95314071 5 Pb (Lebanon)

ISBN 1 84277 564 2 Hb (Zed Books)
ISBN 1 84277 565 0 Pb (Zed Books)

Contents

Acknowledgements

The book draws on a great deal of material from the Public Services International Research Unit (PSIRU), University of Greenwich, London. Sincere thanks in particular to David Hall and Emanuele Lobina of PSIRU, and to David Boys of Public Services International (PSI). Thank you to Fredrik Runsiö and Inga-Lena Wallin of the Swedish Municipal Workers' Union; the LO–TCO Secretariat of the International Trade Union Development Cooperation; editor Ursula Berge of the publisher Agora; Madi Gray, for translation work; and to Robin Gable, for painstaking editorial revision.

Abbreviations

ADB	Asian Development Bank
AfDB	African Development Bank
ALCA	Área de Libre Comercio de las Américas (FTAA)
AMI	Subsidiary of Générale des Eaux
APSF	Aguas Provinciales de Santa Fe (Argentina)
CBO	Community-based organisation
CSD	UN Commission on Sustainable Development
CUPE	Canadian Union of Public Employees
DBSA	Development Bank of South Africa
DFID	Department for International Development (UK)
EBRD	European Bank for Reconstruction and Development
ECOSOC	UN Committee for Economic, Cultural and Social Rights
EIB	European Investment Bank
ETOSS	Ente Tripartite de Obras de Servicos de Saneamiento (regulatory agency in Argentina)
EEIF	Emerging Europe Infrastructure Fund
EU	European Union
EUWI	EU Water Initiative
FCC	Spanish-based water and waste management subsidiary of Veolia Environnement

FFOSE	Federacion de Funcionarios de las Obras Sanitarias del Estado (Uruguay)
GATS	General Agreement on Trade in Services (part of the WTO)
GAWU	General Agricultural Workers Union in Ghana
GNUC	Greater Nelspruit Utility Company
GWP	Global Water Partnership
IADB	Inter-American Development Bank
IBRD	International Bank for Reconstruction and Devolopment (part of the World Bank)
ICFTU	International Confederation of Free Trade Unions
ICSID	International Centre for Settlement of Investment Disputes (arbitration, part of the World Bank)
IDA	International Development Association (part of the World Bank)
IDB	Inter-American Development Bank
IFC	International Finance Corporation (part of the World Bank)
ILO	International Labour Organisation
IMATU	Independent Municipal and Allied Trade Union (South Africa)
IMF	International Monetary Fund
ISODEC	Integrated Social Development Centre (Ghana)
ISPA	Instrument for Structural Policies for Pre-Accession
IUF	International Union of Food, Agriculture, Hotel, Restaurant, Catering, Tobacco and Allied Workers' Association
IWA	International Water Association
MDGs	Millennium Development Goals
MIGA	Multilateral Investment Guarantee Agency (part of the World Bank)
NAFTA	North American Free Trade Agreement
NCAP	National Coalition Against Privatisation (Ghana)
NGO	Non-governmental organisation
OECD	Organisation for Economic Co-operation and Development

Ofwat	Office for Water Service (England)
OSN	Obras Sanitarias de la Nación (former state-owned water utility in Argentina)
PMU	Programme Management Unit (regulatory agency, Jordan)
PPIAF	Public–Private Infrastructure Advisory Facility
PPP	Public–private partnership
PSI	Public Services International (global trade union confederation)
PSIRU	Public Services International Research Unit
PSP	Private Sector Participation
PuP	Public Public Partnership
PUPN	Public Utilities Protection Network (Thailand)
RPR	Rassemblement pour la République (French political party led by President Jacques Chirac)
RWE	German-owned utilities multinational
SAMWU	South African Municipal Workers Union
SEEG	Société de Exploitation des Eaux de Guinée (private water company in Guinea)
Sida	Swedish International Development Cooperation Agency
SONEG	Société Nationale des Eaux de Guinée (regulatory agency in Guinea)
SWD	Swedish Water Development
UN	United Nations
UNCTAD	United Nations Conference on Trade and Development
UNDP	United Nations Development Programme
UNESCO	United Nations Educational, Scientific and Cultural Organization
USAID	United States Agency for International Development
WCW	World Commission on Water for the 21st Century
WWC	World Water Council
WHO	World Health Organisation
WTO	World Trade Organisation

PART I

Water as a global commodity

I

Mountain water:
a commodity for Saudi businessmen

Dikanäs is situated in the northernmost part of Europe, in a remote Swedish wilderness, a sparsely populated area with high peaks and pine forests, frosty nights, extreme cold, and frozen lakes in winter. I grew up there, by the Vojmån river.

In winter, my father drilled holes in the ice to reach the still water. We scooped up water from the round dark hole and drank. I would lay a reindeer hide on the ice, lie down on it, press my head to the edge of the hole and at the same time slide down a fishing line. After a while I could see how curious trout swam around the hook, the water was so clear. The excitement was unbearable, not least when a fish snapped at the hook. I would tug on the line and, suddenly, a trout lay flapping on the ice.

As spring approached, water trickled playfully from small brooks up in the mountains, tumbling down to the Vojmån, which occasionally overflowed its banks. In summer, the water danced along so swiftly that watching the torrents made me dizzy. Timber logs swirled wildly among the stones and sometimes got stuck.

Water – the river – was omnipresent in our lives. In the woods we found a cold spring with wonderfully fresh and pure-tasting water. It crossed no one's mind that, in other parts of the world, there were people who did not have access to clean water. This was in the late 1950s and the world extended no further than the trips we made to the dentist in Vilhelmina, a community 110 kilometres away. Goods trains chugged through, and I never missed an opportunity to watch the railcar passing by, carrying people southwards.

Times change. The large salmon in the Vojmån, which might once have weighed over ten kilos, have disappeared. The Vojmån flows into a river on which a dam was built. This meant that salmon from the Baltic Sea could no longer make their way so far upstream. At the time, I had no idea that this was not unique, or that there was a similar impact on salmon in the Columbia river in the USA, for instance. Today there is not anyone in the world who remains unaffected by global developments, not even in Dikanäs. In my childhood, no one could possibly have imagined that some enterprising individuals might begin to sell water from the ski resort of Kittelfjäll, 24 kilometres from Dikanäs – but it happened.

It was not a success. Several tried, but gave up. The last to try in Kittelfjäll was a firm partly owned by Saudis. There were even Arab sheiks present, when the project was officially opened. The firm pumped water from Kittelfjäll and sent it all over the world. The mineral olivine makes the water in Kittelfjäll very clean, with a clear, good taste. There is a story going round that when the suppliers failed to deliver the water, the distributors simply used tap water. True or not, such behaviour would not be surprising. It has happened in other countries.

An American environmental organisation, Natural Resources Defense Council, estimates that a quarter of the bottled water in the USA is common tap water, which has sometimes been treated with a few minerals, sometimes not.

The small firm in Kittelfjäll went bankrupt. This was nevertheless a drop in the ocean, compared to large multinationals like Nestlé Waters, which now owns the mineral waters Perrier, San Pellegrino and Vittel. Nestlé Waters has established itself in 130 countries with 70 brands across the world, from Pakistan to Lebanon and Argentina. Drinking habits have changed in some countries. In France, Germany and Poland bottled water is now the first choice among soft drinks. Bottled water has rapidly become a major global industry.

To my surprise it appears that the distribution of ordinary drinking water has also become a major industry. Water, common tap water – a basic human right for survival – has become a commodity, delivered by private global companies.

The time came when it was no longer enough to look longingly at the railcar at the station in Vilhelmina. I climbed in and thereby began my life's journey out into the world.

For me, water was still cheap and it was natural to have access to it. I didn't even think about who supplied me with water, or about the men in orange overalls, working for the municipal water utility, who fixed leaks, dug new pipes into the ground and treated the sewage. It was nothing remarkable. It was only when I went to England, to Yorkshire, that I realised that the water utilities had simply been sold off to private interests.

2

England and Wales:
where it all began

In 1996 I met Frank Crampton. He was wandering around a nursery in the town of Collingham in Yorkshire, selecting hardier types of plant for his garden. Frank was not allowed to water his beloved plants because of a serious water shortage, and many plants had died. An entire reservoir nearby had completely dried out. Dead fish lay on the sandy bottom. Tony Jude, a nursery owner, was luckier, since he had his own well, but he was critical of the private water company, Yorkshire Water. 'People here have to pay more than ever before for water. To top it all, the service is rotten', he said.

The shortage of water was so serious that Yorkshire Water was forced to buy water from Newcastle, from the French multi-national enterprise Lyonnaise des Eaux, which had taken over Northumbrian Water, with England's largest reservoir. Night and day, water was transported to Yorkshire. Residents were up in arms! As if the scarcity of water was not enough, further huge quantities were lost through leakage. At the same time, the directors of Yorkshire Water awarded themselves huge salary increases and bonuses. The newspapers were full of angry comments about the company. One in particular sticks in my mind: 'Repair the water network instead of handing out profits to shareholders!'

In the middle of summer, people were forced to fetch water in buckets from standpipes, since there was no water in their own taps. They were not even able to take a shower. A chief executive of Yorkshire Water announced that he had been using a bowl to wash himself for three months. In fact, he was going to his mother-in-law's house to have a shower every night. This further infuriated the people of Yorkshire.

The Labour MP Frank Dobson expressed his anger. Although private water enterprises could not be held responsible for the lack of rain, he observed, the same could not be said about the loss of over 30 per cent of the available water, which had simply leaked away. For years, there had been no maintenance of the infrastructure. 'The Conservative government gave the water industry away', Dobson claimed.

Water prices are set on the basis of expenses worked out by the water companies themselves, and include the cost of capital investments to reach EU standards. The changes following privatis-ation were dramatic. For seven years, prices rose twice as fast as the rate of inflation. From 1989 to 1994 the average water bill increased by 55 per cent. Previously a 'Mr Water' could be found in every residential area, an inspector on call to deal with even the smallest leak. This job was cut when water was privatised.

Several other companies had problems with water shortages that year, but the management of Yorkshire Water was particularly arrogant. This, at least, was the experience of John Kidd, regional branch secretary for the trade union Unison. The employers said they had no money left for pay increases. It turned out that the company had spent £37 million on transporting water from Newcastle and elsewhere.

In Newcastle I met Dave Ericksson at the sewage treatment works. He told me that half of his colleagues no longer belonged to a trade union. The private company had built up a culture which resembled that in the United States. Employees were expected to be loyal to their employer's principles and goals. The company had formed a forum with employee participation, but the majority of the representatives were non-trade unionists. The sole union representative, who was graciously permitted to attend, was completely ignored.

The employees' situation improved somewhat when the French company Lyonnaise des Eaux bought the plant in Newcastle. A workers' council was formed, with at least 20 per cent of the seats to be occupied by trade union representatives.

The great water theft

In the mid- to late nineteenth century, municipal authorities invested heavily in water services in Great Britain, in a bid to come to grips with diseases like cholera and dysentery. It was pointless to rely on private companies to solve the problems. Politicians were compelled to take action long before the Labour Party was created. The Liberal Unionist politician Joseph Chamberlain, in particular, campaigned for state management of water and sewerage. Subsequently it became the natural responsibility of government to operate water services.

In 1974 publicly owned regional water authorities were set up to regulate and manage water utilities within ten regions. However, under Margaret Thatcher's Conservative government and her ideological overvaluation of privatisation, the Water Act of 1989 led to the privatisation of these authorities. In Scotland and Northern Ireland water utilities remained in public ownership.

In England and Wales, water and sewerage services were meant to become more efficient and competitive. The UK had to follow the EU's various environmental directives. This required major investments in the water industry, which was out of date compared to systems in Western Europe. Costs were to be reduced and inflation kept at a low level. As early as 1976 the IMF demanded that Britain should limit its public borrowing if it wanted assistance from the fund.

Before privatisation, the government wrote off all the debts of the water authorities, to a value of over £5 billion. In addition, they received a start-up incentive of £1.6 billion. The ten public authorities were not given an opportunity to raise the capital they required. Instead, they were sold off to private business at bargain prices, some 22 per cent below market value. These sales included large properties with significant cultural and natural assets. The private companies became owners of the entire infrastructure and the buildings. They were to run the water supply and sewerage system for twenty-five years. So much for competition. Nor was there any question of a tendering process.

Companies were to be transformed into profitable, efficient, client-friendly businesses. Directors in particular were expected to think in business terms and were given generous salaries to do so. The directors, popularly known as 'fat cats' were granted fringe benefits and preferential share options.

Pre-tax profits of the privatised companies rose by 147 per cent between 1990 and 1998. Newspapers called it 'the great water theft'. After-tax profits for 1994/5 were £1.7 million, 45 per cent of which were distributed to shareholders. As many as 2.7 million people became shareholders in a kind of popular capitalism. Anyone could buy shares cheaply. Many soon sold their shares, making a tidy profit. In the first six months alone, the number of shareholders halved.

A public authority, the Office for Water Service, Ofwat, was set up to regulate the water and sewerage industry. Its functions included ensuring that water companies deliver good service, looking after consumer interests, and placing a limit on how much could be charged for water. At the same time, water companies had to be guaranteed the economic resources they required to be able to provide a good service and make investments. By 1996, however, it seemed that the government viewed Ofwat's most important function as ensuring that the water companies made sufficient profits.

Companies were permitted to raise charges, but they did not always invest as much as was initially intended. If the water utilities had remained in the public sector, it would still have been necessary to raise charges, because major investments were required. Yet the private companies overestimated the capital costs needed; later it was shown that they had not spent as much as they had led Ofwat to believe. This, however, did not lead to lower water charges; instead dividends to shareholders were increased, according to Robin Simpson of Consumers International. Consumers paid $28 billion to the water companies between 1989 and 1998. Of this sum, about £10 billion was additional money from price increases. Almost the same amount (£9.5 billion) was distributed in profits to the mother companies.

Difficulties arose for the trade unions and the employees. Between 1973 and 1989 the number of employees fell from 80,000 to 50,000, partly due to automation and increased use of computers. From 1990 to 1999 the workforce was further reduced by almost 8,600 people. Employees were given the option to buy shares, but at the same time the trade union Unison had to struggle for workers to retain the pension rights earned from their former public sector employers.

Some people could not afford to pay their water bills. Increasing numbers had their water supplies cut off when they could not pay. In early 1994, for example, nearly 2 million households had not paid their bills and at the end of the year a million were still in arrears. Indignation was aroused even in parliament. Labour MPs cited cases where customers were particularly badly affected: one woman with seven children had her water cut off; an elderly handicapped woman had to rely on neighbours to supply her with water. The water companies were criticised not least by the medical profession. Since water is the basis for health and hygiene, it was argued, all people should at least have access to clean water. The response of the companies that were criticised for cutting off water was to install meters where a card is used to prepay for the water used. (It is notable that as more water for domestic use is being provided in South Africa, a growing number of prepay meters are being installed.) In Britain, the 1998 Water Act stipulates that it is illegal to cut off water or to install this particular type of meter. Hence, the companies no longer have the option of cutting off the water in cases of non-payment.

Water: a global commodity

The system of contracting out the operation of water services to private companies began to spread quite quickly around the world. In the wake of the neoliberal wave that swept the world in the latter part of the 1980s, the private sector was regarded as the most effective means of supplying people with water as it could provide the necessary capital.

In 1992, an international water conference was held in Dublin, organised by the United Nations. Four principles were adopted:

1. Fresh water is a finite and vulnerable resource, essential to sustain life, development and the environment.
2. Water development and management should be based on a participatory approach, involving users, planners and policy-makers at all levels.
3. Women play a central part in the provision, management and safeguarding of water.

4. Water has an economic value in all its competing uses and should be recognized as an economic good.

The conference was a big breakthrough for market solutions.

In addition, the International Monetary Fund (IMF) and the World Bank had already made privatisation a condition of finance for water projects. It is hardly surprising that the Dublin Declaration was announced in 1992, three years after Thatcher privatised water in Britain, and one year before the enormous water and sanitation system in Buenos Aires in Argentina was contracted out to large foreign firms.

The Dublin Declaration postulates that if water is free, people do not regard it as valuable, and so waste it, while the shortage of water in the world is growing. Operation, maintenance and investment should therefore be covered by the payments made by consumers and not by state subsidies. This means, in turn, that citizens must pay more for their water.

It is important not to waste water. Water is not an infinite resource. There are some who seriously maintain that water may become as expensive as oil in the future. Who is wasting water? Without thinking about it, West Europeans take a daily shower, thereby using 30–60 litres of water, while in the USA the trend among the middle classes is to sink into an outdoor hot tub filled with 1,200 litres of water. It is worth reflecting that 30 litres of water is more than a poor family in a barren country like Ethiopia, Mauritania or Chad can manage to obtain in a day to use for everything – for drinking, cooking and keeping clean. Nor is it certain that such a family would have the cash to pay for something as basic as water.

Today 1.2 billion people in the world lack access to clean drinking water, while 2.4 billion have no sanitation facilities. Many city dwellers throughout the world lack even rudimentary toilet facilities. They have to defecate in open spaces or into waste paper or plastic bags. The population growth of the world is outpacing the provision of potable water, especially in the cities. Less than half the population in most large cities in Africa, Asia and Latin America have piped water in their homes.

The world's governments and international agencies have committed themselves to the UN Millennium Development Goals. At the summits held in 2000 and 2002, world leaders decided that by the year 2015 half of the people who presently lack drinking water should have access to it, and that the number of people who live in unacceptable sanitary conditions should be halved by 2015. Long before these decisions were taken, though, private companies were already engaged in providing many cities with water and sewerage – on condition that they could make a profit.

3

Two global giants

In 1993 I met Stephen Collier, an elegant managing director from London. He turned up in Sweden and attempted to persuade local politicians in the capital of Stockholm that S:t Göran's hospital would do best if it were privately owned. He represented AMI, a subsidiary of Générale des Eaux, a private water company established in France in the mid-nineteenth century. It was surprising that this company, given its name, was not solely concerned with water. AMI's headquarters were in London, where the company ran private hospitals. Stephen Collier explained to me that although he did not recognise trade unions in Great Britain, he would of course recognise the Swedish union and adapt to the country's norms.

To cut a long story short, the company never established itself in Sweden. Hospitals were not sufficiently profitable. Like water, however, waste management is profitable. Thus by 1993 Générale des Eaux was already a giant within the refuse collection business in the UK, through its subsidiary Onyx, and remains so today. At the time Onyx took over operations from the municipality in London, refuse collection workers in Camden told how they were forced to accept lower wages and more demanding work.

Overtime pay disappeared. New employees had to accept poor conditions of employment.

Générale des Eaux gets second wind:
Vivendi and Veolia

Générale des Eaux has grown and developed into one of the largest water multinationals in the world. In 1996, Jean-Marie Messier became managing director and chairman. The company changed its name to Vivendi in 1998. Vivendi had already begun to transform itself into a gigantic media company, Vivendi Universal, which included Vivendi Environnement, that part of the company concerned with water, waste management and transport. Messier sidelined this part of the operation in his eagerness to develop the media business, including a film company, Canal Plus, music channels, telecommunications, Internet portals and book publishing. For a while Messier was the golden boy, at ease sitting on a comfortable sofa for interviews in inoffensive French Sunday television programmes. In addition to a salary and bonuses worth €5.1 million a year, he had a huge luxury apartment in New York.

However, Vivendi's expansion was achieved on the back of buy-outs. The company's financial performance soon deteriorated. In July 2002 Messier was forced to resign. The board accused him of causing the decline of the company's market value. Most of the debts were due to the asset write-down of the companies he had purchased. Share prices plummeted following allegations about the company's accounting practices. In 2002 the company owed €34 billion. Since then it has been working on steadily reducing its debt burden. Vivendi Universal retained only 20 per cent of the shares in Vivendi Environnement. According to Veolia's 2003 annual report, the company's shareholders are, in addition to Vivendi Universal, the French companies CDC, Groupama and EDF. There are also a large number of individual shareholders.

On 30 April 2003 Vivendi Environnement changed its name to Veolia Environnement. Veolia was trying to break free of the taint of being a Vivendi company. The name Veolia was taken from Aeolus, the Greek god of wind, always in motion, clean and open. Veolia Environnement has a total of 302,000 employees around the world and supplies 110 million people in over a hundred countries with water. One of its longest contracts is for fifty years, with the city of Shanghai in China. In addition to Veolia Water and Onyx, Veolia Environnement includes Dalkia (energy provision) and Connex (transport). These companies have contracts all over the world. For example, a Czech engineer at a water plant in Prague and an engineer in Niger in Africa both work for a subsidiary owned by Veolia Water. Connex operates trains in Great Britain, Australia and New Zealand, buses in Sweden and the underground system in Stockholm. The list is long and growing.

In 2003, some 36 per cent of Veolia Environnement's income came from Veolia Water, 22 per cent from waste management, 17 per cent from energy services, 14 per cent from transportation and nearly 11 per cent from a Spanish-based company, FCC. FCC is Spain's number-one waste management operator and also a major force in the water and construction markets. In 2003 more than 95 per cent of revenue was generated in industrial countries like Europe and the USA. Veolia's revenue was €28.6 billion in 2003. The company is investing heavily in both China and Australia.

Suez: shareholders before the poor

Veolia Environnement has only one major competitor, the multi-national corporation Suez. Suez is the largest water multinational in the world outside France; within France, Veolia is larger. Suez chairman and chief executive officer Gérard Méstrallet has long maintained that he is struggling to provide water for the world's poor. Nevertheless profit is indisputably the main goal – the shareholders would accept no other priorities. Suez was formerly Lyonnaise des Eaux, which began operating as early as 1880. It merged with the company that had built the Suez canal, hence the name. It has now acquired major water contracts in cities across the globe, including Buenos Aires, Manila, Casablanca, Jakarta, Johannesburg, Paris and Sydney. It also has a special division in China. Unlike its competitor, Suez has not risked its capital in questionable investments in media and communications. This sector plays an insignificant role in the company, and interests are being sold off. The company employs some 172,300 employees around the world. Ondeo, Suez's water subsidiary, supplies 125 million people with water. Degrémont, another Suez company, specialises in the design, construction and operation of water treatment plants. There is also a waste management company, SITA. SITA's lorries, which one day appeared on the streets of Stockholm, operate in several countries, for example Portugal and Thailand.

Of Suez's revenue in 2003, some 67 per cent came from energy provision, and 31 per cent from water services and waste management. In 2003 the company earned over €39.6 billion. Most of the revenue, 90 per cent, comes from Europe and North America. Shareholders include Groupe Bruxelles Lambert, Employee Shareholders, Crédit Agricole, and CDC Group. The biggest shareholder is General Public, which owns 74.3 per cent.

In 2001, Veolia Environnement and Suez together had a turnover that was nearly four times as great as that of the five other major international water companies combined (RWE/Thames, Saur, Cascal/Biwater, Anglian Water and IWL).

And then there were two

Today, 5 per cent of the world's water utilities, which were formerly operated by the public sector, are being run by a tiny number of private companies. The rest are still run by the state and by municipalities. This proportion may sound small, but the fact is that the enterprises involved have expanded enormously over the past decade and a half. In 1990, 51 million people were supplied with water by these companies; today the four largest supply over 330 million people. Over two-thirds of that private water market is controlled by Veolia and Suez.

Sometimes Suez and Veolia behave as aggressive competitors, at other times they cooperate. In Buenos Aires, for example, the water consortium is jointly owned by Suez, Veolia, Britain's Anglian Water and a few other companies. In France, where the private sector controls some 77 per cent of the water market, the two corporations have joined forces in several towns and regions. The Anti-Trust Council has ruled that the subsidiary companies of Suez and Veolia have between them created a joint monopoly, and requested the minister for the economy to order the two companies to modify or terminate the agreements whereby their resources are joined within joint subsidiaries.

It is not easy for other companies to survive among the giants. Two companies, Thames Water and Saur, are now attempting to compete with Suez and Veolia. Of the seven large companies operating in the international private water market, Thames Water and Saur together accounted for 17 per cent of total turnover in 2001, while Veolia and Suez together claimed 78 per cent.

Thames Water is a British company now owned by the German company RWE, an energy giant. It is the third largest private water multinational in the world, with 70 million clients in a number of countries. Thames Water is joint owner with Veolia Environnement of Berlin Wasser. In Budapest, Thames Water cooperates with Veolia in sewage treatment and with Suez in water distribution.

Saur is the third largest water company in France and the fourth largest in the world; it is also involved in construction, energy and waste management. Saur has over 23 million clients.

It is owned by the building company Bouygues, which has expanded into eastern Europe with contracts, for example, in Gdansk in Poland. It has also established itself in Africa, including Senegal and Mali.

There are some smaller companies operating in the water supply sector. International Water was jointly owned by the large American building enterprise Bechtel and the Italian company Edison. Water distribution is a relatively insignificant part of Bechtel's portfolio, and indeed the corporation has sold part of its holding to the European Bank for Reconstruction and Development (EBRD). Cascal comprises the English company Biwater and a municipal company from the Netherlands. Other players include the British companies Severn Trent, Anglian Water and Kelda; and the Spanish firm Aguas de Barcelona, which is partly owned by Suez.

One company that has disappeared from the global market is Azurix, which was started by the energy company Enron. In July 1999, Azurix took over the provision of water services in the seventy-two suburbs of Buenos Aires. The company paid $438.6 million for the contract. It was contracted to remain in Buenos Aires for thirty years, during which time it would invest, improve and expand the water system. In October 2001 Azurix announced that it was withdrawing from the contract. It accused the regional government of 'serious breaches' of contract and demanded compensation of up to $600 million. By this time there had already been problems with the poor quality of service provided. The provincial government, in turn, has claimed the same sum from the company for not fulfilling its contract. The lobbyist for Enron was Marvin Bush, brother of President George W. Bush, and the company supported the president during his election campaign. Enron is, of course, infamous for its creative bookkeeping and for the fantastic salaries of its management. The end came when the company filed for bankruptcy in December 2001.

Meanwhile, the concentration of companies continues. In 2002, Suez bought the American business US Water, while Thames Water bought American Water Works in 2003.

Focusing on the poor?

Over the years, some extraordinary information has emerged concerning the way the private water enterprises do business, regardless of where in world they are.

In 2000, a second world water forum was held in The Hague. The large water multinationals talked about how they would focus on the poor. They distributed impressive brochures and invited delegates to elegant receptions. From the podium, a Suez director detailed how the company had supplied the population of Manila with water. Then a union delegate from the Philippines, Ferdinand Gaite, went up to the rostrum and showed the audience a plastic bottle containing yellow sludge. He said, 'I filled this bottle from my tap just before I came here. I invite Suez to drink this water!' Suez was forced to defend itself, saying that the company would need a little more time in Manila to get things right.

On another occasion I met Hans Engelberts, secretary-general of the global trade union federation Public Services International (PSI). He complained indignantly that it was the ultimate triumph of global capitalism to gain control over something as basic as people's need for water. 'To say that the public sector cannot afford to finance these services, or that the job is best done by the private sector, is a smokescreen to limit the role of the government, and place public services under the control of the market and open the services to for-profit corporations', he explained.

PSI has been fighting privatisation of water since trade unions all over the world turned to the federation when water and sewerage services were allocated to private companies. Neither trade unions nor people have felt able to exert any influence whatsoever. They have simply been confronted by a fait accompli.

Shortly after, I read an article by an American journalist, Jim Shultz, about a private company that at the end of 1999 had taken over the management of the water utility in Cochabamba in Bolivia. The cost of water was raised so high and the resultant protests so strong that they led to a water war. Others subsequently retold the story Shultz had broken. Some claimed that only one person had died in the confrontations; others mentioned several deaths. Each story differed. So I decided to travel there myself to try to establish the facts. Could things really get that bad when a private company supplies people with water?

4

The water war in Cochabamba

A towering statue of Christ stands on a mountainside above Cochabamba. Christ stretches his vast arms as though to embrace the 700,000 inhabitants of the city centre as a single community. The 40-metre statue was erected by the mayor, Manfred Reyes Villa. To satisfy his vanity, he ensured that it was larger than the Christ standing above Rio de Janeiro.

Cochabamba seems to be a town engaged in constant struggle. On Plaza de 14 Septiembre, there is intense activity. Some young people have set up a banner to demand fewer pupils per class. At a little bookstand, a woman in her fifties is standing and selling a brochure calling for protests against the free-trade agreement ALCA, Área de Libre Comercio de las Américas. She is convinced that the agreement will give foreign companies an advantage. 'Compañera', she says, handing me a brochure. We are fighting for the same thing, irrespective of which countries we live in, she tells me. I have not said a word. I am astonished at all the books with pictures of Fidel Castro and Cuba. It is like moving back in time from 2002 to the late 1960s. An old man, leaning on a crutch, holds a microphone in his hand and calls out something about *la lucha*, the struggle against imperialism. On the square, the inhabitants demonstrated their fury and lack of power because the foreign private consortium, Aguas del Tunari, had ventured to move in and lay claim to the country's water.

On this morning, the leader of the coca-leaf farmers, Evo Morales, arrives in the town to meet the president. He demands that the farmers should be allowed to cultivate coca, so that they may, at least, subsist. Prior to 1998, Bolivia was the world's second largest producer of coca. Then punitive action, supported by the USA, was taken against coca cultivation. The population has used coca since time immemorial in tea and other medicinal brews. Now coca-leaf farmers from Chapare have come together in the town. I hear vivid stories of how they were brutally assaulted when the military destroyed their plantations. Furthermore, they have not succeeded in selling the bananas, pineapples, and papaya, which they had to plant instead of coca. They fear that, if the ALCA free trade agreement is implemented, it will become more difficult to sell their products, as they will be forced to compete with foreign companies.

Evo Morales addresses a seminar in a hall that is packed so full that people stand along the walls; others sit on the stairs; outside some Indian women in white hats sit down directly on the ground. Some diligently take notes when Evo Morales says that the gas fields should be returned to the state. They have already recaptured their water resources. The coca-leaf farmers were key players in that struggle.

Regaining dignity

In September 1999 Aguas del Tunari was awarded a forty-year contract to manage water supplies and sewerage services in Cochabamba. The only company to bid for the contract, it began operations in November. The consortium consisted of International Water (which was at the time jointly owned by Bechtel and Edison), Abengoa, a Spanish engineering group, and several Bolivian construction companies. The contract was between the regulatory body La Superintendencia and the consortium; the government was not a signatory.

A regulatory body is needed to control, supervise and negotiate with the private companies. Some developing countries still lack such a body. In other countries, the regulator is weak. Such was the case in Cochabamba. In April 2000, La Superintendencia broke the contract. An outright water war had broken out between citizens, politicians and the consortium. 'The reason was that water bills increased by between 35 and 400 per cent', Oscar Oliviera now tells me, when we meet in his office. He is head of the factory workers' trade union; his office is a stone's throw from the lively square. 'A pensioned teacher living on the equivalent of US$80 a month was shocked that his bill increased from $5 to $25. Water bills rose by an average of 43 per cent for the poorest and 57 per cent for the upper middle classes', he explains.

Tanya Paredes, mother of five children, supports her family by knitting clothes. Her water bill rose by so much that it was the equivalent of the cost of food for the family for one and a half weeks. The connection fee apparently rose by over 30 per cent. An ordinary worker earning about $220 a month was expected to pay over $130 for a connection. How, then, could a worker who earned only $100 afford a connection?

Oscar Oliviera was one of those who led the protests. He informs me that 'Union activists, teachers, workers, environmental groups, students and farmers with small water cooperatives in the countryside joined hands. Together we formed La Coordinadora de Defensa del Agua y la Vida, a fellowship in defence of water and life.'

The concession contract had granted exclusive rights to the private consortium for the provision of water services and control over water resources. The Water Service Law of 1999 had caused great anxiety among small farmers. They saw the law as a threat to their established rights: that they would henceforth be charged for irrigation water; that they would not be permitted to dig their own wells or obtain water other ways. That would, at a stroke, end the ancient tradition active among a large section of the Indian population. What was seen to belong naturally to Mother Earth would suddenly be at the disposal of an unknown foreign consortium.

'Yet we regained our dignity', said Oliviera. He is a quietly spoken man, originally a shoemaker, now a trade union activist. Framed photos of Fidel Castro and Che Guevara cover the wall in his office. Oliviera explains, with deep emotion, 'It was like a civil war. People had stones and cudgels and set tyres on fire. We were united, town and countryside. Soldiers replied with rubber bullets and tear gas.'

In January 2000 people blocked the highway for four days. During the many confrontations, Oliviera was imprisoned and put under house arrest. Finally, the demonstrators' demands were met. Water charges would be reduced so that they would became affordable. The contract itself would be reviewed. Two days later, however, the regulating body La Superintendencia announced that charges would rise. Time after time the government would intervene and La Superintendencia accepted the government's de-cisions instead of supporting consumers. The people duly prepared for further protests. La Superintendencia then cancelled the price rises. Thus the stand-off continued.

On 3 March a carnival was held. La Coordinadora, the organisa-tion for the defence of water and life, organised a demonstration. People paraded papier-mâché dolls, representing mayor Manfred Reyes Villa, among others. They also symbolically killed Aguas del Tunari and sent it on its way by burning a coffin. 'The strug-gle culminated on 8 April when we mobilised 100,000 people, blocking a highway and the city centre. We organised a general strike and the schools were closed. Riot police and government soldiers confronted us. A captain dressed in civvies killed a boy of only 17 years. Over 100 people were wounded', says Oscar Oliviera. In the end, as a result of the social upheaval, La Superintendencia announced that the contract would be cancelled. Operation of water supplies was duly returned to the public water utility.

Fertile ground for water protests

Several overlapping causes served to upset the people, from the very poorest sector to businessmen who saw their interests threatened. They were not solely concerned with water charges. Being confronted by police on motorcycles and later by the military was too vivid a reminder of the old dictatorship, the ruling regime of 1971–78. Furthermore, people had already been badly affected by the intensive privatisation of publicly owned companies. The foreign water consortium established itself in the country at a time when protests against privatisation had begun to grow.

The political elite in Bolivia is heavily influenced by the USA. In the 1980s, the well-known Harvard economist Jeffrey Sachs paid a flying visit. His recipe for creating growth in the country was to halt hyperinflation, change economic policy and liberalise the market. Today he admits that although Bolivia succeeded in beating hyperinflation, it has not succeeded in achieving economic growth. At that time, however, his views had the support of the International Monetary Fund. As a result, the mines were privatised, and many miners lost their jobs. Some moved to Chapare, close to Cochabamba, where they began to cultivate coca.

Privatisation of other sectors of the economy quickly followed. Oscar Oliviera is unequivocal in his judgement of the global foreign companies: 'They exploit our natural resources and profit by this. They have stolen our aeroplanes, railways, roads, communications, factories and mines. They believed that they could even steal our water, together with the mafia in the government.' He adds that privatisation does not seem to have led to any major advantages for the country. Poverty has not been reduced and people still lack jobs. The trade-union movement has been under pressure and does not play as important a role as it once did.

Olivera explains that the outcome of the water war is the first victory for the Bolivian people against the neoliberal model in fifteen years. He perceives this as a test of strength between David and Goliath – a struggle for democracy: 'The governmental mafia and the foreign company did not respect the Indians' traditional ways of supplying themselves with water.' Despite the victory, he is still far from satisfied. 'We have inherited a hugely indebted public utility that is in poor shape technologically. Aguas del Tunari is also demanding compensation of US$25 million, which the consortium claims to have lost from a contract that guaranteed it a 15 per cent return on capital invested.'

The water war has radically changed Oscar Oliviera's life. He now travels the world sharing his experiences. In March 2003 he attended the Third World Water Forum in Kyoto. He appears lost in thought. He has been considering the possibility of setting up a cooperative. He wonders whether it would be possible to establish a world fund for public-sector water investment.

A few days later I meet one of many researchers in Cochabamba, Carlos Crespo. He says that one of the greatest mistakes was not to involve the population in decisions on water services. The government consulted the political parties but went no further. 'The privatisation of water created fertile ground for social conflicts, which could not be handled by the state in a democratic way', he says. He points out that it is of no account that these questions were debated in parliament, since the population does not trust parliament. Its credibility suffered further when the government maintained that the rise in charges was only 35 per cent, while newspapers showed increases of at least 100 per cent. Some 70 per cent of the population of Bolivia live below the internationally recognised poverty line. Coca-leaf farmers were already disaffected: the programme against coca cultivation, promoted by the USA, had driven them into the towns, where they had difficulty in finding jobs. The government did not even want to negotiate with the protest movement La Coordinadora, which some claimed was supported by drug dealers.

Andrew Nickson, another researcher, has analysed what he calls 'the most dramatic failure to have hit a company'. There was no faulting the ambitious nature of the contract: every year a quota of new households would be connected to the water network; by the year 2039 everyone in the country would have running water. Aguas del Tunari wanted to change the pricing system, which it considered old-fashioned: those who used most water – like industry and owners of luxury houses – paid the least. Under the new management those with high incomes would pay three times as much as those with low incomes for the first 12 cubic metres of water, and twice as much for additional consumption. Had the poor been able to afford the connection fees, they might have won under this system, since those unconnected must buy from expensive water sellers. Higher charges could subsequently have been introduced gradually, and preferably once consumers had registered real improvements, Andrew Nickson points out.

The size of increase in water bills varied in residents' accounts partly as a result of a new rising scale system of charging for water services. Residents were reclassified in different categories depending on the kind of dwelling. Some faced increases of over 200 per cent. Oscar Oliviera estimates that the residents of Cochabamba collectively saved over \$3.4 million by escaping the price increases of Aguas del Tunari after the contract was broken.

The folly of Misicuni Dam

The Misicuni Dam Project contributed to the civic unrest. The World Bank had granted a loan for a lower-cost option, the Corani Project. The projected costs for the construction of the Misicuni Dam were three times the estimate for the Corani Project. However, in spite of this, mayor Manfred Reyes Villa, decided to force the Misicuni Dam through. It is said that he in turn was subject to pressure from engineers and a local building contractor, owned by one of the most influential men in Bolivia. They expected to make big money.

The municipal utility, Semapa, which had previously managed water and sewerage services, had never had the funds to invest in constructing a dam. Its budget was not sufficient even to maintain the water mains. The contract with Aguas del Tunari entailed a formal increase in prices by an average of 35 per cent immediately and a further 20 per cent in 2002, when it was expected that the dam would be completed. The price increases were also intended to pay off a debt run up by Semapa.

It was not long before the managing director of Aguas del Tunari declared that the dam project could not go ahead without further price increases. That is, the costs would have to be paid in advance – by consumers. According to Jeff Berger of Bechtel in the USA, joint owner of Aguas del Tunari, the company's management had at an early stage questioned the expensive dam construction and recommended its postponement. The priority in his view was to repair the water network. In this way, access to water would be improved and prices would not need to be raised as much. Nevertheless, local politicians demanded that the construction of the dam go ahead during the first years of the contract. Some maintain that engineers at Aguas del Tunari lacked both empathy and a sense of what was politically and socially acceptable. Their view was that if people did not pay, their water should be cut off.

Back to square one

On the outskirts of Cochabamba, I meet Edwin Oquando Oranda, a water seller. He fills his truck with water before departing for the hospital in Cochabamba. Even the hospital has a shortage of water. 'Our country is so rich in resources, but people do not even have water in their homes', he says. He prefers to believe that God has a greater capacity to solve the water problem than do Bolivian politicians. Sometimes people buy only a few litres of water from him. They cannot afford more. If he were to give credit to the poor, he would soon be bankrupt.

He also participated in the protests against the private consortium. His water sales were threatened, since the company was to have a monopoly on all water resources. The municipal Semapa managed water services from 1967 until the arrival of the private consortium. Now everything has reverted to the status quo ante. Some consumers still have water for only one or two hours a week. The 43 per cent who are not connected must rely on water sellers. To make matters worse, the pipes are so bad that half the water disappears in leakage. An engineer, Ricardo Ayala Antezana, is the temporary manager of Semapa. 'We do not need a Veolia, a Suez, or any other private company, but we do need money to be able to reduce water leakage. We have the technology', he says.

Aguas del Tunari left debts in its wake, and subcontractors are still sending bills to Semapa. 'A flaw in such a contract can be expensive for the government', Antezana says, and points to a clause in which the government promised to reimburse Aguas del Tunari in case of a breach of contract.

It is early in the morning; the corridors at the water plant are swarming with employees. Antezana would like to dismiss half of them to make the utility more efficient, but the trade union is against him. Indeed, the union president Jorge Cortéz maintains that another twenty employees are required.

Jorge Cortéz sits at his desk in an office at Semapa. In a corner cupboard, football trophies are displayed. Along a wall sits a shabby red leather sofa. Above it hang the obligatory Che Guevara picture and a crucifix. He tells how staff were transferred to Aguas del Tunari and then threatened with dismissal. The company asked for police protection for the management at the peak of the unrest. Cortéz intends to prevent Antezana from continuing.

The trade union has a representative on the new democratically elected board of Semapa. Other members, in addition to the mayor, include a representative from the municipality, one for the engineers and three for the citizens. Some say that in Cochabamba the seeds of something new are being sown, by the residents themselves. Cochabamba demonstrates that the water supply is considerably more complicated than a private company simply establishing itself and raising charges. A whole series of interconnected factors contributed to the water war.

The struggle continues

The US journalist Jim Shultz is persevering in his struggle against Bechtel, a partner in Aguas del Tunari. He has organized a global Web petition. Bechtel's lawsuit against the Bolivian government for US$25 million, will be heard by the International Centre for Settlement of Investment Disputes (ICSID) at the World Bank in Washington. In the petition, over 300 citizens' groups from forty-one countries requested that the public be present in Washington at the hearings. These include representatives of trade unions and environmental groups, researchers, and writers from countries including Canada, Japan, Zambia and the USA. But their requests have all been denied.

Every case before the court is decided by three members. Bechtel appoints one arbitrator, the Bolivian government another, and the third is the president of ICSID, who in turn is appointed by the president of the World Bank. Naturally, there is criticism, since it was the World Bank that demanded the privatisation of Bolivia's water system. 'US$25 million is what it costs per year to employ 3,000 doctors in the rural areas, 12,000 teachers or to connect 125,000 families to water', says Shultz. In a letter, he writes:

> Although there is evidence that people received much higher bills, Bechtel claims that only ten per cent were affected. The World Bank certainly did not approve of the Misicuni project – but in February 1996 the mayor of Cochabamba was informed that if water was not privatised, the World Bank would not make any contributions.

Jim Shultz and others have duly protested against Bechtel being contracted to build schools, water utilities and other facilities in Iraq, citing the company's behaviour in Cochabamba.

A social-political question

Few projects have been as closely scrutinised as the 'water war' in Cochabamba. Those who advocate private alternatives claim that the increase in tariffs was a consequence of the need for Aguas del Tunari to repair leaks in the water system, which enabled residents to gain access to and thus consume more water. This may have played a role, but it is far from the whole story. The company began operations in November 1999, the protests started as early as January 2000, and the contract ended the following April.

It would be somewhat surprising if residents in Cochabamba used that much more water in such a short time. After all, the Indians in El Alto in the capital La Paz have reduced their usage in comparable circumstances. There, a subsidiary of the French company Suez runs water supplies. Higher charges have seen a drop in consumption from 110 litres to 87 litres per person per day; in response, the company has been considering a campaign to increase water use, according to the World Bank. When I was there, the manager of the company confirmed that it is indeed a problem that the Indians use so little water, which reduces the company's profitability. The Indians have traditionally collected rainwater, a practice they have not given up even though water is now supplied from a tap in the yard. Following a general strike demanding the return of the water system to public control, the government in January 2005 issued a Supreme Decree for the termination of the contract.

A report written by Raquel Yaksic Antezana from Cochabamba, a student at the Royal Institute of Technology in Stockholm, describes current developments in Cochabamba:

> Semapa's board continues to try to involve users in its operations for both social and environmental reasons. In the long run, Semapa is hoping that consumers will feel that they are part-owners of the company. Through the democratically elected board they can exert control over what is happening.

In practice, this process has not been straightforward. It is claimed in the local press that relatives of Semapa employees have been favoured, indeed that some have even found jobs through knowing someone on the board. Furthermore, it is estimated that over 50 per cent of the water pipes are still leaking. At the same time, Semapa is planning to extend the network, above all in the poor southern districts.

Under the terms of a $3.9 million loan from the Inter-American Development Bank (IADB), the utility has committed itself to a certain reduction in the number of employees on its payroll. When this goal has been achieved, a further $14.5 million will be released.

With residents participating in self-help programmes – for example, digging water mains – people on low incomes can be reached. Yet if greater citizen participation is to become viable, there is a need for 'more dialogue and more education and also more dialogue between the employed within Semapa. Citizens are not even aware of the meaning of having an influence, since they have virtually never had the opportunity of contributing their views', Antezana notes. The idea is also to involve local businessmen to a greater degree and to develop technical support through public–public partnerships, which in this context means obtaining support and know-how from well-run public water utilities, for example in Brazil.

Antezana has interviewed citizens, politicians and employees on their views of the water supply service. She has concluded that a certain quantity of water should be free of charge to users; thereafter there should be a rising charge for those who consume more. 'Water should not be seen only as a technocratic and commercial issue but also as a social-political question', she writes. Over 90 per cent of the women in the southern part of Cochabamba, an area to which water and sanitation have yet to be extended, are interested in participating and gaining influence over how the service is run. First they must acquire the tools to enable them to exert that influence.

The people do not have much confidence in the information they get from the politicians. Surveys show that only 9 per cent trust the municipal government and only 3 per cent the national government; 28 per cent prefer to rely on the information they get from television; 23 per cent trust the information from Semapa.

There are also major differences between what the citizens want and what the politicians propose. Whereas the majority of the people, especially in the southern part of Cochabamba, reject privatisation as a long-term solution, 62 per cent of the politicians interviewed are in favour.

Thus a major challenge remains to develop civic participation. 'All decisions concerning water privatisation were taken without participation by the citizens and local organisations. If they had been allowed to take part, the privatisation might have ended in a different way', Raquel Antezana writes.

5

Tucumán, Argentina:
the watershed?

It is October 2002. In the provincial town of San Miguel de Tucumán in northern Argentina, Jacaranda trees are in flower and fallen lilac decks the streets. It is drizzling; the temperature is 25°C. I arrive after a two-hour flight from Cochabamba. En route, we landed in Santa Cruz in Bolivia, where the water supply is operated by a well-run consumer cooperative, which has been praised by the World Bank. Although this might seem to offer itself as a good example for other water utilities, the World Bank prefers to focus on private solutions.

Outside the children's hospital, El Niño, in Tucumán, an ambulance stops suddenly. A crying woman climbs out. She rushes in to the hospital with her baby, who is nothing but skin and bone. When we next meet, she is in a ward with several other mothers and babies. She holds a mask to her small son's face so that he can breathe in oxygen, at the same time as she rocks him back and forth. The ward has twenty-five beds: a small child, fighting for its life, lies in each one. A very young mother is being helped by her aunt to fill a bottle with something that resembles gruel. It feels intrusive, just standing there and asking what the children are suffering from. I can see how undernourished they are. There are three-month-old babies weighing just 2–3 kilos Some are dehydrated; others have bronchitis, difficulty in breathing, cramps, diarrhoea, or another illness.

A cleaner passes by with a dirty mop and some rubbish bags. Then the clink of porcelain is heard. Two men with masks over their mouths push a trolley with food. Suddenly there are many people in the ward. Everyone gathers here – older brothers, mothers and aunts, indeed everyone who helps with the nursing – because at lunchtime they get a plate of food.

The walls are covered with brown marks where paint has peeled, but there are also crucifixes and colourful posters. The easy chairs are in need of repair. One of the doctors says that there is a shortage of beds; sometimes they do not even have sheets. The director of the hospital, Lorenzo Santiago Marcos, is a worried man. The budget has been cut to a third of what it used to be due to the drop in the value of the currency. He wears a white shirt with a Dior logo; and on the desk stands a diploma from Rotary. He does not even have enough money in the budget to pay the staff their full salaries.

The year is 2002 and Argentina is suffering from the aftermath of a major economic crisis. During the year, fifteen children have died of malnutrition here in the hospital, in a country that previously was regarded as among the world's richest. Lorenzo Santiago Marcos maintains that malnutrition is a direct result of globalisation. Argentina was not ready for competition on the global market. 'We were inundated by foreign goods, but here people lost their jobs. Without work, poverty knocks at the door. With better living conditions, nearly all illnesses are preventable. It would at least be possible to avoid diarrhoea and other diseases if people had clean water and if hygiene was better', he says. Some of the children might have survived if they had grown up in homes with clean water. Instead they were exposed to water from polluted rivers or from rusty old water pipes.

As early as 1995, politicians in the province of Tucumán decided to improve accessibility to water and improve the quality. A subsidiary of the private French company Générale des Eaux (now Veolia) won the contract. It ended with a conflict between the governor and the company, which decided to rescind the contract in August 1997, but was forced by the governor to stay until October 1998. When the economic crash came in Argentina at the end of 2001, the same miserable conditions still existed in Tucumán. It is a complex matter to provide a population with water in another country, one whose conditions, culture and policies differ greatly from those in France.

Mud in the pipes

The residents of the capital of San Miguel de Tucumán remember well Aguas del Aconquija, the French-owned company that raised charges for water to the point where, in the end, people refused to pay. In a café sit five men. Their present concern is not water. One of them is restless and worried. He does not feel well and is not as brave as the other four. Several months ago the Swedish vehicle manufacturer Scania laid the men off. They knew that they would never get their jobs back. They feel affronted and so furious that they have burnt tyres outside the Scania factory. After twenty-five years of faithful service, they have been shown how little Scania thinks they are worth. Now they are trying to sue the company. The man who is unwell is doing his best to keep up with the more pugnacious of his unemployed colleagues, but can he manage? His only wish is to support his family and regain his dignity, to get a job. Official figures show that 17 per cent of the population in Argentina is unemployed; privately embassy officials and politicians believe the figure is much higher.

I came here to write about water, so I ask the men, 'What happened with that French company?' 'Well, we could not afford to pay for water when the company increased charges so very much', one replied. 'Now it costs exactly the same as it did earlier.' They return to their discussion of Scania.

The state water company Obras Sanitarias del Tucumán is housed in a shabby blue building. Outside, people queue to pay their water bills. While they wait, people are happy to talk about Aguas del Aconquija. Maria de Valle tells me that when the French company was there, she paid three times as much for water and sanitation – for water that was dirty! An elderly man says that his bill jumped from 24 to 59 pesos. Others say they had to pay up to 90 pesos. These water bills cover two months' use. They are very high for people who earn so little. The unemployed, for example, receive 150 pesos a month. An auxiliary nurse in Tucumán earns only about 300 pesos a month. In the face of people's protests, the company was finally forced to leave, although the contract was for thirty years.

Those in the queue are becoming eager to talk to me and gather around me in a large ring. 'The company did not make any investments; they only raised the charges', one person tells me. As many as 5,000 complaints were sent to the consumer ombudsman.

Inside, one flight up, I find the interim director, Oscar Adolfo Torres, sitting alone in an office furnished with a single desk. He is despondent. He tells me that the water utility has debts of over US\$6 million. His initial appointment to run operations for six months was extended for another six months, and that is how has continued. The water system is operated by the province, which is the majority shareholder; 10 per cent of the company is owned by the workers' union, Obras Sanitarias de Tucumán. Before the arrival of Aguas del Aconquija there were 2,700 workers. Following the retrenchment of the workforce it is now down to only 850. 'Unfortunately they may become even fewer, given the current demanding economic situation', Torres says. When the French company arrived there were 12.5 employees per 1,000 connections; the average figure in France is 4 per 1,000 connections.

Public Prosecutor Benito Garzon, whose office is in the premises of the provincial government, is the most knowledgable on the subject. He says that Aguas del Aconquija was supposed not only to manage the operation of the existing water and sewerage system but also to extend the network. Yet it was not long before the company wanted to renegotiate the contract and reduce its investment. The pipes are seventy years old. The intention was that the company would invest $180 million over thirty years, but the pipes were in such bad condition that they needed to be replaced immediately. Also the company wanted to invest in the town, not in the surrounding province, as was agreed in the contract.

'Aguas del Aconquija only wanted the best part of the cake, as the company understood that it was more difficult to ensure that people in the countryside could afford to pay their water bills', says Garzon. A further problem was that payment discipline was poor. 'Aguas del Aconquija had been informed that at least 40 per cent usually paid their bills. In reality, only 20 per cent bothered to pay and, in the end, this dropped to only 9 per cent. Why should people pay? When it was hottest here in Tucumán, mud oozed out of the pipes. The water was undrinkable', Garzon says.

Even the politicians lacked discipline. The French government even intervened and tried to persuade the Argentinian government to create order in Tucumán, but that failed. Tucumán had a new political leader at this time, General Antonio Bosso. He used the issue of higher water charges to ruin his political opponents by urging people to protest on the streets and to stop paying. Bosso had participated in the military coup in Argentina, as head of the army in Tucumán in the mid-1970s. He was thus responsible for the disappearance without trace of 500 people who had dissident political opinions. Despite his reputation, he was elected governor of the province. Today he claims to work against corruption, although it is rumoured that he has a Swiss bank account. He does, however, appear to be working to improve roads and access to water for the population.

Garzon continues: 'We are a people who respect rules and regulations, on condition that they are implemented in the right way. We could not pay for service that was so poor. The company made many mistakes. People demonstrated right outside here.' His window overlooks a square, where nowadays public servants demonstrate because they do not receive their pay on time. The economy is that shaky. Garzon tells how entangled the judicial process between the province and the company became. The company declared that its reputation was damaged and refused to accept the loss of millions of dollars on the investments it was to make under the contract, which would later have turned to profit. Here details are in dispute. Who was it that broke the contract, the province or the company? In Tucumán I am informed that it was the province that broke the contract, later demanding millions of dollars in compensation from the company.

The whole business ended up in Washington at the International Centre for Settlement of Investment Disputes – just like the case of Cochabamba. With the help of experts in Tucumán, Garzon is involved in the search for fresh evidence for a new prosecution. At some stage, he says, the court proceedings must come to an end. He concludes with a message to decision-makers in the European Union: 'The EU should have better control over what their companies are doing.'

Privatised water supply was not a success in Tucumán, I observe, but one should not automatically assume that all private companies are alike. In the province of Santa Fe, further south in Argentina, another private company is running the water services. There a non-governmental organisation has held a referendum to decide whether to get rid of the company. I want to know more about this, and so I catch a bus to Rosario in Santa Fe.

6

Water and the poor of
Rosario and Buenos Aires

Rosario in the province of Santa Fe is Argentina's second largest town. On the outskirts, poor people are building informal settlements. Hoping to start a new life here, they have decided to turn their backs on unemployment in the north, where they were born. I can still see in my mind's eye the woman squatting on her knees with a pile of dirty clothing on the ground in front of her, outside the tin shanty that is her home. A green carpet and some rubber tyres lie on the roof; a small flowerpot hangs on a wall. Directly behind the fence is a water tap. The woman washes the clothes in clean water.

To ask the woman if it feels good to have a water supply is like asking a hungry child if it is good to eat. She is very shy. She is happy that she has water, though has no idea who has provided her with it – probably the nun Maria Jordán, who is devoting her life to supporting the inhabitants of in the slum area. She also teaches them how to fix leakages in the water mains. But Maria Jordán does not know either which company came there and built a water pipeline. More then one planned main pipeline never materialised. Sewage-polluted water flows in the ditches. An over-full rubbish dump slopes down to the dried-out riverbed. A boy stands among the garbage holding a catapult.

A little further away many other informal houses are being built, extending the settlement further. There is no water at all there. Thus children go several hundred metres to fetch water from a communal tap in a section of the shanty town that does have water. They fill plastic containers and lug them back home. One man has dug a small kitchen garden and is patiently watering it with a tin can with holes drilled in its base; water streams down over small lettuce leaves. Others, however, have given up. Maria Jordán says that in some shanties there are mothers with eight children, who no longer manage to make the effort to find food for them.

Members of the Association for the Right to Water (La Asamblea Provincial por el Derecho al Agua) accompanied me to this place; one would not visit alone. Nevertheless a social worker emphasises that behind these tin walls is not only misery but also joy. Olga Rosso, a middle-class pensioner from the organisation, sees things differently: 'Here in the slums, people are unemployed and do nothing. They should definitely have water, but it should not be at our expense; nor should a French company earn enormous sums on it.' She cannot herself afford to pay for sewerage pipes to be connected to her house. Life is not as it was previously. The government has reduced pensions and she now only has the equivalent of US$60 a month to live on, having worked for thirty-four years. Olga Rosso regrets that she cannot afford a flush toilet of her own. Official figures show that during the year 2002, 100,000 people fell from the middle classes into neo-poverty.

Water supplies and sewerage services in the town are run by Aguas Provinciales de Santa Fe (APSF). The French company Suez owns over half of the shares via its subsidiary, Ondeo. In 1996 the Inter-American Development Bank (IDB) contributed with loans amounting to $85 million; the total cost of the project was

$219 million. The Association has organised a series of protests against the company.

Alberto Muñoz is an electrician and one of many committed people. He maintains that the company has provided the informal settlements with water only because the municipality made a financial contribution. The company does not bother to develop the sewerage system because it is not profitable enough, he adds. Muñoz worked for the public water utility. When it was privatised, he left. Water charges are estimated according to the size of buildings. Alberto Muñoz wants no part in a system where people are forced to pay more for water and sewerage when their homes have been renovated or enlarged. Those who have henhouses also have to pay more. Owners of small shops are forced to pay for water even if they do not use it. He shows me a photo of himself standing before the Eiffel Tower in Paris, protesting against Suez, which has its head office in the city. The next time we meet he has gathered some thirty people from consumer and neighbourhood organisations – ecologists, students, pensioners and ordinary workers. However, there is no representative from the trade union at the water company; the employees, its members, own 10 per cent of the shares. Everyone has a story. Gloria Fumagelli owes over $140 because she has not been able to afford to pay her water bills since they were increased. She was suddenly asked to pay for water in a garage with a tap, which is never used.

APSF established itself in Santa Fe in 1995 with a thirty-year contract. Since then the contract been renegotiated, water charges have increased, and there has been less investment than the contract specifies. In addition, charges for installing both water and drainage have increased sharply. 'If people do not pay their bills on time, they are liable to pay fines.' Indeed, Muñoz maintains that the company can take possession of the house of a debtor, though I cannot get confirmation of this. Nevertheless, the company has made some improvements. In 1995, 1.6 million homes were connected to water and 0.8 million to the sewerage system. In 2000, comparative figures were 1.8 million and 1.2 million respectively.

In December 2000, agreement was reached with the government to increase charges by 10 per cent by 2005, and to defer investments. This meant, in turn, that expansion of the sewerage network would not proceed as first envisaged. And this despite the fact that connection fees for both water and sewerage have increased. In 2002, APSF claimed it had invested $250 million in the first six years, but according to the original contract, the company ought to have invested $356 million. Investment was thus close to 30 per cent lower than first specified.

In the end, the Association for the Right to Water had had enough and acted: 7,000 activists campaigned for a referendum to get rid of the company. They then organised the voting, overseeing 1,500 ballot boxes. The result: 230,000 people wanted the company to leave, and only 434 voted for its retention. Alberto Muñoz regards referenda as a valid means of putting pressure on politicians. He talks warmly about a publicly owned water company in Porto Alegre, where people participate in decision-making. This is what he wants in Rosario.

The settlements of Buenos Aires

I travel on, to the capital city of Buenos Aires, 300 kilometres south of Rosario. In the twilight the sun glows red over the pampas. The grassy plains are vast, impressive and desolate. As we drive into the city, tin shanties line the highway; just behind them rise tall skyscrapers, huge office blocks and luxury hotels. Poverty and riches coexist cheek by jowl. Three out of ten Argentinians still lack running water in their homes, while the rich of Buenos Aires easily consume an average 500 litres a day, twice as much as in Europe. In the outer suburbs of Buenos Aires, informal settlements without water are growing, although some areas are now beginning to be connected to the system.

A consortium of mainly foreign companies, Aguas Argentina, operates the water and sewerage services in Buenos Aires. The largest shareholder is Suez. In the early years of privatisation, Aguas Argentinas made no effort to provide the poor with a water system. However, forty projects, under the leadership of Alexandre Brailowsky, are now under way in low-income settlements. Brailowsky has a medical background and he has previously worked for Médecins sans Frontières in Guatemala, Mexico, Kenya, Angola and Haiti. In Haiti he worked for a French organisation that gave technological support to the public water utility. Since the year 2000, he has been employed by Aguas Argentinas.

He says it is easy for Europeans who have access to water every day to come and criticise, and claims that Suez has even contributed to democratisation in the country. Before Aguas Argentinas took over operations, clients would phone the public company over and over again without anything happening. It took a long time for them to fix a fault.

We travel to a poor area, Quilmes, on the outskirts of the city. The road is so poor that the car tyres sink deep into the mud. There have been floods here. People sought shelter in a church, when their homes disappeared under water. If they had not been so poor, they would never have built their homes here. As we squelch around in the mud Brailowsky comments: 'The alternative people had previously was illicitly to connect pipes from private wells that might be polluted.' He has developed a network of contacts with small non-governmental organisations, including one called the Mothers of Success.

Maria Zaragoza is a member of this organisation. She invites me to a small, draughty house. She has a small kitchen with a fridge; a bookcase acts as a room divider to create a living room of a few square metres. The room is soon filled with curious neighbours. Maria has water now; she offers us maté, which tastes like bitter tea. A cup with a straw does the rounds and in the cold room the warmth from the drink spreads through the body.

On the floor stands a box containing the powdered milk that Maria distributes to families with children. Maria Zaragoza is an energetic woman, and the water project has raised her consciousness. Many of the men are unemployed. Some of the women get a few hours' occasional work as maids. Maria and other women sew, knit and cook food, and sell their produce to finance projects to develop the neighbourhood.

The Suez water project involves cooperation between the municipality, the province, non-governmental organisations, and the company. The citizens have themselves dug and laid the water mains. They pay through their own work and thus reduce the installation costs. For larger projects a firm is employed that is paid by the province and works under the management of Aguas Argentinas. Households repay the costs of the connection to the province over five years, a little over US$200 each. Those who cannot afford to pay the full water charges receive a subsidy.

Aguas Argentinas has been given tax breaks; the revenue the company would have paid is instead invested in the water network. Members of non-governmental organizations collect the money that consumers pay for the water. For this, they get paid. You could risk your life, going in as a stranger and demanding money for water.

'A connection to the water system means so much to the people living here that they are really reliable in paying their bills', says Alexandre Brailowsky. He is without a doubt very committed to his projects. The public authorities have tended to ignore these informal settlements, according to Brailowsky, not least because inhabitants have illegally occupied land. To extend water provision implies endorsement of their land occupation.

I later learn that people in the community had to fight for water supply. Local politicians, non-governmental organisations, inhabitants all contributed, and many put in work themselves. A report from UN–Habitat confirms that after a long struggle several low-income settlements were successful in negotiating water provision. They were assisted by NGOs and in some cases were supported by the local mayor.

The British NGOs WaterAid and Tearfund have written a report on three very vulnerable women in other informal settlements in Buenos Aires and of their hard struggle to get water. One of them is Elisa. Her father abandoned the family when she was 8 years old. She was harassed and beaten by her brothers. She had a child when she was 16. She and her husband then occupied a piece of land in San Fernando in the municipality of San Martin, 35 kilometres from the centre of Buenos Aires. Here 400 families live in wretched houses. The inhabitants of the informal settlements live by the Reconquista river. It is browny-black with refuse and pollution from households and an abattoir in the vicinity. The river is lined with rubbish. When it rains, the river overflows its banks. Effluent runs in the ditches.

Elisa has enormous strength and willpower. Despite humiliation and persecution, she succeeded in getting the municipality and Aguas Argentinas to provide the settlement with water. She did this by organising a neighbourhood association that demanded that the municipality install water. So far as the city council was concerned, San Martin did not even exist on paper. Elisa also had to struggle against management at the nearby abattoir and meat factory, which wanted access to the land. She was threatened by telephone and persecuted, but did not give way.

When she approached the municipal offices she was treated like dirt, she says. During one visit, a representative of Aguas Argentinas screamed at her: 'You do not know the value of every drop of water nor the cost involved for the company.' Elisa calmly replied, 'We do not want you to give us water. Sell the service to us; we want water, since without water we cannot live.' The company regarded it as too risky to supply water to the squatters without guarantees from the municipality. In the end, Elisa and her associates threatened to sue the municipality. They won the day. Alexandre Brailowsky later informs me that Aguas Argentinas is extending the water network to one area after another and has started working with a cooperative, Tenth December, in San Martin.

For those who live in informal settlements, access to water is still a serious problem. The families who occupy land are often not registered and have no address. Private companies use this as the pretext not to install water and sewerage. Yet the reverse can also occur: the company will select an informal settlement and install water. Residents then have a greater chance of obtaining legal tenure. However, this is producing a situation where the company, rather than the municipality or province, takes the decisions regarding how and in which way the city should grow.

A private company may also decide whether to extend the network early or at the end of the contract, which is operative for a thirty-year period. There may be good reasons to delay new investments. Slum areas usually lie far from the established water networks. Houses are erected in higgledy-piggledy fashion, without any town planning. The company may be unsure of the viability of investments.

The flagship of privatisation is sinking

Alexandre Brailowsky explains that he plans to continue his projects. Aguas Argentinas is now working at a loss, unlike in previous years, and it is questionable whether the company will be able to complete the extension of water supplies and sanitation to the informal settlements. The losses racked up in Argentina are a dark spot in Suez's annual results for 2002. Nothing worked out as envisaged. The managing director, Jean Bernard Lemire, appears to face a daunting task. He must reorganise the company's finances in the utter chaos of an Argentina in which people demonstrate and smash shop windows in sheer anger and frustration, at a time when the domestic currency has lost its value.

'Those who are against globalisation do not think that we should make any profit. Yet profits are necessary to be able to undertake any investments. No bank will give credit if you are not able to repay. Our profit is a guarantee for bankers of our ability to repay in the future', Lemire says. When I later meet him at the magnificent water utility in Buenos Aires, he tells me to be careful about what I write, as the activists can manipulate information.

In 1991, a domestic currency board was introduced, pegging the peso to the dollar. This link was abandoned in January 2002, after a devaluation crisis the previous month. Domestic consumers pay their bills in pesos, which lost 70 per cent of their value after the crash. Aguas Argentinas has to pay its debts in dollars. A clause in the consumer contract states that in the event of a currency change Aguas Argentinas will still be paid the dollar value. Thus the currency risk is transferred to the user, thereby safeguarding the company's profits. The 2002 economic crash was so serious, however, that it was not possible to implement the clause.

In the wake of the crash, food prices have risen and increases in electricity, telephone and water tariffs are likely. That is what the IMF has demanded if Argentina is to be granted more loans. It is also what Aguas Argentinas requires if it is to reorganise its finances. If the company does not resolve the issues, it will have trouble with its shareholders.

We should remind ourselves that this is the very project that the World Bank had hitherto regarded as an overwhelming success – a model for private company control of water distribution and sewage treatment. Aguas Argentinas took control of the management of the public water utility in Buenos Aires, one of the largest in the world, in 1993. Situated close to Rio de la Plata, the works boasts impressive buildings and fine architecture. The sand-filled basins through which water is filtered in the cleaning process are enormous. However, the pipes are rusty, and grass is growing on the cracked stone steps. Steam-driven machines from 1913 have been saved for posterity; French and German water pumps have been renovated. Water flows from the River Plate through enormous pipes. In a technologically advanced control room, information on the water supply and pipe system for the whole of Buenos Aires is displayed and monitored.

An engineer explains what it was like before 1993, when there was but a single computer: 'Twenty-six of us competed for access to that computer. The cars were in an abysmal condition. There was an old Ford Falcon, which was always breaking down. The pipe network was so worn out that it was not always possible to close off the water to make repairs. The state-owned water utility, Obras Sanitarias de la Nación (OSN), was run by politicians who pumped money out of the utility rather than making investments. Top management appointments were political.' No one want to return to those times.

Winners and losers in the frenzy of privatisation

Given the scale of the contract, only the largest companies in the world were eligible to bid: 10 million people had to be supplied with potable water and the winner had to have a proven track record and be financially secure. Aguas Argentinas won the contract. The company promised to reduce water tariffs by 26.9 per cent. Before the tendering process, prices had sharply risen twice, by 25 and then 29 per cent. This made it easier for the company to reduce them later.

Suez is the majority shareholder in Aguas Argentinas, but Aguas de Barcelona, Veolia Environnement (Vivendi), Banco de Galicia, Anglian Water and International Finance Corporation (IFC), part of the World Bank group, all have holdings. In addition, 10 per cents of the share are owned by the employees, administered by the trade union.

The public company was not given the financial support to manage the utility. Aguas Argentinas, on the other hand, was guaranteed substantial loans from the World Bank's IFC, and from other banks. The Argentinian government acted like the Thatcher government in Great Britain: it withheld investment from the public sector. Consequently there were no resources to maintain the water network.

Under the old dispensation, a great deal of water was wasted. The wealthier consumers used an average of 352 litres of water per day, compared with 173 litres in Santiago in Chile, for example. Some 20 per cent of bills were never paid. The company was overstaffed: there were eight workers per 1,000 connections in Buenos Aires, compared to only two per 1,000 in Santiago.

There are many examples of badly run public companies during this time. An Argentinian friend tells me he had to wait four months in 1987 for a telephone line to be installed. He spent a month complaining, without result. In the end he took advantage of the black market: a line was installed in a few hours, once money had changed hands.

Critics maintain that the government, with President Carlos Menem at the helm, intentionally permitted public companies to decay further, to ease the way for privatisation. There was no direct opposition to privatisation when Menem came to power in 1989, and polls showed only 16 per cent against. By 1997 this figure had increased to over 50 per cent. Menem privatised public companies at a rapid rate: a national circus, state-owned supermarkets, cinemas, churches, airlines, railways, and the oil company. Many public servants lost their jobs. During the first five years, jobs fell by 60 per cent in the public sector, while those in a position to enrich themselves by buying and selling shares did so. It was the same pattern as Great Britain. An example is the Soldati group, a family that earned huge sums by the early buying of shares in privatised companies and selling them once values had risen. By buying into Aguas Argentinas in this way, Soldati earned $100 million on the sale of its stock, according to the official regulatory agency ETOSS (Ente Tripartito de Obras de Servicos de Saneamiento – Tripartite Entity for Sanitary Services).

Even World Bank experts expressed surprise that the process of privatisation of water supplies and sanitation in Argentina should be so rapid. In Chile and Peru, for example, politicians took more time. Peru had intended to put the water services in Lima under the control of a private company, but then changed its mind. In the period that witnessed this rethink, Menem had already privatised the telephone company, electricity and gas; only water and sewerage remained. Privatisation was expected to generate new capital and reduce debts in the national budget.

'A certain flexibility must exist in a contract'

Those who gained most when Aguas Argentinas decreased tariffs in Buenos Aires were those in the high- and middle-income brackets. Those without water could not afford to install it. The company offered the latter group a two-year loan to cover the infrastructure charge, to be repaid monthly at an interest rate of 12 per cent. This worked out to about US$44 per month, an enormous sum for people with an average monthly income of between $200 and $245. Consequently, many still could not afford the connection. Instead they fetched their water from contaminated wells, where the water was unfit for human consumption; this then increased the spread of waterborne diseases. Hitherto there had been no infrastructure charge: society had borne the cost of new connections.

Furthermore, the scale of tariffs was so complex that the company could exploit it to its own advantage. As in Rosario, charges were determined by the size of apartment, its position, the type of building and its age. It became quite impossible for the consumer to assess whether the tariff was correct. Buildings were photographed and classified, adding to the cost. The regulator ETOSS became critical of the process. Nevertheless, the company succeeded in reclassifying apartments: 425,000 users received higher water bills. Then meters were installed, which increased the costs for households on low incomes with a large family.

As early as 1994, Aguas Argentinas made a bid to renegotiate the contract. There are those who suggest that private companies deliberately make a low bid to win a concession, calculating on small gains at the beginning while banking on being able to renegotiate the contract later. Managing director Jean Bernard Lemire rejects this notion on the case of Aguas Argentinas. He claims that the information available during the bidding process was inadequate: Aguas Argentinas was not informed of the poor state of the water company, so the reality greeting the managers came as a complete surprise. This is why the situation developed as it did. 'A certain flexibility must exist in a contract', he says. The story of subsequent to-ing and fro-ing could fill a book.

Though ETOSS was intended to regulate the company and ensure it lived up to its commitments, the organisation was weak, and rent by internal division. It was a new public authority staffed by officials from the previous public water utility, who had little insight into the functioning of a foreign profit-making company. It also meant that ETOSS sometimes intervened arbitrarily. In addition, the organisation was subjected to political pressure. For example, the mayor of Buenos Aires wanted to build a highway, so he promised to resettle the residents of a shanty town blocking the route of the highway. He demanded that Aguas Argentinas extend the water and sewerage networks to the new settlement. The company in turn demanded an increase in the water tariff to cover the unforeseen costs.

The first rise in tariffs, of 13.5 per cent, came in 1994. Connection fees and charges for water and sanitation increased further, which ruled out the possibility of the poor being able to access clean water. ETOSS succeeded in reducing the level of charges, but the new prices were still regarded as too high.

Within three years, Aguas Argentinas declared that its revenues were $217 million lower than anticipated and that they again wanted to renegotiate the contract with ETOSS. Since Aguas Argentinas had not made the stipulated level of investment, ETOSS levied penalties on the company. The company's response was to wriggle out of paying the fines. When the parties were unable to agree, two federal ministries reached a deal directly with the company, bypassing ETOSS.

The renegotiation led to replacement of the charges for extending the water and sewerage network with a general solidarity tariff for those already connected. An environmental fee was also levied, with a 19 per cent increase in bills. The move was not popular. Some consumers took the company to court. For those in the slums the new tariff system was more acceptable. A reduced connection fee was introduced; new consumers were able to take out a loan for this, with a repayment of only $4 per month.

At the same time, the company reduced its obligations, cutting expansion targets for the first five-year plan by about 15 per cent for water and 13 per cent for sewerage. The fines levied by ETOSS were cancelled. The original concession agreement had stipulated that the company would be paid only when it had expanded the network and the work was complete. Under the new agreement, the company was paid in advance!

In 1998, when Aguas Argentinas demanded a further tariff increase of 11 per cent, both the public and ETOSS again raised objections. The government intervened and set a ceiling of 4.6 per cent. The debate began to make waves in the press. Complaints from consumers have certainly increased, although this is partly as a result of improved channels of communication. In 1992, 43,800 complaints were received. In 1995 the figure was over 143,000. Dealing with complaints, however, now takes much less time: whereas previously customers might wait for a month, complaints are now dealt with in 48 hours.

Continuing losses and profits

Prior to the bidding for the contract, the workforce was reduced
by 1,670 through 'voluntary redundancy' combined with a retire-
ment package. Aguas Argentinas then cut a further 2,000 staff in
the early period of the concession. Jean Bernard Lemire claims
that the public utility used to lay down five kilometres of pipes
every year. With a considerably reduced workforce, Aguas Argentinas now achieves this each day. The employees were simply
unproductive under the old system, according to Lemire. When
Aguas Argentinas took over, all former employees were asked to
report for work. Some 500 apparently never turned up; among
these a number were found to be fictitious.

What, then, has Aguas Argentinas succeeded in doing? First,
it has set up a more efficient system for bill payment. Following a change in the law, water supply can now be cut in the
case of non-payment. Second, according to Suez, the number
of people with access to drinking water has increased by more
than 2 million since 1993, and 1.1 million more are connected
to the sewerage network. Do the company's claims stand up?
Well, between 1993 and 1998 Aguas Argentinas did indeed extend
the water network. However, only 54 per cent of the consumer
connections stipulated by the concession actually took place;
only 43 per cent of the promised connections to the sewerage
system were fulfilled. This failure to achieve targets is revealed
in a report by the Public Services International Research Unit
(PSIRU) in London. Although the company had undertaken to
invest about $1,289 million, the total spent was less than half
that, only $543 million.

On occasion, the French ambassador has seen fit to intervene
when the company has been facing difficulties. In February 2002,
for example, the ambassador Paul Dijou and the management of
Aguas Argentinas had a private meeting with the deputy minister

of finance. Suez wanted to postpone investments that had been negotiated as recently as 2001.

Jean Bernard Lemire is determined to resolve the financial crisis of Aguas Argentinas: 'We have taken risks by investing. Future profits are necessary, otherwise we cannot succeed', he says. 'In 2003 we need to raise 400 million pesos to bridge the gap between revenues, costs and investments. This is supposed to be covered by a slightly higher tariff. The impact of inflation and devaluation, however, is likely to increase the gap to around 1.7 million pesos.' 'If the operating conditions are so rigorous', I ask him, 'is there any likelihood of your company remaining?' 'Yes, this is the basic assumption', he replies. The chairman and CEO of Suez in Paris, Gérard Méstrallet, had given him the task, he tells me. 'I asked him, "Do I go to Argentina to close down the business or to develop it?" He answered, "Within 4–5 years, we should be able to say that we went through a crisis and that we are world class experts in resolving such crises, notwithstanding the difficulties."'

The crisis has forced the company to negotiate with the banks to pay interest only on its loans; to ask the government to compensate it to the tune of 70 million pesos for unpaid bills; and to propose further tariff hikes. Aguas Argentina wants to concentrate exclusively on operations and maintenance, with investment postponed. 'We are in big trouble if the government does not pay', says Lemire. He tells me that the water bills are in fact lower than all other services, like the Internet and cable television. Nevertheless, he says he understands consumers' reaction, since food prices have risen so much, and at the same time that salaries have been frozen. He also concedes that the company has failed to communicate with its customers. 'They need to understand the problems we face.' On the positive side, he concludes, 'a public survey indicates that 80 per cent of our customers are satisfied with the service.'

The employees, for their part, seem to have a tough time. There have been no lay-offs, but the company has refused increased wages. As they are partners in the company, the trade union's hands are tied. Carlos Ries, deputy secretary of the union El Sindicato de Trabajadores de Obras Sanitarias, defends the policy. 'We had to make major compromises when our state-owned utility went private', he says. 'When the government decided to privatise, what could we do? A special manager in the company represents the workers' interests. His goal is to make a success of Aguas Argentinas. That is also the union's goal, otherwise unemployment will increase.'

Ries agrees that there is a conflict of interests, since the union's role is both to defend its members' interests and to take responsibility for the company's growth. He does say that he will not accept any more job losses, or a further rise in water tariffs.

Shortly afterwards I meet Julio Godio in the government building Casa Rosada. He is a well-known researcher and adviser on labour market questions and has written several books on Argentina's labour movement. He talks with empathy about the economic, social and cultural crises in Argentina, and observes that the political parties are not particularly well organised. He adds that the context is a global crisis in which the Bretton Woods treaty of 1944 has been forgotten – that is, the World Bank and IMF were created to contribute to international economic development. 'The original idea disappeared en route. Private companies must understand our situation. If they are to remain here, they must contribute to development in the country.' He says that there can be no return to the old order.

The current agenda demands that new policies relating to private companies be drawn up. 'They must participate in development of our labour force, through growing production and reasonable wages. Only then can they discuss raising water tariffs. With a population lacking the basic necessities of life, I don't know what kind of market the companies are expecting.' He maintains that regulation of the companies is poor; they have done whatever they wanted to, on the whole. 'In other countries they cannot behave in this way, since there are functioning political institutions that set limits for them. They must adapt to the existing regulations. Now the water company refers to the economic crisis and says it cannot keep its promises to invest. The fact is that it did not keep its earlier promises, either.'

Julio Godio believes it is important to engage in a degree of self-criticism within the country. 'Over the years the various governments have adopted wrong policies and assumed that a capitalist system would develop the country. In reality, everyone works to promote their own interests, resulting in major economic gaps among the population. The labour movement has a responsibility to mobilise its own forces.'

The story of Aguas Argentina continues. At the beginning of 2004, I read in the *Buenos Aires Herald* that ETOSS has again penalised the company, fining it several million pesos. This has been the pattern every year since 1999. The company is criticised for low water pressure and for providing an unreliable service. The Argentinian government has refused to approve any tariff increases despite pressure, including from the French government. The reason given is that the company previously made high profits and failed to make the promised investments.

The government is awaiting presentation of the company's investment plan. The company, in turn, has launched arbitration procedures at the World Bank's ICSID; it points to a clause in the contract which guarantees it fair remuneration on capital invested. Uncertainties remain in Buenos Aires, according to Suez. An interim agreement relating solely to the year 2004 has been reached, laying down the principles for renegotiating the contract.

Suez has had problems in other places as well. In 2004 in Puerto Rico, the contract between the company and the government has collapsed. Suez's subsidiary Ondeo demanded $93 million from the government after the company made losses due to incorrect information supplied about conditions. The government's response was to restore the water service operation as a public utility. In Manaus in Brazil, meanwhile, three legal cases have been pending against the company, relating to the discharge of untreated wastewater, the invoicing process and price increases.

One is forced to conclude that many problems have arisen following the privatisation of water supplies, even though the companies involved have provided many more people with water. Yet is this not their prime responsibility, given that they receive loans from the World Bank and other lenders in order to undertake a certain level of investment under the terms of the contract? In the period 1994–2000, Aguas Argentinas's profit in Buenos Aires was on average 19 per cent after taxes. The profit margin in the water sector in the USA is between 6.5 and 12 per cent.

Problems in Jakarta and Manila

In its annual report of 2003, Suez states that negotiations led to significant price increases in Jakarta in Indonesia, even though they were contested by consumer associations. The outcome of negotiations to enable the company to meet its profitability expectations under the contract remained uncertain. However, the administration subsequently accepted the proposal from Suez and charges were increased by 40 per cent, according to the *Jakarta Post*.

The British company Thames Water (now owned by the German RWE) also operates in Jakarta. In 1998, in the eastern part of the city, Thames Water and a local partner formed a consortium. There was no bidding procedure. The local partner was a son of the former president Suharto. When Suharto was replaced, Thames Water took over most of his son's shares.

In 2003, the UK ambassador asked the president of Indonesia to put pressure on Jakarta city to allow Thames Water to increase water prices by 20 per cent, otherwise the company would leave the country. According to a report by Endah Shofiani at the Royal Institute of Technology in Stockholm, privatisation in Jakarta had been rushed into, without establishment of an existing regulatory framework. The Asian economic crisis resulted in renegotiation of the contract, as due to the increase in the US dollar exchange rate and high inflation, targets could not be met. Shofiani recommends that future water privatisations must establish an independent regulatory body, which is crucial to ensuring an efficient water supply. They must also improve water production and reduce water losses – critical factors given that revenue collected is based solely on the volume of water sold. The only other means of increasing revenue is of course to raise the water tariffs paid by consumers.

In Manila in the Philippines, Suez attempted to withdraw. However, an arbitration tribunal ruled that the concession contract could not be terminated. The company, called Maynilad, was hit by the currency devaluation, and claimed that it lost 5 billion pesos in late 1997. What is more, it complains that its bulk water supply is insufficient and that it had to absorb the debts of the public authority.

Negotiations have continued, but Suez intends to reduce its stake in the company (currently 40 per cent), which it operates in partnership with the local company Benpres (which owns 60 per cent). The consortium was not permitted by the government to increase tariffs and claims that it can therefore no longer make a profit. The water regulation agency meanwhile ordered Maynilad to stop billing consumers to cover its foreign exchange losses (it was charging an additional 4.21 pesos per cubic metre). The government had hitherto granted permission for six tariff increases and allowed a number of other obligations to be negotiated away. In the end, though, the regulatory authority had had enough.

Before Suez's arrival, the public water company had increased charges from 6.43 pesos to 8.78 pesos. Suez undertook to reduce charges. Nevertheless, by 2002 the tariff had instead increased to 15.46 pesos. The company claims that more than 2 million people have been connected to the water system, but the regulatory agency rejects this figure.

Critics say that the failure cannot be blamed solely on the currency devaluation, pointing to overoptimistic calculations and a lack of efficiency. Maynilad, for example, has failed to attend to leakage, which in fact increased between 1998 and 2002. In five years, the company lost 36 billion pesos due to leaks and water theft, which indicates the existence of a thriving black market for stolen water.

Furthermore, according to Joan Carling, chairperson of the Cordillera Peoples' Alliance in the Philippines, rich communities receive a 24-hour supply, while several poor communities have erratic supplies.

Water and sanitation services were handed over to private companies following a recommendation from the International Finance Corporation, within the World Bank. The World Bank and the Asian Development Bank played a significant role, using privatisation as a condition for further loans, and contracting French consultants to study how the public utility could be privatised.

8

The story in South Africa

It is easy to waste water if it's readily available. I heard of women who would wash clothes at municipal standpipes in an unofficial settlement in Cape Town and chat while water flows over the clothes and out of the washtub. At that time the water shortage in many parts of South Africa was so severe that President Mbeki declared a state of emergency in several provinces. Only 30 out of 180 countries in the world have less water per person than South Africa.

People who allow water to pour from the tap clearly need to be taught how to use the resource efficiently. There is something in the argument that, to further reduce waste, water should have a price – a reasonable price that people can afford to pay, as access to potable water ought to be a human right.

Activists in South Africa ask how the government can afford to buy military planes when it is unable to supply its citizens with water. There are devastating examples in South Africa of what happens when consumers must pay the full cost of water without any state subsidies. The demand for water operators to cover their costs is now applied even within the public sector. With the high unemployment rate in South Africa, many quite simply cannot afford to pay for water and sanitation. There are up to a million fewer job opportunities than in the early 1990s; they have been lost mainly in mining, agriculture and industry.

David Shezi found himself in a prison cell a while ago. He had stolen water for his eight children in KwaZulu–Natal, as he could not bear the humiliation of seeing his children having to beg for water. A water seller reported him. Shezi earned 100 rand a month selling fruit and vegetables. He managed to save 500 rand to install water, but later could not afford to pay the bill, since he also had to pay for food and school fees. His water was cut off, but he made an illegal connection to the supply pipes, which was later discovered.

There is a history of poor payment rates for public services in South Africa, a pattern that cannot be changed overnight. Consumers often cannot or sometimes choose not to pay; so water meters have been installed in many areas. (Such meters are prohibited in Britain.) Customers buy water in advance with a card, input a code in the meter, and are credited with a certain number of litres of water. When the credits on the card are used up, they buy a new one. Some meters have been vandalised; others no longer work. People have become so angry that they have burnt tyres and thrown petrol at workers from the company who have come to cut off their water. To reduce intimidation by the community, water company employees are sometimes accompanied by security guards.

Researchers have shown statistically that 10 million people have had their water cut off since 1994, some for a short time, others for several months. This has led to a lively debate. The research was condemned by Ronnie Kasrils, minister of water affairs and forestry between 1999 and 2004, who called the researchers 'foolish revolutionaries'. To cut off access to water for those who do not pay is one way of trying to force them to do so. Some, however, resort to fetching water from a nearby source, like a

dam or river, which is often contaminated. Others reconnect the
water themselves – illegally, at night.

In 2000, a cholera epidemic broke out in rural areas of
KwaZulu–Natal. It left 265 people dead, and 120,000 seriously
ill, according to the official figures. Unofficial sources claim many
more were affected. Hospitals were full; the cost was high. If it
is a choice between food and water, people choose food and
hope that water from rivers and other sources will not be too
polluted.

Minister Kasrils admitted that people are so poor in many
areas that they cannot afford to pay, if water operations are made
to cover their own costs. 'I saw a woman, a baby tied to her
back, digging a hole near the bank of the river to fetch water.
She could not afford to use water from the tap', he said in one
speech. This influenced him in 2001 to introduce a lifeline: to
distribute 6,000 litres of water per household per month free
of charge. Municipalities have difficulty in implementing the
new regulations, however. By the end of 2002, 57 per cent of
the population had access to free water, but only a third of the
poorest had a supply.

This is despite the fact that it is enshrined in the constitution
that everyone has the right to water. The inequalities in South
Africa are noticeable, and relate to whether people are black or
white. Those who lack sanitation are all black households. In
former times, 60,000 white farmers consumed 60 per cent of the
country's water assets, while millions of blacks had no potable
water. According to Kasrils, 12 million people had no water
supply in 1994. 'Some faced the terror of fetching water from
crocodile-infested rivers – on the other side of the fence white
South Africans had sources equal to the best of Europe, full flush
toilets, baths and taps, and even swimming pools. We were two
worlds in one country', he said. Since the ANC came to power in
1994, more than 7 million people have been provided with piped

water. This means that at least 5 million people are still fetching water from unacceptable sources like rivers and springs.

Solidarity out of suffering

The following story shows that it is not always easy to provide consumers with water and sanitation. Steve Bloomfield and John Kidd from the British trade union Unison visited employees at South Africa's water and sewage treatment plants in 2002 to demonstrate their solidarity and develop cooperation between the two unions. The trip was a joint undertaking with representatives of War on Want. This is how they describe their visit in a booklet published by War on Want and Unison:

> The type of poverty we witnessed was typified at Embalenhle Sewerage plant in Mpumalanga, where a community of 4,000 people live almost on top of the plant. Embalenhle consists of thousands of 'houses' – scraps of rusting metal and wood. Sanitation is provided by the 'bucket system' – 14 members of the local community are responsible for disposing of the human waste generated, using only buckets. When the tractors that pick up the buckets break down, they are not repaired immediately. Some of the buckets are broken. It was clear that the system was greatly in need of further investment, but in a community where more than 75 per cent of adults are unemployed, with no source of alternative income, it is impossible to construct an economically viable case to raise more funds from the community.

Water and sanitation had been privatised, but community pressure forced the local council to retake control in 1997.

> Standpipes had been installed but they were fitted with washers which cut off the water if the particular standpipe was being over-utilised.... Following privatisation, pension fund and medical entitlement were cut, and workers were de-unionised. Although the union successfully sued the company for pension

cuts, the workers only received one-quarter of the amount awarded when the company liquidated.

Their account continues:

> The really distressing fact is that just half an hour's drive away, some of the richest corporations in the world own lavish buildings shaped like diamonds, aeroplanes, even the Taj Mahal. White people enjoy a western lifestyle, complete with swimming pools and unrestricted water access.

The group journeyed on to Nelspruit, further north, where Biwater (now Cascal), a British/Dutch multinational, had signed a thirty-year contract to operate water and sanitation. Participants describe their experiences:

> Many people complained to us that under the new system they were being charged very high tariffs for water and sanitation, without even enjoying a constant supply of water. As an example, when we arrived, the Zwelitsha community was on its fourth day without water, and Matsulu community members were forced to hire cars to drive 5 km to collect water. Nearly 60 workers at a plumbing company – a Biwater subcontractor – were found to be earning only R150 (roughly £11) per week, while being forced to work in ragged clothing, not being paid proper insurance and not receiving payslips.
>
> Workers complained of no uniforms or safety clothing – many workers wore worn ripped t-shirts and worn out trousers. Many workers were employed on temporary contracts. Sub-contracted/temporary workers could not be unionised. Cutting off water had been sub-contracted to a local operator. In terms of pay, most workers received R1,380, (£98) per month, but temporary workers received R600 (£43).

At another water depot, the men met a worker who had been working for three years as a temporary employee, and thus was not entitled to sick pay or other benefits.

John and Steve continued with the group to Odi on the outskirts of Pretoria, where water distribution and sewage treatment are operated jointly by the state and the municipality. This was also not functioning. In one school with more than 700 pupils, the teachers had been forced to shut the toilets.

The school owed around 96,000 rand (roughly $7,000) in water bills. Pupils had been told to bring their own water to school, but many did not have water at home. Although the South African constitution specifies that everyone is entitled to a basic water service, set at 6,000 litres, residents said that they are not receiving this and had been forced to make illegal connections.

The next stop was Johannesburg, where Suez–Ondeo had been awarded a five-year management contract for the water utility.

Whilst working conditions were visibly better, employees stressed that since profit became the bottom line, cost-cutting wherever possible had become normal. The results were obvious enough – pipes visibly spewing water into the street, sometimes for several weeks, ultimately costing more than was saved. Another worker told us: 'They don't provide the necessary tools for the job', every additional item had to be bargained over.

This was only a small part of the group's story.

In Newcastle, employees of Northumbrian Water have begun to build up contacts with colleagues in Johannesburg, a twinning arrangement between union branches. All work for Suez. The idea is that if companies operate on a global level, then workers must cooperate globally, so that their rights cannot be undermined worldwide. Since then, Suez has sold 75 per cent of its share in the company in Newcastle to improve its accounts.

Ability to pay comes before need

In South Africa, six contracts have been signed with private companies since 1992. This has led to difficulties for users, employees and the company itself. Details are given in a research report on the Nelspruit Water Concession, undertaken by Dr Laila Smith and others within the Centre for Policy Studies. They describe what has happened in Nelspruit.

From the mid-1970s onwards, local authorities have been expected to provide consumers with cheap, good-quality water while having to cope with cuts in fiscal transfers from national governments. When the municipalities failed to supply people with water, increased private-sector participation was seen as the solution. The private sector has been expected to provide new capital, to reduce costs, and to extend services. Liberalisation has led to a new approach to water supply. Formerly, to get access to water, need was the vital factor; today the ability to pay is crucial.

In 1999, the Nelspruit Local Authority contracted the British-based multinational Biwater to provide its water services for the next thirty years. This was the first and most extensive privatisation of water in the country. It includes large sections of Mpumulanga province. Here, in the former 'homeland' of KaNgwane, many people are very poor. In some areas 40 per cent of households have incomes below 6,000 rand per year, which is below the poverty line. In addition, there is high unemployment, often over 30 per cent.

To extend services, the Development Bank of South Africa (DBSA) estimated that it would cost local authorities about 250 million rand, a huge sum in comparison with the 8.5 million rand allocated to water and sanitation in the council budget. Municipalities in the Nelspruit area applied to the provincial and national governments for economic support, but were turned down. The DBSA stepped in, to help prepare the tender documents. The contract was signed with Biwater despite community, labour and political opposition.

The company took on the existing employees, but new staff are recruited only on temporary contracts. Two trade unions represent

the staff. One is the Independent Municipal and Allied Trade
Union (IMATU), which traditionally represents white employees,
often managers. The other is the South African Municipal Workers Union (SAMWU), which has historically represented black
labourers. SAMWU opposes privatisation, regards water as a human
right, and has expressed the fear that a private company would
try to make undue profits; it accordingly conducted a campaign
against privatisation, while IMATU supported it. SAMWU also
demanded, in connection with the bid, that a public option
should be included and compared with the company's bid, but
the union was ignored. SAMWU members say that the council's
promise that employees would be involved in wage negotiations
during the first five years has not been kept.

Biwater set up a 'labour forum', where employees can voice
their complaints rather than involve their union representatives.
Both trade unions perceive this as a company attempt to discourage
strong unions. The forum serves to create an environment where
workers are reluctant to voice their concerns publicly, they say. For
example, in July 2002, no Biwater employees joined a nationwide
strike against privatisation, despite many having grievances about
wage negotiations.

Cascal, a joint venture between the British Biwater and the
Dutch Nuon, holds 48 per cent of the shares in the Nelspruit
Water Concession. Sivukile, a black empowerment group, bought
a 10 per cent holding. Although Biwater promised to invest, most
of the financing comes from the Development Bank of South
Africa, through a loan of 150 million rand over a seven-year
period.

The greatest challenge for Biwater is that most consumers do
not pay their bills. To persuade them to do so, Biwater cut off water
supplies and removed water meters to prevent illegal reconnections.
This had the opposite effect: more illegal connections were made.
Biwater has subsequently realised that this is the wrong approach

and has begun to adopt a subtler tactic: to reach consumers with information, which has had a more positive effect.

The government's decision to introduce 6.000 litres of free water per household caused the company to react. The provision of free water was not part of the contract. Biwater was thus awarded 2.2 million rand a year in compensation. Nevertheless, when consumers did not pay their bills for use above the free quota, Biwater itself came close to breaking the contract. The company refused to invest in the extension of services to new areas. In one area, for example, only 8 per cent of consumers pay their bills; in another only 35 per cent. Yet not all non-payees are indigent. Civil servants, for example, owe the company 1.3 million rand, since many have chosen to prioritise other expenditures, though they can afford to pay their utility bills. Politicians prefer to focus on other sectors and have not regarded it of prime importance to regulate the concession through the Compliance Monitoring Unit.

To improve communications, a water forum has been set up with consumer representatives, Biwater staff, and local councillors. Why do so many customers not pay their bills? The reasons are complex. Some are dissatisfied with the quality of the service. Others have received an unexpectedly high bill that does not correspond to what they think they have consumed, or complicated billing that does not show how much has been consumed above the free quota. In some areas, consumers are quite simply too poor to pay. When interviewed, pensioners said that they struggled to save water, and still the bill was high. Many are willing to pay, if they can afford it. Others do not pay as an expression of civil disobedience. They are angered by the concessionaire's methods of cutting off water and removing meters. Still other users believe that a basic need like water should simply be satisfied free. They are backed up by political forces who, for ideological reasons support non-payment by consumers, since they agree that water should be free.

The fact that well-paid civil servants do not bother to pay has led the company to talk of a 'culture of non-payment'. The phrase is also applied to the poor, even though through no fault of their own they simply cannot afford to pay.

The report suggests that among the lessons to be learnt is that in communities which have been denied services for decades it may take them more than one generation to understand their responsibilities as users and also the rights they have as citizens.

If communication with the township residents does not improve, a continuing payment boycott would likely mean that the company will implement its threat to withdraw. This would leave the local authority liable for the 50 million rand debt incurred by Biwater through its loans from the Development Bank of South Africa.

It is risky to sign a thirty-year contract when a country is undergoing massive transition, much of it at the local level. For instance, the area included in the new Mbombela local authority, of which Nelspruit is a part, has doubled since the contract was signed, which means that the concessionaire is plagued by an increasing number of illegal connections by those who are not officially covered by the concession.

The writers of the report stress the importance of creating a climate of trust between consumer and the service provider. It is important to improve communication between the local authority, the utility company and consumers by involving customers in the process of water delivery. This can be achieved by cooperating with existing community structures such as women's groups, churches and other organisations. Water bills must be clearer to meet the informational needs of low-income service users. Furthermore, the local authority should identify who cannot afford to pay and earmark subsidies just for them.

Part of the problem lies in a mistaken idea of what private enterprise can achieve. It is expected to take the commercial risks, but the local authority is not free from responsibility, if conditions change and the company can no longer recover costs. Technical solutions do not resolve the problem of poverty. This is a political issue, the report notes. The concessionaire is expected to meet the needs of the poor, but profit and efficiency are not easily reconciled with the patience and the flexibility that are required to ensure that the indigent get water. The private company is not a suitable service provider of water supplies and sanitation in areas of great poverty, the report notes.

Biwater, for its part, describes the concession in Nelspruit as a success story. Traditional political protests have led the company to seek new methods of persuading consumers to pay, from meetings with elected representatives to street theatre. It is gradually being accepted that one should pay, and payments are steadily increasing, says Biwater.

The company says that in the first two years it laid down 91 kilometres of water pipes in urban areas and 8 kilometres in rural areas, 18 kilometres of sewerage pipes in urban areas, and 17 kilometres in rural areas. A growing number of households are being connected to water supplies.

Can the private sector offer a solution in South Africa? Currently feelings are mixed, not only in Nelspruit. Some politicians in the richer cities like Johannesburg and Cape Town are disillusioned with long contracts with private utility companies like electricity and water suppliers. Such contracts see the income from a profit-making operation go to the company rather than be ploughed back into the local authorities. There is a growing awareness within the municipalities that they do not yet have the capacity to regulate and control the companies. Local authorities have in the main simply rid themselves of a difficult area of service delivery without possessing the ability to take appropriate action when the concessionaire does not adequately meet the needs of the poor for water.

Is the pendulum swinging back?

In 1995 a subsidiary of Suez won a ten-year contract in Nkonkobe in the Eastern Cape. The contract was cancelled following a legal judgment in 2001. The mayor explained in a letter to the government that it was impossible for the municipality to pay the 400,000 rand a month in management fees demanded by the foreign company to operate water supplies and sewage treatment. This unreasonable burden prevented the local authority providing service within other sectors. By breaking the contract, the municipality would save over 19 million rand, the mayor explained. It could do so as the council no longer had to pay the management fees during the remaining contract period. The contract could be cancelled because it had not been made public before it came into effect – there was no transparency. Indeed, it contained a clause that prevented public knowledge without the company's agreement. The mayor concluded his letter with the following words: 'The municipality firmly believes that its continued compliance with the terms of the contract would be reckless in the extreme and would amount to an imprudent utilisation of available resources.' The mayor expressed his joy over the High Court decision to nullify the contract.

The fight against privatisation of water supply continues in South Africa. 'We are prepared to die to save water from being privatised', said a union delegate from South Africa at the Third World Water Forum held in March 2003 in Kyoto, Japan. Lance Veotte from SAMWU said in March 2004, that at this stage there have not been any further cases of privatisation. He says that even though it is said that workers are not being affected by privatisation, there has been a clear reduction in the workforce through natural wastage and the engagement of contract/casual staff who can be hired and fired at will.

SAMWU campaigned for free water and got it: 6,000 litres per month for each household, about 25 litres per person per day.

'We are campaigning for 50 litres of free water per person per day and will continue to campaign and mobilise', he says. 'We have a big problem at the moment, as pre-paid water meters are still installed in the poor areas and this is a problem as it allows the councillors to abdicate their responsibility. If you don't have money to pay, you don't have money.'

Mike Muller, director-general of the same department, gave a speech in November 2002 that attracted considerable attention. He spoke of some private concessions that have met with mixed success. He added that, on the other hand, there were some interesting public–public partnerships, where public utilities share their experience and knowledge with those water utilities that need to become more efficient. Another model he discussed was community-based organisations (CBOs), which can undertake management, particularly in small, isolated rural communities. 'Business as usual will not achieve our [UN Millennium] goals', he insisted. He concluded that people were generally willing to shoulder their responsibilities, but too often 'if the "no payment, no access" line is held, people resort to other, unacceptable water sources because they simply cannot afford to pay.'

Muller also maintains that it is more expensive and harder to extend water supplies and sewerage services in poor countries in the Third World than in industrialised countries. The principle that water supplies and sanitation should cover their own costs is a greater challenge in poor communities. Labour is cheaper, but labour costs are usually a relatively small proportion of the total cost. Household incomes can be a hundred times lower in developing countries than in the First World, while consumption is less by a factor of only ten. Muller adds:

If we are going to achieve the Millennium goals we cannot accept as an iron rule that the poor must pay for their services. Now this is a heresy and many will point out that the principles, which I have just torn up, have been internationally agreed in

places such as Dublin. Here we need to be self-critical …
the international water debate has been largely driven outside
the formal multilateral system and the key conclusions reflect
largely the views of the donor community.

A little later he counsels: 'We must not be distracted by that
mind-boggling US$60–160 billion annual additional financing.'
For these figures include funding for far higher levels of service
than those required by successful Third World cities and were used
to promote the potential role of the private sector. He explains:
'Unfortunately, that number has distracted us from the critical
issue of addressing the basic needs of the poor.' He suggests that
some US$10 billion may be needed annually.

Substantial funding flows, which should go to the poor, are
intercepted in favour of the less poor. Meanwhile the aggressive
push by international water and financial interests for private
engagement, has been working to their ultimate detriment.

The pendulum is swinging against too great involvement of
the private sector. Resistance to private engagement is the result,
in part, of the oblivious failure of the private initiative to address
the core challenge of the unserved.

There is a vital role for private expertise and resources in
providing water services. Unfortunately, if that role is literally
forced down the throats of the potential beneficiaries, they often
choke.

Muller suggests that 'Donors and lending agencies should cease
from making private sector involvement a precondition for water
sector support.' Most governments try to make their own decisions.
'Help them to make sound choices, their own choices.' With this
focus, he thinks, 'we may well create conditions in which more
appropriate – and more successful – private intervention may be
developed.'

Mike Muller advises 'OECD countries, their companies,
preferably both, to call for water services to be taken off the

table in GATS and related trade negotiations. This would help to make the point that we are serious about achieving the global objectives and not just pursuing our trade objectives under a benevolent guise.'

PART II

Private solutions:
for and against

9

Companies and their strategies

The model adopted in England and Wales is full privatisation: a private company purchases water assets and runs the operation as a business on a permanent basis. It is not particularly common. Chile and to some extent New Zealand also operate in this way. The French model is the most widespread, and what most think of when the term 'privatisation' is used in connection with the water industry. There are various types of contract:

The *concession contract* operates, for instance, in Buenos Aires in Argentina and in Nelspruit, South Africa. Here a private contractor manages the whole utility, and invests in the maintenance and expansion of the system. The company supposedly takes the commercial risks while the municipality retains ownership of the assets. Such contracts may run for twenty-five, thirty or even forty years or more. In reality, however, a company will ensure that it minimises its risks – for example, by renegotiating the contract before it is due.

Another type is the *lease contract*. Here the revenue is determined by the tariffs. The contractor collects the tariffs, pays a lease fee, and retains the difference. With a *management contract*, responsibility for operation and maintenance transfers to a private company.

The company does not take the risks, as the public sector retains responsibility for investment and expansion. The public sector may also choose to keep control of billing and revenue collection. Such contracts generally run from five to ten years. The municipality pays a fee to the company. A *service contract* is a short-term agreement. The private company takes responsibility for specific tasks, such as installing meters, collecting bills and repairing plumbing. Under a *build–own transfer contract* a private company constructs, say, a sewage treatment plant, and then manages it. At the end of the contract the assets may remain with the private company or be transferred back to the government. The *joint venture*, common in the Czech Republic and Hungary, sees a private company working together with the public sector. A *consortium* works by several companies and interested parties joining together to run a utility. In this way, they do not compete with each other.

When private industry takes over water distribution and sewage treatment, it is as a rule introduced with fanfare and impressive plans regarding the scale of investment and improvement. However, something usually happens to derail the plans, and changes to the contract or agreed schedules follow. A common tactic for a company that wants to enter a market is to make a low bid. The company may even promise to provide service at a lower cost. On occasion, the government will raise charges before the company takes over. This makes it easier to lower the price at the beginning of the operations. The reduction in charges is, however, only an interim measure. After a while, the company will demand to renegotiate of the contract, claiming that costs have arisen. This in turn leads to a rise in water charges. Installation of sewerage facilities is likely to be postponed. A company may have been overoptimistic regarding consumption levels. If it does not make as much money as estimated, it will try to increase charges.

On taking over a contract, companies tend to reduce staffing levels. In Ecuador, for instance, International Water first dismissed all the workers and then hand-picked those it wished to re-employ. This was despite an initial agreement that it would take on most of the employees and train them. It simply changed its position once it had control.

Such employees are often cast into unemployment without social safeguards. In other cases, companies have given severance pay. Although it is true that some state enterprises have indeed been overstaffed, it is equally the case that a smaller payroll means higher profits for companies.

In some cases a contract may have been approved due to bribery. Some municipalities require a form of 'entrance fee' – a practice that has now been forbidden in France. In Budapest, for example, a consortium consisting of Suez and RWE were awarded the contract, not because they were cheapest, but because they agreed to pay 3 billion forints to the city. Their charge for household water was 3 forints per cubic metre higher than another tender. In Latin America, it is also common for a company to pay annual fees.

Logics of the 'free' market

The water industry generally does not invest very much of its own capital. It comes instead largely from the World Bank, development banks and foreign aid agencies. In Buenos Aires, Suez contributed about $30 million at the beginning of a thirty-year contract with Aguas Argentinas. The water company promised to invest $1 billion on improvements. Most of this was raised through loans from the International Finance Corporation of the World Bank, and from other banks, according to a report published in 1999 by the research unit PSIRU. In many cases, in fact, privatisation is undertaken in response to conditions set up by international institutions, such as the World Bank, the IMF and other development banks.

There is very little competition within the water sector. The private contracts signed in the Czech Republic, Hungary (Budapest excepted) and Poland prior to 1997 were not preceded by any tendering process. Likewise, in 2000 Suez was awarded a 25-year contract in Romania without any tendering. In several cases companies have been simply awarded a contract with no other companies invited to submit a tender. There tends to be even less competition when a utility is to be built or renovated – the contract will usually go to a building firm within the same conglomerate. In the meantime the concentration of the market continues, the focus now being on the USA. There Suez, Veolia and Thames Water have bought up American companies.

A contract may cover a period of forty years. During this time the municipality or town loses its control over water utilities. It is often difficult to end a contract early, since companies may demand millions of dollars in compensation. One of the longest contracts to date is in Valencia, Spain. There a private company took over water operations as early as 1902. The contract was for a 99-year period. The huge French company Saur subsequently took it over. When the municipality tried to retender the contract, the company threatened to sue the city. Had Saur lost the contract it would have demanded €54 million as compensation for investments made. Negotiations continued, with one proviso: the winner should pay €54 million to Saur's subsidiary. In these circumstances, not surprisingly, no other company made an offer. Saur will thus continue to run operations, jointly with the municipality, for another fifty years.

Companies receive economic support from public authorities. For example, a new water utility was built by the South African government with Portuguese support. The plant was handed over to the British/Dutch water company Biwater, which also took out a loan from the South African state-owned development bank.

The terms of a contract may be unclear. What, for instance, is the position regarding the extension of the water and sewerage networks to encompass low-income areas if people are living there illegally? A private company may claim that connection to the networks does not necessarily mean water is supplied to every home, but can legitimately involve a connection to a water post, to which residents can go to fetch water, or to a pipe in the yard. The municipality in such a case may say that the company has not met the terms of the contract, while the company claims to have done precisely that, according to the letter of the agreement. Clashing political priorities, along with sudden currency changes, may make it difficult for a company to keep its promises.

Numerous other administrative problems may be present from the outset, or may arise in the course of the contract. For example, a regulatory authority, to check that companies fulfil their commitments, may be too weak or not even exist. Municipalities and government may lack the knowledge to negotiate and draw up a contract. Poorly trained civil servants are often expected to hold their own against highly paid well-educated lawyers from multinational companies with enormous resources at their disposal.

In some cases, consumers may be excluded from the processes that will serve to change their lives radically. In July 2001, for instance, residents outside Kampala in Uganda were surprised when they were woken by the sound of a building contractor's drill digging a well. This represented progress, certainly, but it was very confusing for the people, who had received no prior information. They might have wanted to participate, perhaps to decide on the location of the well, and what type would be most suitable for their needs and living conditions.

The profit a company makes in the water sector may be used to invest in other areas, for example, TV channels or Internet portals in France, as in the case of Vivendi (see Chapter 3).

A contract may contain guarantees to compensate a company if it incurs losses. In Hungary, for example, certain contracts stipulate that if the water charges levied do not provide a certain level of profit, the municipality must compensate the company for the shortfall. This of course shifts the risk to the consumer. If consumption falls or the rate of exchange deteriorates, companies demand automatic increases in charges. In other cases, municipalities undertake to buy a specified volume of water, irrespective of demand.

Instead of supporting the local companies in a given country, large multinational companies often use their own subsidiaries to deliver material or for construction. For example, the water company Aguas Andinas in Chile, which is partly owned by Suez, was awarded a contract for $315 million to build a new sewage treatment plant. It was built by Degrémont, a subsidiary of Suez/Ondeo. Major companies also benefit directly using their own suppliers of chemicals and materials.

Bribery

Globalisation has created a climate that encourages the practice of bribery to secure contracts. This has been exposed in the water industry on a number of occasions. The most infamous case of bribery occurred in Grenoble in France. There is a French saying: 'A clean French mayor ensures that a private water firm also presents the local citizens with a new swimming pool as part of the deal. A corrupt mayor ensures that he gets a swimming pool on his own property.' In the case of Grenoble, a subsidiary of Suez was given responsibility for water operations. The mayor, Alain Carignon, received over 19 million francs in bribes. Among other things, the company supported his election campaign and gave him gifts. Carignon was a member of the ruling Rassemblement pour la République (RPR) party, where the secretary-general from 1976 to 1978 was Jérôme Monod, subsequently chairman of Lyonnaise des Eaux, now Suez. Carignon was sentenced to a term of imprisonment as well as fined. The court also sentenced two executives from the subsidiary to prison. Five years of negotiations followed, before the contract was finally terminated and operations returned to the municipality. Now citizens pay less for their water than they did previously. Suez also paid a high 'entrance fee' – several million dollars – to get the contract. As a result of this case, it is no longer permitted to charge 'entrance fees' in France, and in 1999 the Grenoble tribunal declared it illegal to recover such fees from customers through raising tariffs.

In another case, 1996, Jean-Dominique Deschamps, a director of Vivendi (now Veolia) was sentenced to eighteen months' imprisonment and fines of $27,000. He had donated money to political parties in exchange for water contracts. Similarly, in 1997 the former mayor of Angoulême, Jean-Michel Boucheron, was sentenced to two years in prison and fined the equivalent of $172,000 for having accepted bribes from companies that submitted tenders. Vivendi was one of them. Other cases have been dropped due to insufficient evidence of bribery to go to trial.

Several companies have close contacts with the French government. Evidence indicates that the French water industry has given economic support to Chirac's party, the RPR, in exchange for contracts in fields as diverse as water and maintenance of lifts. Building contracts in the province of Île-de-France were also involved. Both employees of these companies and party representatives have made admissions. Suez subsequently sold the subsidiary implicated and now prides itself on its code of ethics and good reputation in the world. President Chirac simply dismissed the affair out of hand. In Italy, too, a newspaper has revealed that a Vivendi (Veolia) official planned to bribe local politicians in Milan to win a contract for operating a sewage treatment plant. The council president Massimo de Carolis and the Vivendi manager Alain Maetz were convicted and sentenced to prison.

Bribery is of course not confined to these water companies. In 1989 a Swiss subsidiary of ABB paid money to competing firms so that they would not submit tenders for a major sewage treatment project in Egypt. ABB was obliged to pay the equivalent of $53 million in fines, according to a report from Unicorn. In another case, an academic study interviewed people who stated that Aguas Argentinas had bought the support of local councillors with free trips to World Cup football matches in France in 1998. There is, however, no unambiguous evidence that this occurred.

In yet another case, in May 2002, a court in Lesotho found a former director of the Lesotho Highland Project guilty of accepting bribes. He had received some $3 million from multinationals in Canada, South Africa and Europe, among them subsidiaries of major water companies. In exchange, the companies were awarded contracts worth hundreds of millions of dollars.

The water industry, for its part, claims that it does not condone corruption and maintains that it follows international ethical regulations. Neverthess, it is clear that severe penalties and more stringent laws are required in support of these principles. Some moves are under way. The Organisation for Economic Co-operation and Development (OECD) has introduced an Anti-bribery Convention against Corruption and is monitoring adherence to in practice. Also international trade unions created a global Unions Anti-corruption Network, Unicorn. Its overall mission is to mobilise workers to share information and coordinate action to combat bribery globally.

10

Public funds, private solutions:
the World Bank and the IMF

The World Bank is of great importance when it comes to supplying people with water and sanitation. Although the Bank declares that it no longer puts pressure on countries to undertake privatisations, critics insist that the coercion continues.

In February 2003, the World Bank adopted the New Water Resources Sector Strategy, in an effort to increase growth and reduce poverty. In this strategy, the World Bank notes that through partnership between the public and private sectors (PPP), people will gain access to water and sewage disposal. Private companies will continue to play a significant role. Nevertheless that the World Bank is committed to being more attentive to the wishes and aims of local communities.

Steve Commins is one of the authors of the World Bank's *World Development Report 2004*. He says the report does not start from the premiss that private operation is best. Yet nor is there an assumption that public control is always best: 'The public sector often fails, but so does the private sector. "What is the best way to supply the needs of the poor here and now?" is the question to ask in each situation.' The trade unions, for their part, have reacted to what they perceive as contempt, expressed in the report, for public-sector employees, who are regarded as lacking the capacity and will to do a good job.

Of the 276 loans that the World Bank granted for water projects between 1990 and 2002, 84 called directly for privatisation, the majority during the last seven years. Furthermore, the World Bank has acted as adviser in many countries and has supported private companies by offering loans. The International Finance Corporation, part of the World Bank Group, owns, for example, a percentage of the shares of private water companies in both Argentina and Bolivia. The Bank even seconded a manager to assist Aguas Argentina in Buenos Aires to negotiate with the government about increasing water tariffs. This, though, was before the economic crash in Argentina. The World Bank also offers tips – a 'toolkit' – on its website advising governments how to go about privatising.

Mats Karlsson, director of the World Bank in Ghana and former vice-president of the organisation, nevertheless says that there really has been a significant shift in the Bank's approach during the last four years. It now has a more balanced attitude in regard to who should operate water and sanitation services. 'We are not so dogmatic that we believe that the private sector does everything better', he says. He admits that during the 1980s and 1990s there was strong support of the private sector. 'We recognise that it is not always so simple. Private companies did not always deliver what they promised', he says. He maintains that the debate concerning the World Bank is out of date. 'We are aware that we must change our way of working. To rely on the state to provide water and sanitation did not function in the 1970s; nor did the subsequent solutions proposed by the IMF and the World Bank. One must analyse each individual case.'

The UN and the World Bank increasingly work towards the same goal: to reform the state and make it more democratic, claims Karlsson. 'There must be a very strong public sector, which lays down the rules and can negotiate with private companies, and this has been missing', he concedes. 'I'm a great believer in making good use of the resources existing in local communities. We still have a top-down perspective. This must change.' He speaks of mutual respect and shared values – far from the conditions operating in the past, which proved to be so limiting when working together with local communities. Karlsson cites the example of a woman doctor at a clinic who pioneered surgical treatment for a stomach condition, but who had no operating theatre. With determination and a creative approach, she was able to get the operating theatre built. 'Perhaps this doctor shows us the way – an entrepreneurial spirit in the public service. She did not wait. She had the will and strength to act.' In conclusion, Karlsson observes that those who protest against all forms of privatisation have an oversimplified view; nevertheless protests can still make a difference. 'Without protests, after all, it would not have been possible to reduce the burden of debt', he notes, referring to those African countries that have qualified for debt relief according to the HIPC (Heavily Indebted Poor Countries) Initiative established by the World Bank and the IMF.

Imposing conditions

At a conference about fresh water that took place in Bonn in 2001 the decision was taken that development banks should not make privatisation a condition for granting loans to countries. As this agreement was not binding, it is fairly easy to ignore it.

I learned that Nepal was planning to privatise its water, and asked the journalist Prakash Khanal in Kathmandu for the reasons. He replied that it was not the state of Nepal that wants to privatise drinking water; it is an unconditional demand from the Asian Development Bank for granting loans of several million dollars to a large water project at Melamchi. The problem is that Nepal finds it extremely difficult to attract any serious companies with knowledge and experience. The government has no money of its own to implement the Melamchi project, which is the only way the demand for water in the Kathmandu valley in the immediate future can be met. In the beginning, eighteen companies were interested, but they dropped out due to the uncertain and unstable political situation. In addition, many claimed that the bidding process was so complicated that they could not understand it.

The situation in Nepal is not unique. In Nicaragua, Tanzania, and a number of other countries, for example, the International Monetary Fund has insisted on privatisation of water and sanitation services before it will grant a loan.

Cooperation or coercion?

The World Bank dates back to the immediate post–Second World War period. At the time, its primary aim was to assist Europe with capital for reconstruction. The Bank was formed at the same time as the International Monetary Fund. The decisions were taken at a conference in Bretton Woods in the USA in 1944. The World Bank is owned by 184 member countries and gives loans to middle-income countries and creditworthy poorer countries to reduce poverty. Member countries must join the IMF. Their voting power is determined by the size of their economies. The five major partners are the USA, Japan, Germany, France and the UK, each of which has a representative on the board of directors. China, Russia, and Saudi Arabia are also represented.

The World Bank Group comprises the following:

- The International Bank for Reconstruction and Development (IBRD) lends money to poor countries.
- The International Development Association (IDA) gives advantageous loans to the poorest countries in the world.

- The International Finance Corporation (IFC) supports private investments in the form of loans and capital. Its turnover has grown substantially in recent years. The IFC owns shares in a number of companies. In practice, this means that public funds increasingly go to large multinational companies.
- The Multilateral Investment Guarantee Agency (MIGA) encourages foreign investment and gives guarantees to investors and granters of loans so they are insured against risks of all kinds, from broken contracts to the outbreak of war.

  Over the past two decades, loans and guarantees from the IFC and MIGA have increased more than sevenfold, from 3.3 per cent in 1980 to 25 per cent in 2000. In 2000, for example, MIGA paid $15 million to the US company Enron for an energy project in Indonesia. It was subsequently cancelled. MIGA then insisted that the Indonesian authorities should repay the money, otherwise MIGA would not offer any further guarantees to new companies in Indonesia.
- The International Centre for Settlement of Investment Disputes (ICSID) is an arbitration court in conflicts between companies and states.

The International Monetary Fund, according to the homepage of its website, is 'an organisation of 184 countries, working to foster global monetary cooperation, secure financial stability, facilitate international trade, promote high employment and sustainable economic growth, and reduce poverty.'

Like the World Bank, the five major partners of the IMF are the USA, Japan, Germany, France and the UK. Together with China, Russia and Saudi Arabia, they wield most of the votes and thus have the greatest power. According to the IMF, financial stability requires privatisation and cutbacks in the public sector.

Thus both the IMF and the World Bank are controlled by their major donors, which means the richer West. Traditionally, the

European countries elect the IMF president and the USA elects the president of the World Bank. Neither organisation has ever had a president from Asia, Africa or South America. Decisions are not taken through a vote, but by consensus. Agendas and minutes are not made public. The UNDP, part of the UN family, is one of the organisations demanding more influence in the IMF and the World Bank for developing countries.

From public to private monopoly:
Ghana and Guinea

Private-sector involvement in the public sector is known as PPP: public–private partnership. In the water industry, however, the reality is that a private 'partner' operates the water supply and often the sewerage system as well, instead of the public sector.

Now it is Ghana's turn to experience PPP. Mats Karlsson, director of the World Bank in Ghana, believes the private sector is needed if order is to be imposed on water distribution in this African country. 'Ghana has for a long time been planning to reform the water sector', he says. 'Between 1985 and 1995 the country received millions of dollars from the World Bank for investments to improve water distribution and make the public water utility more efficient. This has not led to the desired results. How can one then find a solution?' he asks.

Karlsson observes that in the West the assumption is that the public sector acts in the interests of the people, but this cannot be taken for granted in countries such as Ghana. The state fails to provide the population with the services it requires. 'The public sector is absolutely necessary for Africa, but it must be reformed. Three out of four jobs are found there; 43 per cent of Ghana's income is spent on wages to public-sector employees, so there is little available for other expenditure.'

In 2000, elections in Ghana brought a new government to power. As part of its poverty strategy, it wants the private sector to participate. Karlsson acknowledges that opinions differ on whether water distribution should be operated privately or publicly. Nevertheless he says he has not met with much opposition. He concedes, however, that private companies show little interest in investing. 'We assume that we in the World Bank and other donors from Great Britain and Denmark will contribute so that the water system can be extended. It is most important to us that the poor pay lower charges than today.' He points out that the poor pay ten times as much per litre for water from water sellers than do those who are connected to the public water system. Under the new dispensation those who cannot afford to pay will be given a lifeline: up to a certain level of consumption they will pay a very low tariff, while those who are better off will pay more. 'It is a good, proven solution', he declares. Karlsson insists that the World Bank does not regard the private option as the only solution in all countries. However, in the case of Ghana the public company did try to reform itself and failed.

Picking raisins from the cake

There is, however, an undercurrent of dissent in Ghana regarding the principle of foreign ownership of water resources.

'I'm not against privatisation in principle, but if foreign companies are to run all the work that comes about as a result of development cooperation, then foreign companies will run our lives.' These are the words of Charles Abugre, head of Ghana's Integrated Social Development Centre (ISODEC), a voluntary organisation working in poor areas. ISODEC believes that, instead of privatising, the government should strengthen public service. Its representatives consider it unlikely that foreign companies will provide the new capital needed for investments to renovate and extend services. They are there only to pick the raisins from the cake.

Jan-Erik Gustafsson, Associate Professor at the Department of Land and Water Resources at the Royal Institute of Technology in Stockholm, has followed developments in the Ghana. He tells how the water services have been split in two: a profitable sector in the cities that has been put out to tender to global water companies; and a sector covering the rural areas and many villages that Ghana itself must supply. At the time of writing Ghana had no efficiently working sewage treatment plant. Furthermore, only 32 per cent of the population have access to sanitary toilet facilities. 'The sanitation sector is not profitable. So local authorities, or districts, must deal with this. In Europe, in general, the situation differs. Water supply and sewage treatment are jointly operated and the income we make from supplying water we can invest in sewage treatment', observes Gustafsson.

Already in 1988, the World Bank was recommending that Ghana's government should transfer responsibility for drainage and sanitation to the local districts, which had duly happened by the mid-1990s. Mats Karlsson of the World Bank regards such local operation as a way of decentralising power. 'We have good experiences of people in local communities who are involved and participate in different projects', he says.

Jan-Erik Gustafsson disagrees. 'The World Bank regards the national state as corrupt and says that there should be more local influence. Thus, it recommends that the government should decentralise the services to local units, which, however, lack competent personnel and economic resources. Then it becomes easier for private companies to take over water operations in case they find it profitable.'

He points out, 'Before water services are tendered out to private companies, water tariffs are increased so that it will not be so embarrassing for private companies to increase them further, after they have won the contract. Price increases have already occurred more than once in Ghana. When tariffs are further increased, it is up to the government to support the poor in some way, through subsidies or other means.'

A tendering process took place during the tenure of the previous government. However, a deal was cut with Azurix, owned by Enron, whereby it would only need to pay a low price for taking over Ghana's national water company in exchange for making certain investments. When a newspaper revealed the entire affair in March 2000, protests arose. The World Bank stopped loans to Azurix. The company was suspected of having paid $5 million in bribes to a senior civil servant.

Nevertheless, instead of the government asking the public sector to improve water and sewerage services, a new round of tendering was organised. In the data made available to the bidders, Western consultants determined the conditions of the pending contract over the heads of Ghana's government, according to Gustafsson. 'If one were to privatise at all, officials from Ghana ought to have been included. There is a risk of losing all the knowledge about water and sanitation that exists in the country', he said.

Jan-Erik Gustafsson emphasises that Margaret Thatcher in Britain and Ronald Reagan in the USA pushed privatisation so zealously that their policies also left an indelible mark in other countries. 'In certain countries the World Bank's officials even write the documents for the procurement process and the programmes that are adopted by largely corrupt parliaments', he says. 'These programmes then weaken the right to national self-determination.' In the USA, funds have been created to subsidise companies directly and put pressure on development banks to do the same. 'Why don't development agencies help to build up national competence in the water sector in developing countries instead of uncritically accepting privatisation programmes supported by the World Bank, the IMF, other banks, the EU commission and WTO/GATS?' asks Gustafsson.

Gustafsson believes that the World Bank's strategy of private solutions is undermining the negotiating powers of poor countries. In plain language, this means that those countries that are willing to remove obstacles for foreign investors also have greater opportunities of receiving loans. The World Bank adapts itself to the global system of trade. This entails removing trade barriers and thereby making countries even more vulnerable to foreign interests. Gustafsson adds that criticism of private companies has, however, left its mark. 'A representative for Suez said at a recent conference that it is a human right to have access to water. One did not hear the company saying this in the past. Ironically, this human right is still supposedly achievable only through private initiatives.'

In 2002, a number of organisations, including the Christian Council, the Trade Union Congress, the Ghana Catholic Bishop's Council, the African Association of Universities, along with members of civil society, invited an international delegation to study the proposed private-sector initiative. The delegation consisted largely of British and North American academics and representatives of different organisations. Lawyers, a Liberal Democrat Member of Parliament, and a representative of the British trade union Unison were included.

The delegation duly met representatives of governments, the World Bank, several non-governmental organisations and members of the public. It concluded in its report that Ghana's 'current Private Sector Participation (PSP) proposal is not the optimal option for ensuring expanded access to clean and affordable water for the people of Ghana', especially not for the very poor, who lack a direct water supply. Identified shortcomings of the water reform plan included:

- There is no plan to ensure access for the poor.
- Investment priorities and lack of capital are likely to privilege wealthier communities.
- The lifeline tariff is not a contractual obligation.
- In its programme, the government has paid insufficient attention to improving the sanitation system, which is fundamental for controlling the spread of disease.
- Loans increase Ghana's burden of debt while the private water companies make guaranteed profits on water without incurring any particular risks.
- Planned talks with the trade union representing water and sanitation workers have not taken place. The trade union was instead presented with a fait accompli and left to negotiate severance pay for half the workforce.

Ghana's blue-collar trade union confederation supports the National Coalition Against Privatisation (NCAP). NCAP is not opposed to the private sector providing services – for example, payment collection or water pipe installation. It is, however, critical of a system that has been deliberately designed to grant foreign companies privileges. According to lawyer Rudolf Amenga-Etego, coordinator of NCAP, it was first agreed that the private companies would invest $70 million. This was then reduced to only $30 million. Later the question arose as to whether they would invest anything at all. Amenga-Etego argues that privatisation displays arrogance and insensitivity to the cultural and religious values and norms that are equated with the ownership and use of water in Ghana. To the ordinary Ghanaian, privatising water is not a simple case of economics: it goes far beyond that. It amounts to their lives being sold to a private entity for profit; it amounts to saying 'You are good for nothing, you can't even manage your life'. It strikes at the very collective psyche of the nation.

The powerful coalition that emerged to challenge the water privatisation agenda was completely ignored, according to Amenga-

Etego. Its alternative proposals for community management and control of water delivery in partnership with the Ghana public water utility were not even considered. The lawyer blames bilateral donors for pressuring Ghana to open up its water and electricity industries to private companies. Both the Department for International Development (DFID) of the United Kingdom and the United States Agency for International Development (USAID) have been active financiers of the reform process with a view to influencing the process in favour of multinational water services companies from their own countries.

Amenga-Etego says that in Ghana, a country where over 50 per cent of the population earns less than $1 a day, the increase in water rates to achieve full cost recovery levels is already making life difficult for a significant proportion of the population. Some people have had their water turned off because they could not afford to pay their accounts. Amenga-Etego fears that, given the family care system in Ghana, where a worker takes care not only of his nuclear family but also of his less fortunate relatives, the rising costs of water and electricity may very well be sentencing more people to poverty and an early death.

Forced privatisation in Niger

In Niger, which is north-east of Ghana, the French company Veolia Water is already ensconced. Stina Hansson, an economic history researcher at the university in Stockholm, visited Niger in 2002. Niger is a former French colony and one of the poorest countries in the world. When Hansson arrived, workers at the water company were on strike. They were furious about the low wages and the neocolonial attitudes of the French management. She says that the French managers keep their own salaries a secret, even to shareholders in Niger. The trade union at first opposed privatisation, but agreed to it after a social contract was drawn up. However, this contract was subsequently broken. Under the contract, the employees own 10 per cent of the company's shares. This holding does not confer power or automatically grant access to information, however. Shareholders left one meeting in protest against the French management, which had refused to reveal the figures for the losses the company had incurred. Hansson, likewise, was unable to obtain access to any financial information about the company. An alternative trade union has recently been formed, with the support of management. The clear intention is to divide the workforce.

Water has historically been common property in Niger, managed by the community. There is a strong sense of cultural tradition. The administrative director of the Veolia-run company tends towards a different view of those who seek to preserve such communalism: 'Not here, but in some countries, people think they do not have to pay for water at all, because water is a gift from God. But God did not build treatment plants, God has not built networks, God has not installed the connections, so someone has to pay for all of this.'

According to Stina Hansson, the World Bank forced Niger to privatise. A French consultant was also involved. As part of the deal, the government was able to borrow money from the Bank. Yet the private company is not investing and refuses to take any major risks, even though the World Bank advocated privatisation as a means of securing investment and underpinning risk. 'They make suggestions, but in fact they are demands. We do not have a choice. They tell us, "Listen, we are going to help you, but you have to privatise", so in reality they force us. We no longer have a choice', a UNICEF representative says about the World Bank's tactics. Two years after privatisation there was still no regulatory authority in place to monitor the company.

Stina Hansson's conclusion is that a market solution in the form of privatisation is promoted, but then the market mechanisms are set aside because they are not viable. In place of private investment, the World Bank provides the money, because private lenders would charge too much interest. Furthermore, the private operator is given contracts for extension of the network free of competition. That is, local companies are not permitted to compete on market terms. In short, a public monopoly is replaced by a private one.

Although the World Bank brings money to the water sector, it routinely imposes privatisation. This is in line with the ruling ideology in the field at this time: private operators are better suited to the task of supplying water. In the case of Niger, Hansson asks: why was there no attempt to reconstruct the water utility instead of privatising it. And, regarding the larger issue of why water privatisation is being pushed so aggressively, she asks: is World Bank policy simply a consequence of the fact that the rich countries with power in the Bank promote their own economic interests above all others?

A failing model

In other parts of Africa, significantly, developments go in the opposite direction. Increasingly, companies have begun to withdraw or have broken off contracts in countries south of the Sahara. Saur has sold its shares in a consortium in Mozambique, for example. Biwater withdrew from a project in Zimbabwe. One reason is that the large companies have reassessed risk following significantly lower profits than projected.

Guinea, on the other hand, is considered a successful example of privatisation in Africa. Here a joint venture was created where foreign owners – Saur, the major shareholder and Veolia (Générale des Eaux at the time) – were responsible for most of the operations. The contract, signed in 1989, ran for ten years. When it expired, however, the government did not want to renew on a long-term basis, preferring annual agreements on account of the high escalating prices and because the contract had not run smoothly. There was no common ground and negotiations collapsed. Saur and Veolia pulled out and left the country at the beginning of 2001. Whereas it is true that water quality has improved and productivity has increased, water tariffs are sky-high – among the highest in Africa.

Conflicts soon developed between the private operator Société de Exploitation des Eaux de Guinée (SEEG), and the state agency, Société Nationale des Eaux de Guinée (SONEG). SONEG's job was to regulate the private company, but it was too weak and was not able to withstand the arbitrary actions of the government. Because SONEG had no access to SEEG's financial reports, when the company wanted to increase the tariffs the regulator had no means of assessing the proposal – it lacked the data to do its job.

In 1986, the water tariff was only 60 Guinean francs per cubic metre. Ten years later, the average tariff had increased to 880 FG per cubic metre. In 1996 the cost of being connected was 90,000 FG (about \$90). Considering that the average income of a senior public sector servant was then about 150,000 FG (\$150) per month, it is unsurprising that even the wealthy claimed that the high prices made it almost impossible to afford a connection.

The private operator SEEG had taken on almost no investment-related risk. For example, loans for infrastructure were the responsibility of the government. There were 31,000 private connections in 1997 compared to 13,300 in 1989, and 130 standpipes installed compared to 40. The increased rate of connection was slower than had been expected.

One reason was that people could not afford the high price of connection. In 1994, 12,000 connections were inactive due to non-payment. Another factor is disagreements between SEEG and SONEG, which slowed the expansion of the water system.

One important lesson to learn from this case is the need for an effective state regulatory agency, with the authority and competence to monitor the private company and accurately assess its performance.

12

Kenya:
the problems of rural water supply

The major global water companies are mainly interested in establishing themselves in cities, where populations are financially secure. Hence the villagers of Kampi ya Moto in Kenya are unlikely to make their acquaintance. It is not so profitable to install water in the countryside.

Twenty orphaned children have been given sanctuary in a children's home in the village. The orphanage does not have its own supply of water; it depends on delivery by a tanker. Sometimes the vehicle does not arrive, in which case a member of staff must cycle 3 or 4 kilometres with a can hanging on either side of the handlebars. The cans, each of which holds 20 litres of water, are filled at a well drilled on a large estate owned by former president Daniel Arap Moi. He charges five shillings per can.

Water absorbs between 10 and 15 per cent of the orphanage's budget. It needs at least 200 litres per day for the household, to be able to launder clothes and keep the twenty children relatively clean. On occasion, when the former president's escort approaches, the water fetchers have been sent away. They are not allowed to be in the vicinity of such a prominent person. On the other hand, the children are now permitted to bathe once a week in Moi's pool.

Jacinta Njoroge-Lahti, who was born in the village, runs the children's home. Her dream is to have a well of her own, and to this end she asks people to donate money to her project. she is currently working in Sweden, taking care of the elderly. Nevertheless, she continues to collect money for the children, and for the well. 'To be without water is a catastrophe during the dry season. There are people who have to live without water for two days or more', she relates. Neighbouring farmers are forced to rely on the rains. They grow maize and beans. If there is a drought, the beans shrivel up and there are no crops, nothing to sell.

The children's home has a tin roof and water can be collected from the roof. Others in the village only have thatched roofs and therefore lack this facility. Every time it rains the orphanage saves water; the money it saves goes towards the children's school fees. The rainwater is stored in two tanks in the garden.

Jacinta makes sure the water is boiled. Its purity cannot be guaranteed. Six-year-old Jane has had cholera, as has eight-year-old George. You can't be too careful. The village school has no water supply. At times it is very hot and airless in the classroom. Fifty children sit close together, in fours, on benches. The children bring in plastic water bottles, which soon become lukewarm in the heat. The water has many uses. For instance, the children must scrub the floors and keep the toilets clean. Cleaning tends to be only perfunctory. They would rather keep their water to quench their thirst. 'We can hardly wash ourselves properly, but everyone can shampoo their hair once a week', says Jacinta.

The toilets at the orphanage consist of two holes dug in the ground, covered by a small shed. Everyone in the village has such drop latrines. When Jacinta grew up in the village she could take a shower and had a functioning toilet at home, but today the water pipes are broken and dry. She lives in her childhood home during her stays, but now flushes the toilet by throwing in a bucket of water. Many in the village share latrines, but they never think of throwing ash down the hole, or of washing their hands. If there is any water over, the women splash it on the earth floor to keep fleas away. Their lowest priority is to use water to clean the toilets. The latrines are therefore dirty and attract flies, which buzz around and settle on food. The lack of clean water and poor general hygiene are the direct cause of many illnesses, from bloody diarrhoea to worms and even blindness.

Twenty kilometres from the village is the town of Nakuru. There the water pipes are old and rusty, dating from colonial times. The sanitation system does not work. The public toilets cannot be used. The water and drainage systems have also fallen into disrepair. Meanwhile the population has grown.

Jacinta thinks it remarkable that while oil can be pumped from Mombasa, people are not supplied with water. 'Kenya has received millions of dollars in support from various countries, but the money has landed in the pockets of individual people. There has been an incomparable system of bribery, even to get a place at the hospital', she says, adding bitterly, 'While some Kenyans own planes and property abroad, poor women must trudge 20 kilometres a day to fetch water.' She speaks of women who are beaten by their husbands because there is no water in the home.

Jacinta has begun the preparations for drilling her well. She heard from the public authorities that there is only a single drilling rig in northern Kenya, and that she would therefore have to wait for several months. First, though, a water engineer must confirm that there is indeed water lying beneath the plot. Then electricity will need to be connected so that water can be pumped up. At the same time, public authorities must have proof that the plot belongs to Jacinta. Papers must be sent hither and thither. Jacinta has been informed that it will cost some $20,000 to drill the well.

She does not yet know how she will find all of the money. She is trying to raise some of it in Sweden.

Julius F. Mwandembom of the Kenyan embassy in Stockholm speaks authoritatively about rural women's drudgery. He knows of women who rise at five in the morning to fetch 20 litres of water; it is two in the afternoon before they return. A family may consist of six children; this water must suffice for all. The women waste their time and exhaust their energy just to provide the family with water. Were there a water supply nearby, they would be able to work longer in the fields and produce more crops.

The situation is a little better in the towns. There are other problems though. For example, there is a racket whereby people make illegal connections to the water pipes and then sell the water illicitly. These illegal connections reduce the flow of water in the pipes.

Mwandembom raises the issue of widespread corruption. Ministries and other public authorities tend not to bother to pay for water, for instance. Some have not paid for twenty years. Should a manager from the water company venture to demand payment, he might earn this response from a person in high office: 'How dare you? I'll make sure that you lose your job.' Or perhaps the head of the water utility was given his job as a thank you for voting for the right politicians in the elections. Further down, those who read the water meters can be bribed to register a lower reading. Someone on his way to cut off water may similarly be bribed not to do this. Mwandembom doubts that a public sector that is so corrupt could reform itself.

On the other hand, Mwandembom is aware that a private company, by charging a high tariff, may make it harder for people to pay for their water, although he believes the government ought to permit differential charging in which the poorest pay less than others. Expert advice is needed to rethink the billing system, so that those with a decent income pay for the water they use. To be fair, the new government does try to deal with the corruption and to seek remedies for the badly run water operations. Mwandembom says that on balance he would rather have a domestic company running the water supply than a foreign multinational. 'The French own the large water companies, but do not themselves let any foreigners in. Why, then, should we be forced to? There ought to be another way, but what?' he wonders.

Kenya is not the only country in Africa with these problems, of course. A report by UN–Habitat tells horror stories about the struggle to get water: people fighting for their pitiful quota of water at a pump where access is allowed for only a few hours a day; others, having stood in a queue for hours, being shouted at because someone considers they have taken too much water, or being treated as an interloper, for trying to source water from an area that is not their own. The girls must often fetch and carry water rather than go to school. Boys rarely miss school, as they carry water less often. They are learning to be men – not to carry water.

Women's organisations, internationally, fighting for women to get access to water, maintain that if more women participated in decision-making bodies the task of supplying the developing world with water, toilets and washing areas might move ahead more speedily. Access to water and sanitation is crucial to human dignity and the shape of a person's entire social being. Unfortunately, some houses are so cramped that there is not even space for a toilet. People must therefore use public toilets. This often involves long queues and then subjection to the personal remarks of those waiting in the queue. One option is simply to find somewhere to squat outdoors. Another crucial issue, of course, is that women would no longer need to spend time at the hospital with children who have become ill from a contaminated water source. Thus, more than being simply a personal issue, an inadequate and unsafe water supply represents a waste of resources and labour power, with all the social and economic ramifications of this. Water and sanitation would be a revolution in the lives of these people.

The situation, then, is complicated: yes there is corruption, but there is also the serious problem of a shortage of potable water in thousands of villages. There is no point in saying that a private company from France will resolve this, since they seldom reach villages in the countries where they operate. Likewise it would be equally mistaken to believe that the public sector can resolve the situation if it is corrupt and inefficient, and in the absence of adequate funding.

Water wars?

Water shortages increase the risk of conflict between nations. Iraq, for example, threatened to bomb a Syrian dam in a disagreement over the water of the Euphrates river that flows through Turkey, Iraq and Syria. In 2003, Kenya pulled out from an agreement on cooperation on the Nile. The Egyptian minister for water resources described it as an act of war, since Egypt is dependent on the Nile, the source of which is Lake Victoria. Kenya wants to use the water for its own development. Boutros Boutros-Ghali, former Egyptian foreign minister and ex-secretary-general of the UN, has predicted that the next war in the region may be about water. Meanwhile, the USA fears that drinking water may be sabotaged by terrorists.

In the Middle East, the water resources of the River Jordan are shared by four states: Israel, Jordan, Lebanon and Syria, as well as by the Palestinian administration. Conflict over this water was one of the causes of the Six Day War in 1967 between Israel and its Arab neighbours. As the victor, Israel strengthened its strategic position in regard to water. Significantly, Israel is dependent on the West Bank for its water. Some claim that as much as 82 per cent of the West Bank's water goes to Israel and the Jewish settlements, leaving only 18 per cent for the Palestinians on the West Bank.

Water can, however, also lead to cooperation. For example, Iran has signed a thirty-year contract with Kuwait to supply it with water; this involves a 540-kilometre water pipe from Iran.

Water: the facts

- Ocean covers 71 per cent of the earth's surface. Of all water on the planet 97.5 per cent is salt water. Of the 2.5 per cent sweet water, the greater part is in the form of glaciers and snow; only 1 per cent is surface water. Of the surface water, over half is in lakes.
- Human beings are 70 per cent water. If only 5 per cent of our fluid balance is lost, we feel uncomfortable; 10 per cent reduces mobility; a 20 per cent loss can mean death.
- Water use per person per day in most European countries is between 130 and 180 litres. However, some regions in Italy and Spain see much higher per capita water usage – as much as 372 litres per day.
- The best-case scenario in certain developing countries will see 30 litres of water consumed per household per day. The minimum volume required to sustain life and health is 25 litres per person per day, according to the World Health Organisation.
- In the USA, 65 per cent of the water consumed is used by industry and in the generation of electrical power; 27 per cent is used by agriculture; and only 8 per cent is used as drinking water, in households and for hygiene, according to figures from the World Bank in 2001.

- In Asia, however, only 8 per cent of the water consumed goes to industry; 86 per cent is used in agriculture, 70 per cent of which is for irrigation. The cultivation of just one kilo of rice requires at least 2,000 litres of water.
- Water is a scarce commodity, not least in parts of Africa and western Asia. About twenty countries are already suffering from a water shortage.

The global water club

A network of think-tanks, companies, engineers and lobby groups dominate the debate about how people, especially in developing countries, should get access to water.

The WWC and the GWP

An organisation with a great deal of influence is the World Water Council (WWC). It describes itself as an 'international water policy think-tank' dedicated to strengthening the global water movement to improve management of the world's water resources and services. Its mission is 'to promote awareness, build political commitment and trigger action on critical water issues at all levels, including the highest decision-making level'.

The WWC's president was until January 2005 William Cosgrove, an ex-World Bank consultant. Loïc Fauchon, president and director-general of Groupe des Eaux de Marseilles, owned by Suez and Veolia, is now acting president. René Coulomb, of Suez–Lyonnaise des Eaux, is one of three founding members of WWC and still sits on the board. The Council's office is in Marseilles. It organises a triennial World Water Forum. The third such forum was held in Kyoto in March 2003.

Another influential organisation is the Global Water Partnership (GWP) formed in 1996 by the World Bank, UNDP and the Swedish International Development Cooperation Agency (Sida). The GWP describes itself as a working partnership of all those involved in water management: government agencies, public institutions, private companies, professional organisations, multilateral development agencies and others committed to the Dublin principles. They state that fresh water is a finite and vulnerable resource, essential to sustain life, development and the environment. Water development and management should be based on a participatory approach, involving users, planners and policymakers at all levels. Women play a central part in the provision, management and safeguarding of water. Water has an economic value in all its competing uses and should be recognised as an economic good.

The GWP serves as a mechanism for alliance building and information exchange. The mission is to 'support countries in the sustainable management of their water resources'. The secretariat is in Stockholm. Formerly the office had space at Sida. The GWP's steering committee chair is Margaret Catley-Carlson. She also chairs the Water Resources Advisory Committee, created by Suez in 1999 to guide its Water Resources Department. She is a former president of the Canadian International Development Agency (CIDA). Catley-Carson is one of very few women whose voice is heard at the global level, where policy decisions about water and sanitation are made.

The WWC and the GWP jointly initiated the Camdessus Panel in 2001, to consider solutions to the future global financial needs of the water sector. Chairman of the twenty-member panel was Michel Camdessus, formerly managing director of the IMF and then honorary governor of the Banque de France. The Camdessus

Panel report, *Financing Water for All*, was presented at the Third
World Water Forum in Kyoto. The report says that annual investments in water services need to increase from US$75 billion
to US$180 billion. This is at a time when international private
investment and commercial bank lending have declined.

The report recommends full cost recovery for water projects.
It does acknowledge that public–public partnerships – that is,
cooperation between public utilities – may be a viable option. Yet
it lays far more stress on the great potential benefits of involving
private companies, even if they are not so willing to invest in
developing markets. The report seeks new ways of mitigating
risks for the private companies. It advocates the use of public
funds to pay for the preparation of private concession contracts
and tenders. It also proposes utilising public funds for a 'Liquidity
Backstopping Facility' to guarantee corporate profits in cases of
currency devaluation (as occurred, for example, in Argentina and
in the Philippines). The report also recommends creating mechanisms to lend directly to municipalities, thereby bypassing national
(sovereign) governments. Some say this could result in increasing
levels of debt, which consumers would have to service.

There has been no lack of criticism of the report, not least due
to the composition of the panel. All panel members were men,
except in the case of Thames Water, which had a woman as an
alternate member. The panel included Gerard Payen, former senior
executive-vice-president of Suez, and former chairman and CEO
of Ondeo, the water subsidiary of Suez. Veolia (Vivendi) is another
player. One of its directors, Charles-Louis de Maud'huy, enjoyed
direct informal contacts with Michel Camdessus in connection
with the report. Also on the panel were presidents of regional
development banks, former ministers, two NGOs, and Ismael
Serageldin, former vice-president of the World Bank. The panel's
$1 million budget was funded by the Dutch government.

Revolving doors

In 1998, the WWC together with the UN, certain governments and the World Bank formed the World Commission on Water for the 21st Century (WCW). It presented a long-term view, 'A Water Secure World: Vision for Water, Life and the Environment' at the Second World Water Forum in The Hague in 2000. This again declared water to be an economic and social asset. Just like oil and other natural resources, it maintained, water is subject to the laws of the market and to competition. Since it requires major investments, only private, profitable companies will have access to the capital required, the argument runs. The chairman of the Commission is Ismael Serageldin. Among the members are Suez former executive director Jérôme Monod, Margaret Catley-Carson, and Enrique Iglesias, president of the Inter-American Development Bank, who was also on the Camdessus Panel.

It is no secret that French president Jacques Chirac is enthusiastic about private companies continuing to run water operations. Beyond the direct interest of French water companies is the indirect involvement of the French motor industry. Renault and Citroën deliver vehicles to water and sanitation plants all over the world, where French companies have taken over services. There are strong links between the business and France's political leadership. Jérôme Monod, former CEO of Suez, left the company in 2000 to become campaign leader for President Jacques Chirac. He has also advised James Wolfensohn, president of the World Bank until May 2005, and the government of China, a country where the private companies are expanding aggressively.

The water companies use embassies to increase their influence and make contacts. The French minister of trade, Bruno Durieux, visited Buenos Aires in the early 1990s and lobbied for the bid made by Suez and Veolia (Vivendi), among others. He promised that France would increase its investments in Argentina depending on the number of private contracts awarded to his country. The French ambassador has ongoing contact with the Argentinian government regarding the Suez and Veolia contracts in Argentina. In 2002 the embassy exerted extensive pressure on the Argentine government to pay the contracted fees in dollars, despite the fact that this would have doubled the cost of water to consumers – this during a major economic crisis. The government resisted this pressure, however.

The EU also has close contacts in these circles. The EU's Water Initiative states that private-sector expertise and capital have a role to play, but it requires regulation to ensure that each company fulfils its contractual obligations. The water companies lobby the EU heavily, and Suez hired a former EU commissioner to help in this regard. There is a much-used 'revolving door' between the companies and the governments that help them.

The EU commission advocates that the private sector should become heavily involved in water and sanitation services and that the water sector should be opened to competition. This is shown by its Internal Marketing Strategy for 2003 to 2006.

Connections between the European Bank for Reconstruction and Development and Suez are intimate. EBRD's former deputy vice-president, Thierry Baudon, joined Suez as managing director of the international finance division. Now he is a CEO of Emerging Markets Partnership (EMP), connected to the Emerging Europe Infrastructure Fund. The Fund focuses on countries that have recently joined the EU. EEIF's objective is long-term capital appreciation in equity and securities in infrastructure sector companies that operate in central and eastern Europe. Formerly, Baudon held various senior positions in the World Bank. The EBRD's first loan for water and sanitation in eastern Europe was granted to Suez, to support an investment programme.

In 2004, Kofi Annan appointed a UN Advisory Panel on Water and Sanitation. Among its members are Michel Camdessus, former managing director of IMF; Gérard Payen, former chairman and CEO of Ondeo and Suez; and Peter Woicke, executive vice-president of the International Finance Corporation, the part of the World Bank that deals only with private corporations.

The role of USAID

Another organisation promoting privatisation is the United States Agency for International Development. In January 2004 USAID awarded a contract to the US construction corporation Bechtel to build schools, water utilities and other infrastructure in Iraq. USAID presents itself on its homepage as an independent public authority, even though the organisation engages in foreign and humanitarian activities to promote the USA's political and economic interests. It is in fact the international donor agency of the US government.

A number of wealthy countries advocate the private management of water systems in developing countries. They use a number of mechanisms: their positions as executive directors of the World Bank and the regional development banks, which, through their loans and grants to developing countries often impose privatisation of public services; their bilateral aid agencies, such as USAID or the Swedish Sida, where again bilateral loans and grants are made conditional on privatisation; regional and global trade negotiations, where they advocate increased 'competition' and corporate rights in the delivery of public services.

14

The big players reassess risk

Suez and Veolia both sent delegates to the Third World Water Forum in Kyoto in 2003. The message they delivered was clear: they will operate water and sanitation services in developing countries on condition that someone else takes the financial risks. Both companies have begun to withdraw from developing countries.

Suez's executive director, Gérard Méstrallet, had previously stated that the company was involved in a drive to bring water to the poor. To give everyone access to clean water, a united effort by all the countries in the world, international institutions and private companies would be required. He says he has attempted to mediate between the two sides: those who advocate the private sector and those who are against it. Private companies have adopted a more pragmatic approach. They are eager to point out that they do not sell raw materials, but rather perform a service. Suez, for instance, claims it seeks social as much as economic responsibility. Nevertheless, in its 2002 annual report, the company announced that its aim for 2003–04 was 'to improve and protect profitability and strengthen financial soundness'. This strategy involved withdrawing from Manila in the Philippines and demanding millions of dollars in compensation for investments already made.

Suez runs its subsidiaries from Paris

The headquarters of Suez in Paris are close to the fashionable shopping street Boulevard Haussmann. There, in 2003, I meet its director, Jean-Luc Trancart. The company has employed him since 1993. He was previously a political adviser in the French ministry of the environment, dealing with water and infrastructure. Before that, he worked for Vivendi (now Veolia).

I have hardly sat down before Trancart begins to talk about the problems connected with financing the extension of water systems in developing countries. Each household's connection costs between $500 and $1,000 to install. This expenditure is financed through concession plans and long-term contracts under public–private partnerships (PPPs). The private contractor manages the whole water system and invests in the maintenance and expansion of the system. 'PPP has been criticised, but is very efficient in most cases', Trancart says in passing. He adds that the company invests through debt financing; this has led to problems in both Buenos Aires and Manila. He explains: 'As it was not possible to get loans in local currency we had to take loans in dollars. So our debts are in dollars and today there is a huge difference between the local currency peso and the dollar, due to devaluation. If we are not able to finance the debt, the company will not survive.'

This is also the reason that the company has stopped investing in Buenos Aires and Manila and is thus unable to improve the system. He says the situation would be the same for the public sector: the financial risk is identical. If a municipality needs to improve its water network and there is no market for debt financing in the local currency, the municipality has to take its loans in dollars. It has nothing to do with privatisation.

Trancart says he does not yet know if Suez will withdraw from Buenos Aires. The company is protected against currency risks, but it is currently impossible to increase water charges to compensate for losses. The situation differs from that in Casablanca, where, according to Trancart, everything is working well. Investments there are financed in dirhams, the local currency. Customers pay in Moroccan dirhams; the company repays the banks in dirhams. The poor pay a lower rate for water, while those who have a fairly good income compensate for any water sector deficit by paying higher electricity charges – Suez is also a prominent player in this market.

Were it not for the business climate in Argentina and in the Philippines, the company would have an easier time of it. 'We have long-term contracts in forty countries and only have problems in two of these countries', Trancart says. He refers to the Camdessus Report: 'What Camdessus says and what the World Bank has to do is to try to create a local finance market in the local currency. This is the only way to secure investments.' 'Is it possible to do that?' I ask him. 'Yes', he replies. 'The World Bank has a great deal of money and can ensure all kinds of investments, while local governments can secure private investments by taking loans.'

At the World Water Forum in Kyoto, there were many non-governmental and voluntary organisations, and trade unions, protesting against the private companies. What did he think about the protests? Trancart perceives two levels of protest: those that follow increases in water, energy or transport tariffs, which he considers understandable; and those organised by people who do not want water to be privatised, which he does not consider reasonable. 'Some activists took a very tough stand against us. The position they took was so extreme, that it turned out to be a good thing for us. When people demand that water must be free, most of our clients, politicians, and a host of NGOs, think it is a crazy position. Our status and knowledge are recognised.' He points out that those countries that have decided not to contract a private company to manage their water have made a political decision, which has to be accepted. Then he adds sharply: 'If you don't want customers to pay for their water, you are crazy. Water is not abundant, and if people do not pay anything they will waste water. You need to put a price-tag on water.' He points to the way the water systems deteriorated in Poland, Hungary and Russia, because the population paid so little and stresses the huge task it is to restore the system.

Over the years, Suez has expanded across the globe. However, Trancart does not expect the company to establish much of a presence in developing countries. 'Private companies provide water to between 5 and 6 per cent of the planet's population. If we, within five or ten years, get a further 3 per cent of the market, it will be an accomplishment. It all depends on whether we find a financing system that exposes us to less risk in the future.'

Trancart has no interest in the British model of total privatisation. 'For Margaret Thatcher and the Chilean government, privatisation was a political issue. It was excessive', he says. He thinks it is absurd to buy assets with private money. 'It is not a good way to use money, as it increases the costs. I prefer it when the public water company owns the assets and the private sector operates the network. We are selling organisation and knowledge, but we should not be spending capital.'

'So what is the future for Suez?' The revenue from France is quite high and Trancart is sure that the company will continue to operate in western Europe. Italy, Spain, and Greece are late in adapting to the European directives on sewage treatment. Suez has begun work in these countries to accelerate improvements in the sewerage systems. Trancart also expects the company to expand in the United States. Suez already owns one company there, United Water. Other companies are owned by the German RWE/Thames Water and by Veolia. 'If the Americans want to work with the private sector, they have a choice between one German and two French companies.'

If the financial problems involved in investing in developing countries are resolved, Suez may have a future there as well, although this market is unlikely to account for more than 15–20 per cent of the company's business, according to Trancart.

Water and sanitation for all?

I later meet director Alain Mathys for lunch near his office. He is happy to talk about Suez operations and, in particular, his experience of the inefficient public sector. Before he came to Suez, Mathys worked within the World Bank.

Mathys speaks of Renault cars when it was a nationalised industry, part of the French state. Since privatisation, the vehicles' quality is much higher and the company is more profitable. It is the same in the water sector, he says. The water sector requires a considerable amount of expertise, which is not always available in the public sector. 'Not even in Argentina did the public sector succeed, despite Argentina being South America's richest country in the 1990s.'

Alain Mathys manages a programme called 'Water and Sanitation for All'. He points out that it is not charity; the objective is to develop services for low-income inhabitants, where the public sector has failed. When Suez extends the network to poor areas, it is also concerned with the company's image: it is both a business target and a contractual obligation to extend services to the poor. 'If we say that the private sector is only going to serve rich people, obviously the participation of the private sector will be condemned. If we say that we have an obligation to extend the service to everybody, we are in a much stronger position.' Mathys explains that a large company with a vision cannot forget that it has a role to play in the sustainable development of society. He adds that Suez has no intention of giving up in developing countries, since the company is on the right road.

In El Alto in La Paz, Bolivia, water coverage increased from 50 to 100 per cent of the population and sewerage provision doubled. Yet problems of various kinds persist. For example, consumption among indigenous inhabitants is very low, which impacts on company revenues. As it is not possible to make a profit in La Paz, the company must improve the tariff structure. 'There must be a fair return', Alain Mathys says. The rate of return is indeed very low, in comparative terms, sometimes just 6 per cent, whereas it may be over 15 per cent in the energy and telecommunications sectors. 'If we can raise the rate of return to between 10 and 12 per cent, the private sector will become quite active.'

In terms of urban infrastructure, water supply is the most expensive to install and operate. At the same time, it is the cheapest commodity. A family pays less for water than for electricity and other services. 'This is because water is considered to have both an economic and a social value. So governments are always reluctant to charge for the real cost of water.'

'Some people, but not all, paying a low tariff would be able to pay a slightly higher tariff. This does not mean that water will not be available to the poor', Mathys says. He gives an example: in Jakarta, Indonesia, the tariffs are set in a progressive block system. The first block is low – that is, you pay a lower price for the first 10 cubic metres. The low-income community is subsidised by the high-income community, which pays a higher price. This is better than paying fifty times more for water bought from private water sellers than those who are connected. 'We have never had problems with the poor who are connected, as they realise the value of having water in the pipes', he says.

His conclusion is that protests against the tariffs are actively informed by ideological values. 'Those who have always had water in the home do not realise what it is like not being connected. Normally it is very rare that poor people demonstrate. When people are really poor and cannot pay the full price, you have to develop some form of subsidy. The decision to subsidise is a political decision.'

Several models exist for subsidising the poor. In Chile, subsidies are provided through a fund established by the government. The poor pay say 50 per cent of the bill and the rest is covered by the fund; hence the water company always receives the going rate for the water it supplies. In Bolivia, where the government is always bankrupt, according to Mathys, it is better to embed the subsidy within the tariff. Those who can afford it will pay a surcharge on their water to compensate the company for those who cannot afford to pay the full price. 'The subsidy should benefit only the poor. In some cases, the rich have small families and the poor large families, who consume more water than the rich do, so the poor pay more per cubic metre. This mechanism subsidises the rich more than it subsidises the poor. You must design a new tariff structure that includes a real social subsidy, targeted to the poor.'

Mathys has been working in the water sector since 1981. He observes that during the 1980s the focus was on investment and therefore results were not very good, as no effort or capacity was devoted to maintaining infrastructure. Billions of dollars were spent, but very little progress was made in terms of increasing coverage. By 1986, the World Bank and the United Nations had concluded that public companies had to be reformed.

Before he moved into the water business, Mathys worked for the African Development Bank, which developed reform programmes, tried to strengthen management structures, provided training, studied tariffs and so on. 'The results were not very positive. Management was selected not on the basis of competence, but rather links with those in power, often relatives of the president. A manager might even be forced to hire a cousin of the power-ful person who had appointed him. When a water company generated cash, the government often used the utility to provide it with money, so the company had no resources left to finance its investments.' When a government changed, civil servants were also changed and the experience of their predecessors was then lost. 'This is even more typical at municipal level, when a new mayor is elected', Mathys says.

'All right, a private company takes over, but why does it have to stay thirty years in a country?' I ask. 'This depends on the size of investments.' replies Mathys. 'You invest a lot in the beginning and cannot increase the tariffs in proportion to the investments. We count on recouping our investments later.' He is sure that this will change. The model for private participation will prob- ably involve shorter contracts, maybe ten years, and less direct investment by the operator. 'We will probably separate the role of operator and the role of financier or investor. In Argentina, we played both roles. Our job is to be the operator. We have to develop partnerships with financial institutions to get the funds, while we ourselves will probably concentrate on operation.'

At the World Water Forum in Kyoto, institutions like the World Bank, the Asian Development Bank, the French donor agency and others were very active. Everyone continues to believe that to improve access for the poor to water and sanitation services, they have to partner with the private sector, as this provides efficiency, according to Mathys. All agree that they have to find a new model for the financing of investments to offer more guarantees to the private sector. 'All, that is, except the activists', Mathys says.

Alain Mathys is fairly optimistic. Many initiatives – from the EU, the World Bank, and European agencies – attempt to provide a more secure environment for private investment. 'I am confident that the water sector will continue to evolve positively. New partnerships will develop. In the past we thought that globally the role of the state was diminishing and now we realise that the state and public institutions, like the World Bank, still have quite an important role to play, partly in terms of regulating the environment.'

For four years, Alain Mathys lived in La Paz, Bolivia. He is annoyed by activists who accuse the World Bank of having forced the privatisation in Cochabamba, as the World Bank said no to the huge dam project, recommending a cheaper option. He stresses, however, that it is vital to explain what you are doing to the population. That process was a failure in Cochabamba. 'If you do not explain to the community, you should not be surprised if they do not cooperate. In Cochabamba the company should have explained the costs and benefits far more clearly. It would have been possible to hold a referendum or started a stakeholder committee, to discuss what amount the consumers are willing to pay.' For Mathys, the model is to hold discussions with members of the community and explain the different options: 'If you want a house connection you have to pay a connection fee. There will be another option where you may participate in the work, like digging trenches, which will make it less costly to install water. Or maybe a standpipe not far from the house is the best solution and then you pay according to that.'

The main issue is that tariffs must increase because the company has to invest a large amount of money when it takes over a poorly managed utility where the infrastructure is in bad shape and there is only partial coverage, according to Mathys. Connecting one poor family is often more expensive than connecting one rich family, because the poor are remote from the network, and the company has to invest even more, which is not profitable. The key point is to get a return on invested capital, to generate enough cash to pay the capital interest and the operational costs.

He compares access to water with buying a new washing machine: 'If your parents used to wash clothes by hand and buy a new washing machine, then they invest money in it. Every time you increase the level of the service you have to pay more.'

For the first five years of a contract, the company will normally run at a deficit. Representatives of Suez discuss with financial institutions how to ensure the company has the required cash-flow. There are two options: either the World Bank or another institution can finance the infrastructure by delivering the capital to the community, or the Bank can finance the company's deficit by an agreed amount for each cubic metre sold. The consumer pays one part and the World Bank pays the other part. Every year the part that the consumer must pay increases and the World Bank's part decreases. The operator always receives the same amount, which allows for investments to be made, as there is a rate of return from the first day. This model has already been implemented in some countries. For example, Suez has finalised an agreement with the IFC for Manaus in Brazil where the IFC provides the funds for extending services to 12,000 new connections.

Strong regulatory authorities are important to make the process work. If there is no regulator, the private sector tends not to operate properly. Alain Mathys has come across a number of weak regulatory authorities. He explains what can happen. 'Every five years you meet with the regulator, open your books and say: "This is expenditure and this is the income." We try to decrease our expenditure. We need to increase the tariffs and the regulator will say yes or no. They may say, "Politically we cannot accept a tariff increase because there is going to be an election next year, and if we increase the tariff it is bad for the current governor or the president." In the Philippines, for example, a legal framework exists, but for political reasons the government does not choose to apply it', Mathys says.

I ask Mathys about corruption, which is a major problem in many countries. He points out that it was not the private companies that invented it – even though he is aware that I know about the bribing of the mayor in Grenoble (see Chapter 9). He knows quite a lot about the scale of bribery, especially from the time he worked for the African Development Bank. Zaire, under Mobutu, used to be a bad case. 'Every private contractor had to pay a commission to win a bid, or a government representative would say: "I can sign the contract but you must give me 10 per cent and put it in a bank account in Luxembourg".'

In France formerly, when there was a bid for a public service contract the company that had donated money to an election campaign could well become the winner of the bid. The law now forbids this.

Another form of corruption is the entrance fee, which is quite usual in South America, for example. A public authority agrees to give a private company the contract, provided that the company pays a fee. The company that pays the highest entrance fee wins the concession. 'This is stupid. We paid close to $100 million for the Manaus concession. You cannot then invest this money in service improvements, which would be much better, so in the end the consumers have to pay for it. Mathys thinks that in the future Suez will probably not enter into contracts where there is a demand for an entrance fee.

When the city of Berlin decided to contract out its water and sanitation services, Suez was asked how much they were prepared to pay. 'Vivendi (Veolia) won the competition. Vivendi offered more than $1 billion to manage the water services in Berlin. It was amazing!' he says.

We have no more time to talk about Europe. Before I leave, Alain Mathys points out that environmental directives within the EU are also very strict. Wastewater technology is quite sophisticated and its operation requires considerable skill, he tells me. What he is actually saying is that this represents a potential future market. I have had a good lesson in how private companies think and act regarding water distribution, and enjoyed a good lunch. During the day the phrase 'rate of return' has been a persistent refrain.

I read later in Suez's 2003 annual report that private-sector water operations are growing around the world. In developing countries the company can, however, only maintain its place if solutions are found to avoid risk-taking and if it can be ensured that public authorities are able to honour their contractual obligations, the rates of return. Outside Europe, indicates the report, there will be strict selectivity in capital expenditure. Suez has thus appointed a chief risk operator.

Veolia: lessons learned

The offices of Veolia lie only a few blocks from those of Suez. This is practical, since the companies often collaborate, despite being competitors. I walk to Veolia. I want to know why its subsidiary Aguas del Aconquija has not remained in Tucumán in Argentina. There is a striking difference between the run-down state water utility's offices in San Miguel de Tucumán, with their bare walls, and Veolia's headquarters in Paris. A focal point of the reception area is a vase with a huge floral bouquet. Polite English-speaking young women stand behind the desk. The foyer is furnished with glass cases displaying long slender bronze statues. In one corner, a television set is on, showing uninterrupted newscasts about the latest world events.

Impressive glass doors lead to the offices and to Charles-Louis de Maud'huy, who is adviser to Henri Proglio, president and executive director of Veolia. Maud'huy turns out to be a jovial elderly gentleman. Papers are piled high on his desk. He refers to himself as 'an obsolete engineer who has been faithful to the company for thirty years'. He was for a while a member of the board of the Spanish subsidiary of Vivendi Universal that financed the first film by Pedro Almodóvar. Vivendi was building an empire that included many things besides water. Maud'huy calls the former chief executive officer Jean-Marie Messier 'a strange character', who regarded water, waste management and transport as sidelines.

Maud'huy was chairman of the board for the company in Tucumán. In response to the question of why tariffs for water and sanitation services were raised so high that the residents of Tucumán could not afford to pay them, he replies: 'Tucumán is a very simple story. Rates were not higher than in Buenos Aires. It is, however, true that this local community was poorer. How to recoup the costs of delivering water is up to the political body to decide and the rates were accepted by the provincial administration.'

According to Maud'huy, the new governor of Tucumán, General Antonio Bossi, was the cause of all the misery. It was the first time in the 150-year history of the company that it had to terminate a contract. 'We have survived two world wars, but we could not continue in Tucumán. Governor Bossi rejected our termination of the contract yet later he decided that he was going to terminate it. If you do not like the operator, you do not force a company to stay. Bossi said that we were bad and in addition that we had to remain', Maud'huy says. 'We had to deliver services for several months without revenues.'

The case went before the International Centre for Settlement of Investment Disputes. It is still not concluded. Maud'huy says, however, that in two decisions the tribunal in Washington has declared that the company had reason to terminate the contract. 'We won. The governor used excessive political power and harassed us. Bossi demanded that we both lower tariffs and increase investments, which was impossible.' The province of Tucumán, for its part, claimed that the dispute was about the contract between the province and the company. It contained a clause stipulating that, in the case of contractual dispute, the operator had to appear before the local judiciary. The public prosecutor in Tucumán, Benito Garzon, had explained to me that the company was not found to be in the right. Maud'huy says: 'Last year we won the second decision in ICSID, but the province requested a change in some of the wording.' According to Maud'huy, Veolia is entitled to $380 million in compensation for lost revenues over the twenty-eight years remaining in the contract.

Maud'huy is convinced that no company will want to deal with the politicians in Tucumán and adds: 'Being there was a sad story, but it has shown us that dictators have to behave. One day the governor Bossi said to me: "I understand, Mr Maud'huy, that you still have not understood that the system is stronger than the contract." So everything seems to be centred on the system', Maud'huy starts laughing – it is a despondent laugh, dedicated to Bossi.

Maud'huy is the oldest member on the board of Aguas Argentina in Buenos Aires, of which Veolia is part-owner. He has learnt a few lessons. 'The concepts of Buenos Aires and Manila were not based on a correct analysis. The right analysis does not start with investment needs and then calculate the tariff.' According to Maud'huy, they should start by looking at the capacity of the population to pay, which would enable the company to calculate and recover its costs. Then the company should go back to the elected authority. It is up to this body to decide how much money it wants to invest, what people can afford to repay, or whether it wants to invest more and who should pay for it, either taxpayers or consumers, perhaps through surcharged electricity. This is a political decision. The operator has no legitimacy to take that decision.

He explains that the poorer the community, the more expensive are the investments, and thus the greater are the risks. The costs should be shared on a national basis; the burden should not fall on the poor people in the community.

Maud'huy appears to be a warm admirer of Michel Camdessus, head of the panel that submitted the report in Kyoto on how global water and sanitation services should be financed in the future. Veolia had issued a warning before this, saying that it might be difficult to invest in poor countries. Camdessus supports the company's view. Maud'huy has visited his office to discuss these questions. During the interview with me, Maud'huy referred to the Camdessus Report several times.

Having spent years in Buenos Aires, Maud'huy has realised that it becomes too expensive if private funding is the sole source of financing. He knows that Camdessus has a very strong conviction that, with few exceptions, public funding is cheaper than private funding. Private operators should not be responsible for all the investments and financing. Here he uses the same arguments as the directors of Suez. In the case of currency devaluation, some mechanism should be put in place so that the private companies are protected against risk. If this were done, there is no reason why Veolia should not continue to expand its business in developing countries. Maud'huy points out, however, that the culture of Veolia is based on a very strong belief that 'Our main responsibility is to operate existing systems, to optimise their maintenance.' He stresses that it is very important for municipalities to take responsibility for deciding on the quality of the services, investment plans, and so on. The World Bank should lend them the money. 'It is the local authority who is master over water. We operate these systems when communities ask us to do so. If the result is good, maybe other cities will want us to come.'

What does he think about activists who are against private solutions, I ask. Maud'huy was one of the first to debate the issue with Maude Barlow, a well-known critic of privatisation. She leads a large civil-society movement in Canada, the Council of Canadians, with 100,000 members. He has also held talks with David Boys from the global trade union federation Public Services International. 'It is very important that we discuss. There is a lot of ignorance. At the World Water Forum in The Hague, everyone exchanged insults and nobody listened to anybody. In Kyoto in 2003, we at least listened to each other.' He tells me that there he even kissed Maude Barlow on the cheek! David Boys, for his part, told me later that it is disingenuous for Veolia to say that is regards local authorities as the masters over water. Veolia lobbies for an ISO standard, which means a uniform standard of water quality, and makes other demands of municipalities. For Veolia this will be an opportunity to offer the technology needed to reach the required standard. This is especially the case in Europe.

Only a few years ago, Veolia had a very optimistic outlook. The company was counting on the private market increasing in Latin America from 4 to 60 per cent between 1997 and 2010, in Africa from 3 to 33 per cent, and in Asia from 1 to 20 per cent. Now by contrast – witness its 2003 annual report – Veolia focuses on long-term contracts in Europe, the United States and Asia. It sees strong potential growth in China, South Korea, Japan, Singapore and Australia. No poor country in Africa is even mentioned.

15

The global protest movement

There has long been a chorus of condemnation of top-level managers in the private, international water sector. They are referred to as water barons, who inhabit a world of power, privilege and elegant gatherings, with revolving-door connections to the corridors of government.

In 1998, a group around Portugal's former president Mario Soares launched a *Water Manifesto: The Right to Life* in Lisbon. The *Manifesto* points out that water is vital for both human life and the larger ecosystem. No individual or group has the right to make water private property. 'There is no production of wealth without access to water. Water is not like any other resource; it is not an exchangeable, marketable commodity', the *Manifesto* states.

An increasing number of NGOs, civil-society and non-profit-making organisations are likewise engaged in the struggle against the privatisation of water. The World Bank Bonds Boycott is an international grassroots campaign, launched in 2000 by organisations from thirty-five global South countries and the USA. The World Bank receives most of the resources to finance its lending from the sale of bonds on private capital markets. Bonds are bought by governments, universities, mutual funds, pension funds, life insurance companies, churches and civic groups. The idea behind boycotting the bonds is to threaten the Bank's primary source of funding.

Maude Barlow, president of civil rights movement the Council of Canadians, is fighting against everything that multinational water companies stand for. Her very name gives rise to sighs and groans among private water managers, not least within Suez. She maintains that future wars will increasingly be concerned with fighting about water; that there is a water shortage and that this shortage will increase. She is co-founder of Blue Planet, a project that consists of farmers, environmentalists, indigenous populations, employees in the public sector and others who are struggling for water to belong to the earth and its people. According to Barlow, the industrialised world would be able to supply every single person on earth with clean water if we wrote off the debts of the Third World, increased development assistance, and introduced a tax on currency speculation.

There follow some examples of different places in the world where people are protesting. Many involve trade unions that have water workers as members.

Latin America

In October 2002 in the city of Montevideo in Uruguay, people were busy painting placards to demonstrate against privatisation of water and sanitation services. Among those organising the protests was the trade union FFOSE, which organises employees in water utilities in Uruguay. FFOSE opposed the intended privatisation legislation, and even developed alternative proposals to keep water public, in cooperation with engineers, civil society and municipal managers. Furthermore, in 2004 the union and other organisations arranged a massive petition campaign, successfully forcing the government to hold a referendum on its privatisation legislation.

Two-thirds of voters expressed the view that water and sanitation are fundamental rights and charged the government with ensuring this right by legislation, also demanding that piped water should be supplied exclusively and directly by state-owned entities.

Protests have also taken place in a number of other countries in Latin America, organised by trade unions, environmental groups, political parties and voluntary organisations. For example, there is a strong coalition of consumers, environmentalists, trade unions, local and national politicians and churches in Brazil. They managed to stop the planned privatisation of water operations in Rio de Janeiro in 1999 and continue to pressure national and state governments to support public water. There is growing public dissatisfaction with privatisation globally, but especially in Latin America. According to the World Bank report *Reforming Infrastructure*, in 2002 almost 90 per cent of Argentinians and 80 per cent of Chileans surveyed disapproved of the principle of privatisation.

The United States

In the USA, a Public Citizen Water-for-All campaign has been running since 2001. Suez and Veolia attempted to take over water operations in New Orleans. Members of this campaign persuaded the local authorities to stop privatisation. Mayor Ray Nagin has declared that his city's water privatisation effort is officially dead. The Water-for-All campaign was also active in Atlanta, Georgia, where Suez lost a large contract. In 1999, Atlanta gave United Water Resources (UWR), a subsidiary of Suez, the task of running its water and sanitation services. The company promised to save $20 million per year, thereby reducing the cost of managing sanitation. In the event, only $10 million were saved and charges for sanitation increased. UWR also failed to collect bills worth $33 million, choosing instead to increase tariffs. In January 2003 the city and Suez agreed to terminate the contract and the city has since returned to municipally run water and sanitation services. The mayor, Shirley Franklin, complained that the company failed in its maintenance and repair responsibilities.

In the USA, over 80 per cent of water and sanitation services are still run by the public sector, even in Washington DC, where the World Bank and the IMF have their headquarters. In Washington DC, the infrastructure network was previously in poor condition. Water became polluted. Politicians considered privatisation as a way to upgrade the water system. Yet, after months of discussion and commissioned studies, the city decided to retain water and sanitation services in the public sector. An evaluation had shown that it was possible to improve the utility's efficiency at a lower cost to consumers without privatisation. Improvements were instead financed through the issuing of bonds.

Nevertheless, global water companies remain active. Suez already owns shares in the second largest private water company in the USA, United Water, and has bought two other large water utilities. Veolia and RWE also own water companies in the USA. Through intensive lobbying, they attempt to persuade mayors and local politicians that it is good to privatise. One trick is to persuade the media to publish articles stressing the benefits of privatisation and to take part in the debate at public meetings. The companies may, however, find themselves in hot water if they do not perform well. The USA has a well-developed regulatory system with considerable consumer influence. Indeed, it seems as if the companies are increasingly in trouble. Suez was kicked out of Atlanta, and its concession in New Jersey is in deep trouble.

Canada

The Canadian Union of Public Employees (CUPE) has long been involved in a struggle against privatisation in Canada. Nearly all water and wastewater facilities in Canada are still in public control.

They are owned and operated by local authorities. Municipalities have, however, permitted the water infrastructure to deteriorate and hence CUPE is fighting for more money and resources for water and sanitation services.

CUPE is in the vanguard of Water Watch. It has committees, engages in lobbying, and conducts campaigns got public support. Robert Fox of CUPE says: 'We were sure that we would not be exposed to any private companies in water operations here, but it went faster than we thought possible.' CUPE directs a searchlight on the large companies – Suez, Veolia and Thames Water – as soon as they attempt to take over a contract somewhere. If a contract is awarded, CUPE keeps a watchful eye on them.

CUPE tried to persuade the residents of Halifax to elect a new municipal council, in order to prevent a private company getting a foothold in the town, but failed. Suez out-manoeuvred Thames Water and was expected to operate the sewerage system. Protests occurred concerning the cleaning of harbour water, on environmental and other grounds. During the final negotiations, disputes arose between the company and the council. The project was abandoned. Halifax's mayor told the media that tearing up the contract would save taxpayers millions of dollars.

In Hamilton, adjacent to Lake Ontario, during a five-year period, the town, a local firm, two US companies and, most recently, Thames Water, have all had a go at running the water facility. One of the companies was Philip Services, whose sub-sidiaries gave money to various candidates in the municipal elections. The company cut 60 of the workforce of 128. It was accused of releasing millions of litres of sewage-polluted water. Some 115 people demanded compensation because their houses were damaged. The company refused to take responsibility for the damage it had caused, maintaining that it might have happened anyway. The trade union's point of view was that staff cuts were an important factor.

Those who advocate private solutions consider CUPE a trouble-some union. It is the greatest obstacle to privatisation in Canada because of the strength of its campaigns. The union also objects to the large quantities of water being exported to the USA and demands that this be stopped. CUPE's goal is a high-quality public sector. This requires local authorities investing in the education of their employees, thereby enabling the appropriate level of certification.

Other parts of the world

There have been protests against privatisation of water in Malaysia, in India, Sri Lanka and other Asian countries. In Thailand, the police used pepper spray to disperse protesters during a hearing on the privatisation of the public water company. The electricity workers' and water workers' unions have formed the national Public Utilities Protection Network (PUPN), to fight privatisation and encourage citizens to get involved in decisions affecting Thailand's core public services.

In South Africa protests have been particularly intense. SAMWU, the municipal workers' union in South Africa, regards water conferences throughout the world as circus acts with a lot of empty chatter, run by an international lobby for private solutions, led by people like Ismael Serageldin, former vice-president of the World Bank. Lance Veotte of SAMWU says that, for them, access to water is an issue that is bound up with giving every individual the possibility of developing – like, for example, the little girl who cannot attend school because she must fetch water for her township family who cannot afford a connection.

Europe has also seen protests. For example, 'No profit on water', say the trade unions in both the Czech Republic and in Portugal. In a letter to PSI they say that the struggle to keep water in public ownership must never be abandoned.

The water conference industry

Water conferences are held throughout the world. The Third World Water Forum in Kyoto in 2003 alone accounted for millions of dollars in costs for travel, accommodation, dinners, conference premises and activities. Would it not be better to supply people with water instead – to exchange words for action? Critics tend to believe that water conferences have a function but that they do not translate readily into concrete action plans. The UN's International Decade for Water ran from 1980 to 1990. The goal was to provide access to potable water for all by the year 2000 – a goal which, signally, has not been realised. Since then several water conferences have taken place.

The forum in Kyoto in Japan saw close to 8,000 pre-registered participants, the attendance of 1,000 journalists and 130 ministers, according to the World Water Council, one of the organisers. The water industry and the various organisations that support it in different ways largely dominated the agenda. The organisers of this type of forum regard them as indispensable. 'Our discussions here in Kyoto will have far greater importance for humanity than the current crisis in the Middle East', said William Cosgrove, former president of WWC.

Conferences like that in Kyoto are, of course, occasions for exchanging experiences and information, for placing water and sanitation services high on the international agenda, for exerting pressure on governments to invest more in providing clean water for their citizens. The global trade union federation PSI utilised the Kyoto forum as a platform for repeatedly making a point in the debate and presenting its message: 'Invest in sound public solutions!' Responses varied from cynical smiles to people who listened and grew interested, even though PSI's representatives sometimes felt their words were destined to fall mainly on deaf ears.

16

Taking responsibility
in the developing world

A range of activities are under way to facilitate the continued
expansion of private companies in the world's water and sanitation sector. At the same time, a growing number of reports call
into question the sense in expecting the private sector to solve
all water problems. Local authorities, governments and the water
companies are often simply not equipped or able enough to
manage the changes entailed in the process of privatisation. British
charities WaterAid and Tearfund, note as much in a report, *New
Rules: Does PSP Benefit the Poor?*, which studied the effects of
private solutions in several countries.

For example, when water pipes are repaired and replaced this
often favours those who are already connected to the water
network. The poor, who are not connected, come low on the list
of priorities. When a company complains that a contract needs
to be rewritten, it should know that very few governments in
developing countries possess an adequate overview of their water
and sanitation systems. And it is difficult for other agencies to
obtain this information. In Manila in the Philippines, for example,
the International Finance Corporation of the World Bank group
prepared the basic data for the procurement process. The Bank

underestimated the scale of the water network. It is difficult to provide exact information regarding a network buried in the ground, not least without access to a computer system.

It is not always certain that a private company will wish to establish itself in a particular area. A state water utility in Mozambique began installing water posts in rural areas but was forced to cut back, because donors demanded private solutions. It subsequently appeared that there were virtually no private entrepreneurs interested. The episode resulted in a serious deterioration in the living conditions of the poor.

Sometimes a community will favour a technical solution that they feel will suit them better. A private company installed some hand pumps in rural areas of Mozambique. When the pumps broke down, there were no spare parts. Conclusion: it would have been better to dig a well so the community could draw up water.

What is required, the WaterAid and Tearfund report suggests, is a thorough understanding of how the private sector functions and what the results of private solutions will be. There are two camps: those who do not want to see any private solutions and those who give it almost uncritical support. The latter camp includes donors, banks and the WTO, which believe the private sector has the ability to solve almost anything.

It is increasingly common for responsibility for water and sanitation services to be handed over to the local district or to municipal authorities. Yet the report regards these as being even less competent than central authorities at regulating private companies. It is more important to achieve a functioning management and regulatory system with active citizen participation than to have a free market.

Those with the greatest need for water, the truly poor, are not even visible. They live on the outskirts of towns and cities, sometimes on land they have occupied illegally. They are not catered for in town planning and are excluded from official statistics, and there is nothing to indicate that the private sector would do anything to include them in its plans. If a population is not on side, it paves the way for failure. Riots, like those in Cochabamba, may not be far away.

World Bank figures show that private investors have tended to be drawn to semi-developed countries. Sub-Saharan countries, where water is most scarce, account for less than 1 per cent of investment. Profit-making multinationals cannot be expected to play a leading role in solving the problems of the poor countries of the world. New solutions are required. International donors, aid agencies and development banks must focus on local authorities, governments, public utilities and civil society, instead of being fixated on private solutions in developing countries. 'Each company exists to make maximum profits and not because of any solidarity.' These are the conclusions that WaterAid and Tearfund have drawn.

Jordan: a private oasis

There are no guarantees that private solutions will deliver the desired results, Rebhieh Suleiman, a researcher at the Royal Institute of Technology in Stockholm, reminds us. She worked as a chemist, before changing her career, and was for a while employed as chief buyer at the water and sanitation company in Amman in Jordan. In 1999 a consortium, largely run by Suez, which called itself Lema Water, won the water and wastewater management contract. It gives the company a toehold in the Middle East. Suleiman says: 'Jordan does not have efficient public authorities and institutions and so it does not matter whether a private company does or does not arrive. Irrespectively, one is subject to the bureaucracy that already exists.' The most important conclusion she has drawn is that 'It may even get worse if a country is forced to accept private solutions in order to get loans.' Suleiman suggests that the World Bank should instead engage technical expertise, which could work side by side with a public water utility and assist it for a number of years.

Suleiman's research concerns privatisation in Amman, a city of 1.6 million inhabitants. The object is not to assess whether the private sector has succeeded or failed, but to examine the changes that have taken place since 1999. She has interviewed the various parties affected and studied the documentation.

Jordan is a very dry country. Despite huge investment, it still has problems with water supplies. Of the rain that falls, only 15 per cent runs into the rivers, with 85 per cent evaporating. The water deficit has resulted in the country having to increase its food imports. In short, there is a major water shortage. Jordan shares its water resource – the River Jordan – with other countries. Lebanon, for example, wants to divert more of the water. This has led Israeli Prime Minister Ariel Sharon to make renewed threats of war.

There is an underlying familiar pattern, nevertheless: the country's water and wastewater services are viewed as inefficient. The public water authority has no capital. There is not enough money to improve the water and sanitation systems. Charges do not cover costs. There are 13 employees per 1,000 connections, compared to the 4 or fewer of efficiently run utilities. Figures don't exist on the number of households connected to the sewerage system. Residents in newly built apartments do not get billed. The list of failings goes on.

Since 1993, Jordan has tried to tackle the problems by, among other things, turning to the private sector. This is also the most likely route to acquire capital for investments. Arthur Andersen was duly contracted for consulting services. (It subsequently earned notoriety as one of the US companies that went into liquidation following the Enron scandal.) The World Bank meanwhile helped the Ministry for Water and Irrigation carry out an evaluation to provide the basis for a five-year plan of action. The Bank granted a loan of $55 billion for improving the service and supporting the four-year contract. The contract was awarded to the Suez-led consortium Lema Water over the sole competitor, the former Vivendi, now Veolia.

Lema is supposed to improve efficiency, reduce leakage, repair the network and change meters, maintain and operate the water and sanitation systems, and do the billing. Lema was obliged to retain 50 per cent of the employees for the first year of the contract. It had the right to reduce its payroll by 12.5 per cent by the end of the contract.

Charges for water were formerly low because the state subsidised water and sanitation services. The billing system was changed in 1999. Amman now has the second highest average charge in the whole of the Middle East and North Africa. The state no longer provides subsidies to the poor. However, the system is designed so that the richer inhabitants and industry pay more, and the poor pay less. Indeed, some non-household consumers pay as much as twelve times higher. Tomato factories pay a little less, as they are regarded as a vital part of Jordan's economy. The high tariffs have had unexpected outcomes, such as the fact that large hotels and commercial enterprises have started supplying their own water, taking delivery by water tankers; it is cheaper and the hotels also avoid paying wastewater charges. Most ordinary households are able to pay their bills, except the poorest, who cannot afford the charges. If they do not pay, their water is cut off.

What, then, has been achieved in Jordan? The managing director of Lema Water says that the company has turned former financial losses to profit. Water quality has improved and electricity costs have been reduced. Education, IT and customer contacts also work better. Staff have been encouraged to perform better.

The Ministry of Water and Irrigation, for its part, has set up a special Programme Management Unit (PMU), to monitor the company, and ensure that it fulfils its contractual obligations. PMU staff say that unaccounted-for water was projected as 53 per cent in 1999 and was supposed to be reduced to 43, 36 and 25 per cent during contract years 1, 2 and 4, respectively. What has been achieved is a reduction of only 5–7 per cent. The quantity of water handled is between 92 and 94 million cubic metres, of which 46 million cubic metres are being billed.

A member of PMU staff commented: 'Frankly speaking, it is not possible for Lema or any other company to achieve the stipulated targets before rehabilitation of the whole network. However this company accepted and approved the contractual conditions of the bid at an early stage and they should comply with that. Many companies quit the bid because they knew how hard it would be to reach the targets.'

The government and army owe between $3 and 4 million in unpaid water bills. Lema has not succeeded in resolving this. The company blames the old computer system and says it is waiting for a new one. The staff conclude: 'Many parties influence the decision-making process including the World Bank and the French embassy. The state can bear the risk of losing $10 million in respect of this contract, but cannot afford to lose financial assistance from donors. The turnover of the French company is many times the entire budget of this country, so how can we exert an influence?'

Part of the money from the World Bank loan, some $10 million, is allocated as fixed management fees. Some $24 million are allocated to investment and improvement to the service. 'From this account Lema bought 70 French Citroën and Renault cars. We struggled to limit them to this number, as in the beginning they wanted to buy 150 cars', a member of PMU staff says.

What do customers think? A sixth did not know that a private company ran the water and sanitation services, although it had done so for the last three years. Some 80 per cent claimed that prices had risen, which they thought was unacceptable. With regard to quality and level of service, 60 per cent had not noticed any difference, while 40 per cent thought that they had improved – for example, better access to water and a more rapid response to complaints.

'The lack of insight and information among ordinary citizens is very striking', remarks Rebhieh Suleiman. Notably, the trade unions were given no opportunity to participate; there was no information about an upcoming campaign to persuade people to save water. It followed that there was no reaction, either positive or negative. She concludes that the arrival of the private sector in Amman was not of major importance to people. Amman might just as well have continued to operate the water and wastewater treatment plant as a public service. Of course, this was not possible since the city was not permitted to borrow the requisite money. There was thus no alternative to privatisation. Now more privatisation is under way in Jordan – one of the few countries to use a private water company in the region.

Water in Tunis: an efficient public utility

It is a myth that the public sector lacks the resources to supply populations with fresh water. Tunis, for example, has an efficient public utility that even makes a profit, which then contributes to investment. A comparison with Casablanca in 2000 showed that Tunis has less 'unaccounted-for water' – that is, disappearance through leakage and unpaid accounts – than the Moroccan city has. The significance of the comparison is that Suez runs most of Casablanca's water and sanitation services. The contract is purported to have come about through personal contacts between King Hassan and the then French executive director for Suez. There was no tendering process.

17

Public not private,
people not profit

'We do not oppose the private sector. We oppose operating water for profit. Most of all, we are trying to demonstrate good examples of public water management. We have something positive to advocate, to reform and strengthen the public services.'

These are the words of David Boys, utilities officer of Public Services International, the global trade union federation. Boys, born in Germany but holding a Canadian passport, worked in the trade-union movement in the USA and Canada for eleven years. Nowadays his workplace is the PSI office, which is squeezed into a shopping mall in the small French town of Ferney-Voltaire, close to the Swiss border. For years he has conducted a determined and tireless struggle against privatisation of water.

Boys is clearly not popular with the executives of the private water companies. One Suez director dismissed the opposition coordinated by Boys and others as the work of 'some northern ideologues'. Boys brushes such criticism aside: 'This is a desperate attempt to dismiss all the opposition. It is a sign of weakness', he says. He acknowledges that the public sector has failed to meet the needs of citizens in many developing countries, but rejects the notion that the private sector is the solution. 'This is where the analysis goes wrong. The private companies exist to make profit and the poor are poor because they have no money, so how can you make a profit from the poor? The first investment the companies make is putting water meters in the houses so they can figure out who is paying or who is not.'

Boys accepts that private companies possess good management skills and deploy very advanced technologies and are able to access capital. Hence a well-managed public sector will use the private sector to build treatment plants, to maintain its pipe network, perhaps even to install meters. PSI has no objection to a municipality buying technical services through fair and open bidding. 'What we oppose is the private sector taking over the whole management of the water and sanitation system; that they manage it for profit rather than for social need. We are opposed to using public funding such as World Bank money and other development funds for privatisation, instead of focusing on community development and public water and sewerage utilities.'

David Boys is also convinced that decisions on charges and access to water and sanitation must be made socially and politically and not by the market. 'We resist having water defined as a commodity.' According to information the PSI receives from its affiliated unions, the large private companies concentrate their services in the large cities and therefore do not reach the poor unless governments pay or provide multiple guarantees. 'It would be better if the rich in these countries subsidise their own poor instead of subsidising shareholders in Europe', he says.

Boys is unable to understand the logic of a foreign company managing a water system on a thirty- to forty-year contract. He draws a comparison: 'If I want to get my house painted, I decide what colours I would like to have and when to do it. I check the references of decorating companies, they give me a bid, I sign a contract with one of them, and get the painter to do the work. This does not mean that I let the painter move into my house and tell me how to run my family.'

Boys has attended many of the world's water conferences. He talks about the Second World Water Forum in The Hague in 2000, where PSI tried to get formal recognition, which was problematic. In the meantime, the big water companies spent a lot of money on glossy publications, took stands to display their technology, and organised receptions with food and drink. Ministers from all over the world visited the Forum. 'We were not too welcome. We were regarded as outsiders', Boys says. David Boys headed PSI's delegation at the Third World Water Forum in Kyoto in 2003. 'Water policy decisions are being made by people who do not live in the communities that are affected by these decisions', he points out. PSI is trying to bring a different perspective to these global meetings. He does not understand why the private sector expects to be the only solution for people to gain access to clean water. 'The private model lacks the capacity to reach the goal of half of 1.2 billion people by 2015. Even Suez admits that. One cannot depend on private companies to such an extent. They do not have the capacity, even if they get a lot of money from the international financial institutions. We will be forced to use the public sector, whether we like it or not.'

Boys points out that, since it is not possible to make a profit from the poor, companies invariably run into problems with the contract and governments are then forced to intervene and guarantee profits. The report of the Camdessus Panel on water financing in the future he regards as a huge disappointment. The World Bank, the IMF and other development banks as well as private companies will continue to dictate conditions. 'The panel's report is more or less what I expected: an attempt to save the ebbing fortunes of international water companies. Private companies have been given far too much influence', he says. 'Governments and the large international banks are expected to develop guarantees and insurance systems to protect company profits.' He points out that not a single head or financial expert from a municipal utility participated in the Camdessus Panel.

David Boys believes that there are too many problems with private solutions and is seeking a more balanced and informed debate. This is not so easy in practice, since local authorities cannot afford to spend money on international meetings. He sees no sign that the large banks have any interest in the attendance of, say, an executive director of a municipal water utility in Porto Alegre at a meeting in Kyoto to talk about the positive experiences of publicly run water supply. 'The head of the World Bank, James Wolfensohn, does not ask what might be the opinion of Hans Engelberts, secretary-general of PSI. Nor does he turn to any manager of a municipal water utility in Porto Alegre. He asks Jérôme Monod', says Boys. (Jérôme Monod, former executive director of Suez, has been a political adviser to both President Chirac and Wolfensohn.)

Neither were there representatives of farmers, or of women's organisations, on the Camdessus Panel, although these groups arguably have the greatest interest in access to water. By contrast, private companies were not only represented but also participated actively to ensure that their interests were served. 'The panel even proposes setting up a fund to contribute extra money for preparing contracts and tenders, since the process is quite costly', notes Boys. He fears that this money will go to lawyers and consultants to draw up contracts that the local authorities, unused to negotiations, cannot interpret. He notes how sharply critical the panel is of the public sector and its way of running water and sanitation services, while the companies are treated with kid gloves.

Boys can quote examples of many public water utilities that would like to extend their water services themselves and make them more efficient, but that require international economic support to be able to do so. These municipalities lack access to investment capital. 'They are starved by an international leadership possessed with supporting private companies. Decisions are taken at a global level, where those who are affected, the municipal water utilities, do not exert any influence over what happens. They have never been provided with a platform, the managers have never been invited', observes Boys. 'What is never discussed', he points out, 'is the risk taken by local authorities tied by contracts that may become a thirty-year nightmare, since it costs so much to break them. In addition, the local authority in question loses competence to operate the plant and thus it becomes difficult to take it back. Generally speaking, it is not easy for local authorities to defend themselves against private solutions and to make a municipal bid of their own.'

'Above all', says Boys 'Suez and Veolia have personnel who have developed a singular capacity to lobby, to influence mayors in large cities, environmental ministers and other political leaders. They know that decisions about water are mainly political. They win bids with cheap tenders, convinced that within two or three years they can renegotiate the contracts. They know that governments then will not be able to say "No!" since these companies already run the services. And the companies will hire former ministers, commissioners, regulators, whatever it takes to help them win these contracts.'

David Boys shows me an invitation to a water conference in Bratislava that he happened to come across, which features both use of a golf course and a wine tasting. The speakers include several ministers, bank officials from the European Bank for Reconstruction and Development, and the mayor of Bratislava. The sponsors are Veolia and Suez. The scheduled discussions about water and sanitation services across the world also involve the participation of other interested parties, both within the UN family and from the governments of different countries.

During 2002, the UN Committee for Economic, Cultural and Social Rights (ECOSOC) declared that water should be treated as a social and cultural necessity, a human right, and not simply an economic asset. The right to water is essential to the living of a healthy and dignified life. 'The declaration might increase the pressure on governments to actually supply people with water', Boys believes. At the same time, he thinks that companies are trying to exploit the UN for their own ends. The UN talks about partnership between the private and public sectors as a way of meeting the UN Millennium Development Goals. These partnerships involve multinational corporations and local or national governments. He is very concerned that this is a smokescreen for privatisation. He points out that the concept of partnership between a municipality in a developing country and a multinational corporation does not work. A partnership involves a common purpose between equals. Yet, in this case the one party is much stronger. 'The capacity of the corporations far outweighs that of small municipalities. The corporations have more expertise, more lawyers, more accountants, bigger budgets, more experience.'

Multinational corporations play an increasing role within the UN. Kofi Annan has included them in certain decision-making processes. It was a shock for David Boys to be informed in March 2004 about Kofi Annan's Advisory Board on Water, composed largely of some of the principal advocates of privatisation, among them Michael Camdessus; and including Gérard Payen, connected to Suez. The board also consists of former ministers of countries that have adopted privatisation policies, Mexico, Colombia and Egypt. The board was constituted without consultation, either with civil society or with many governments.

Through the International Confederation of Free Trade Unions, the PSI is involved in the UN Commission on Sustainable Development (CSD). At the annual meeting of the CSD in April

2004 major groups expressed the view that the creation of the Advisory Board was an affront to the multi-stakeholder process going on within CSD and was not acceptable within the UN system. With support from the NGO community, the PSI pressured the UN to add to the Board some representatives from labour, women, slum dwellers, farmers, public utilities and local government. And they did finally make some progress. David Boys is now included on the Advisory Board, as is a women's representative and a public utility manager!

David Boys considers that water conferences in various parts of the globe, organised by the UN and other organisations, fulfil an important role. Ministers from across the world gather to focus on water issues. This in turn makes demands of governments to deliver programmes on how to resolve water problems. He says that the northern hemisphere must give more aid to enable developing countries to invest in water and sanitation services. 'The North does not like to give money without making its own companies richer', he says ironically, and continues: 'The Dutch government is a major player promoting privatisation, and we find that quite hypocritical as it does not allow privatisation at home. Yet it thinks privatisation is best for developing countries and spends a lot of money enhancing privatisation.' Other governments in the North care less, according to Boys. Their involvement is restricted to the odd statement from time to time.

One serious problem is that governments in developing countries are not particularly interested in supplying people with water and sewerage. Typically, only a small fraction of the national budget is earmarked for water. 'Water is not as sexy as having a new highway or ten jet fighters. The pipes are not visible. Water gets no attention from the political elite, even if clean water in the tap results in infant mortality being reduced', says David Boys. He believes that the only way to pressure governments to invest in water is through popular political pressure. This can only occur if communities mobilise their citizens and force governments to change their priorities.

There are viable alternatives to the private sector running water services. PSI has a 'Quality Public Services' campaign. Its objectives include:

- ensuring that public services are adequately funded so that well-trained and properly resourced workers can deliver quality services to all who need them;
- meeting social objectives, especially poverty eradication and people's empowerment;
- ensuring that all public-sector workers enjoy fundamental workers' rights;
- creating a movement of organisations to pressure governments and global institutions to cease the dogmatic drive to privatisation and instead ensure the viability of quality public services.

Boys is adamant that a great deal of effort must be put into creating a good public sector – that it is there that the solution to the water crisis will be found. The campaign is being conducted by trade unions all over the world; environmental groups and many other organisations support it. The major challenge, according to the PSI, is to persuade public water companies to exchange experiences and knowledge to the end of developing better-run utilities.

The PSI set out to cooperate with public managers in order to bring good examples of public water management to the fore at international meetings. Interest is considerable. The problem is that municipalities have no budget for sending delegates to international meetings, so the task is to find ways of funding these managers. At the Water Forums in The Hague and Kyoto, for example, not a single public-sector water manager spoke as an official guest. Discussions were dominated by the private sector.

Nevertheless, the picture is changing: municipal managers from Brazil, South Africa, Japan and Bangladesh are in contact with one another and there is also interest among managers in Spain, Germany and Sweden. Public water authorities and utilities in Brazil are already collaborating with two public companies in South Africa.

David Boys is convinced that a great deal of invaluable knowledge exists in the public sector, but also that it can be efficient, run a high-quality service and stand for regeneration. 'What motives would municipal managers, who are performing well, have for sharing their knowledge with others?' I ask. 'The managers who have begun to share their experiences are very committed', he replies. 'Managers can be motivated for social and professional reasons. It is positive to demonstrate that one is so good that one becomes a mentor for others.'

Another option is for strong public water companies to support weaker ones, with managerial and technical advice, on a non-profit basis. This notion of public–public partnerships is gaining attention. But how should these be financed? 'This is a problem', Boys admits. 'Why would the local taxpayers pay? The water utility is supposed to deliver water to the residents of the municipality, not help a public utility in another country.' There is some reason for optimism, however. Even in the Camdessus Panel there is recognition of the importance of the public–public concept.

Despite everything, Boys believes that banks, including the World Bank and donor agencies, will give more support to public solutions in the future, if it can be shown that they work. A good example is Stockholm Water, which for several years has contributed know-how in the Baltic States.

The PSI has developed proposals for financing water and sewerage services, for example through selling domestic bonds. Another possibility is to invest money from workers' pension funds. 'What can citizens do to influence ministers and other decision-

makers so that they listen and accept the available options?'
I ask. Boys encourages people to persuade politicians in EU
countries to raise their voices in the cause of retaining water and
sanitation services in public control, and to be conscious of the
powerful pro-privatisation forces within the EU, not least in the
European Commission, which advocates liberalisation of water
also in Europe.

David Boys shares with me his vision of the future – or is it
a dream? He believes that within fifteen years the private sector
will have identified its role. Companies may provide technical
services on a temporary basis to local authorities. They will
eventually start to recognise that their best position in relation to
municipalities is as servants not as managers. Their main interest
will be in contracts within industry, providing ultra-pure water
for certain manufacturing processes or cleaning up water polluted in the production processes. They will themselves come to
realise that such areas are where they perform best, rather than
taking over the management and operation of public water and
sanitation services.

Boys believes that companies will continue their privatisation
strategies but in a more cautious manner. Their interest is now
turning to China, in whose market they are already established.
Their opponents there cannot make their voices heard without
risking reprisals. The Chinese government is conducting an active
policy of privatisation.

Public Services International is a global trade-union
federation that represents 20 million women and men working in the public services around the world. It has some 600
affiliated unions in almost 150 countries. PSI is an officially
recognised non-governmental organisation for the public sector
within the ILO. It has consultative status with ECOSOC, and
observer status with UNCTAD and UNESCO.

18

GATS and the democratic deficit

Relatively few people know much about GATS. The General Agreement on Trade in Services is intended to reduce trade barriers. All trade is to be liberalised, including water and sanitation services. The EU Commission regards GATS as a way of creating new business opportunities for European water companies. To this end the Commission has invited companies to discuss their objectives and to identify the obstacles that make it difficult to establish themselves in new markets.

Trade in services is a rapidly expanding market across the world. Each country in the World Trade Organisation lists the services it is willing to open up to other countries. They may be business services, building services, tourism, transport, energy, environmental or other services. Under the Agreement any country can demand of another that services in the public sector should also be opened to other actors, namely private companies, if that country has already engaged the private sector within a particular service. Foreign and domestic companies should be able to compete on equal terms.

The EU coordinates the demands and undertakings of member countries. It has requested the introduction of a new heading under the section in GATS dealing with environmental services: 'Water for human use and wastewater management, wastewater collection, purification and distribution services through mains.' The introduction to the EU's list of demands states that the continued liberalisation of services is an asset for all members, and for developing countries. Most of the EU's proposals have been leaked. We know, for instance, that the EU Commission wants seventy-two countries to open their water supplies to foreign interests. Among these countries are Bangladesh, Bolivia, Botswana, Brazil, Egypt, Honduras, Panama, Paraguay and Tunisia.

The WTO emphasises that countries can choose whether and when they will open public services to foreign competition. Nevertheless, the same countries have often been subject to pressure from banks and governments to call in the private sector. Supporters claim that those who say no to GATS are in effect saying yes to private monopolies. Through GATS, they say, there is competition, which affects consumers positively. In practice, GATS might entail a developing country opening its water sector to competition: the infrastructure requires pipes, meters, chemical products, and other investments. However, a large, multinational corporation may make a low bid, win the tender, and take a loss for five years. It uses its own subsidiaries to supply and deliver products. In this way local industry is knocked out; the next time it will not be there to compete. The corporation can then dominate supply and increase its charges again.

Mike Waghorne, assistant general-secretary of PSI, is clear: GATS is a bad thing. 'If people knew, they would be angry', he says, adding that there is far too much secrecy around GATS. Citizens have not been informed of the demands the EU has made of developing countries. They are not publicly announced. They have nonetheless leaked out. Waghorne is opposed to keeping the negotiations confidential. 'People should be concerned about the secrecy of the process. It is not democratic. The requests by the EU and the offers Europe is making in response to those requests have been handled in secret', he says.

Another aspect of concern is a country's ability to control its own security. Governments can legislate and pass regulations, but they must make sure that the rules are not more burdensome to trade than necessary. A member state has a right to bring complaints to the WTO. A disputes panel has the power to ask the country to undo regulations it has passed. Waghorne raises a third concern: national governments deal with GATS at EU level without consulting the municipalities affected.

The EU demand that certain developing countries open their markets to private water companies is of great concern to Waghorne. For, once contracts are signed, the decision is irreversible. In practice, it becomes impossible for the population to change the policy. 'It is not possible to come later and say that one wants to develop one's own public sector instead. It is too late. For me, this is concerned with solidarity with these countries', Mike Waghorne says.

As part of one protest, trade unions and other organisations sent 'presents' to the EU Commissioner, Pascal Lamy, in Brussels. Hundreds of cartons were sent through the Belgian post office, and the workers there ensured that all the parcels were duly delivered. In all there were several truckloads. The message was: since Lamy had given a present, namely yet more privatised services, it was only fitting that he should receive presents in return. In response to the protests Pascal Lamy agreed to talk with representatives of PSI. He wanted them to hear the full story. Lamy assured PSI that at least education and health care are fully excluded from GATS. As a socialist, he says, he wants to safeguard the public sector, although he believes in competition as a tool to improve the performance of certain public services.

In a letter to PSI in 2003, Lamy confirmed that the EU has made requests in developing countries for access to certain sectors.

These are sectors where either governments have already decided to open up to private domestic suppliers or where experience has shown that competition has improved performance. He also reminded PSI that for many people in developing countries, access to affordable, efficient public services still remains a distant hope. Removing barriers, which either restrict access by foreign firms or discriminate against them, may improve certain public services, he claimed.

Mike Waghorne remains sceptical: 'What will happen in new trade talks? Increasingly conservative governments are being elected in Europe. This could change the whole picture. What will happen when someone other than Pascal Lamy negotiates for the EU? This has not even been finally negotiated. The EU can be pressurised into making concessions.' Waghorne is convinced that GATS is a way of achieving greater security for private corporations. 'The multinationals want guarantees if they make investments in other countries. Such decisions cannot be overturned by some political whim of a socialist government. A company might open a private hospital, and after some years a newly elected socialist government says that it does not want private hospitals. Then the company would have to leave. With GATS they do not run this risk.'

Campaigns against GATS are under way all over the world. In both Europe and Canada there are forces critical of GATS, while others support it. Canada, the USA and Mexico signed a free-trade agreement, NAFTA. Part of President George W. Bush's energy programme includes Canada selling water to the USA. Should Canada later want to stop the sale of water, it could not do so as this would be in conflict with the trade agreement, according to the trade union CUPE. Indeed, such conflicts are already taking place. In 1998 a company in California launched a lawsuit against the Canadian government for $10.5 billion because the province of British Columbia has prohibited the export of water.

CUPE fears that GATS will also make way for cheaper labour. It may be possible for foreign companies to recruit workers in the international labour market, whom they could then send anywhere on temporary contracts.

In South Africa, the government has declared that water will not be included in its GATS obligations.

The **World Trade Organisation** is committed to the liberalisation of trade. It has 140 country members. Negotiations take place in rounds of talks. The WTO regulates what individual countries may and may not do with respect to trade. Yet it lacks the powers to regulate the big players – the multinational corporations.

The **North American Free Trade Agreement** binds together in a trade agreement the USA, Canada and Mexico. It came into force in 1994. It stipulates that within fifteen years customs and other obstacles to trade between these countries should be removed.

Monitoring the private water business

At Greenwich University in London, David Hall regularly analyses the performance of private companies working in the public sector. What does he think about GATS? An automated, driverless train heading for Docklands passes enormous office complexes built during the Thatcher era. Here and there, more or less dilapidated blocks of council flats can be glimpsed behind the luxurious lease-hold flats with private moorings at Canary Wharf. The Docklands train stops in Greenwich, not far from the museum clipper ship the *Cutty Sark* and the university. There David Hall heads the Public Services International Research Unit (PSIRU).

When I arrive, David Hall sits engrossed at his computer, digging out facts about companies all over the world. When he is not here, he lectures all over the world. Yes, he says, he has thought a great deal about GATS. For over thirteen years, private companies have been taking over the management of water and sewerage in municipalities all over the globe. In the West, no one seemed to care very much. Suddenly, however, there is a renewal of interest, fuelled by a rising anger, as the companies busily encroach on a human right: water. 'I believe that this interest is concerned with GATS', he says. Hall is somewhat surprised that GATS, which is so technical and complex, has caught people's attention. He sees it as part of the growing protest against globalisation as a whole, in which water has become a crucial symbolic issue.

Many different institutions in the world are promoting the private management of water services, not least the EU. The EU Water Initiative is an attempt to coordinate aid by the EU countries and to let the private sector play a bigger role in developing countries. Hall finds it somewhat bizarre that countries like the United States, Norway, Sweden and the Netherlands retain their own water within the public sector while promoting through the aid agencies the privatisation of other people's water. The UK government is particularly very interested in promoting abroad business opportunities in the water sector.

David Hall has studied the consequences of water privatisation in great detail. In his many reports he lists the private companies that have failed to keep to the clauses in their contracts. As early as 1984, when the miners' strike was at its height in the UK, he began to study what happens when public utilities are sold or contracted out. That was when I first met him. He told me of the cleaners at Barking Hospital near London who were protesting against the contracting out of the cleaning service to a private company. They were then re-employed under worse conditions, cutting costs. I travelled to the hospital. The cleaners formed a picket line outside in the cold, while the company bussed in strikebreakers. Middle-aged women threw stones and shook their fists in anger at those on the buses, with their boarded-up windows. Nowadays, of course, it is common for multinational cleaning companies, like the Danish ISS, the British Rentokil Initial and the French Sodexho, to clean hospitals all over the world. I have never met a cleaner who doesn't think the work has become more stressful.

It was at this time that Hall and others at the trade union Unison began to develop a database of private companies and how they act, particularly those in areas like energy, waste management, and above all water and sanitation services. In due course, Hall left Unison to develop the PSIRU in Greenwich, which receives financial support from PSI. In the late 1980s Hall was already studying what was happening with water and sanitation operations in the world. Today the unit has five additional researchers. PSIRU gets its information from many sources internationally: from the media, universities, trade unions, policy think-tanks and, not least, from the annual reports of the companies themselves. It is the largest active database in the world monitoring private companies without the involvement of any underlying business interest.

The pressure to privatise

David Hall is no emotional agitator. His opponents are unable to brush him off as an activist, for he and his researchers deal in hard facts. They inform me, for instance, that Veolia had problems not only in Tucumán but also in Brazil.

In 1998, Veolia bought shares in the water company Sanepar in Paraná, Brazil. In 2001, the residents of Itaperuçu in Paraná were hit by diarrhoea. Tests revealed E. coli bacteria in the water. In another area, Curitiba, the water was of poor quality, and smelled and tasted bad. An environmental agency in Brazil levied fines because Sanepar had used groundwater sources without a licence. In another case residents were also forced to use rainwater to cook and drink, when their water was cut off for months at a time because they could not afford to pay the bills.

Veolia is a minor shareholder in the company Domino, a partner in Sanepar. In 1998 Domino appointed the board members to represent regional government; furthermore the company had a majority on the board. This practice has now come to an end. The regional government in Paraná has taken back control of the water company and holds 60 per cent of the shares. The new governor claims that Veolia paid out excessive dividends and neglected its investment responsibilities, a charge that Veolia denies. Strangely, Veolia retains a seat on the board, due to its know-how in the water sector!

David Hall and researcher Emanuele Lobina could continue in this vein for a long time. 'A prerequisite for getting a loan from a development bank is often to privatise, but for poor countries it is not always so easy to attract private investments. Thus governments may be forced to make tax concessions and give companies other guarantees', says Hall. They may have to contract to buy all the water produced, irrespective of demand. In certain countries this may lead to financial ruin when they cannot pay, for instance because of currency fluctuations.

In 1995, for example, Thames Water signed a fifteen-year contract to supply the Turkish cities of Istanbul and Izmit with water. Included in the contract was the construction of a dam. The contract was worth $933 million. When the water began to be delivered, it was so expensive that industries and customers in the municipalities in the vicinity did not want to buy it and chose other solutions. In the end, the government had to pay the company $387 million for unsold water.

Hall tells how, in power generation, agreements exist in which a country commits itself to buying all the electricity produced at a fixed dollar price for up to thirty-five years. Governments agree to such terms to attract investors. Similar demands are now also appearing in the water sector. Clauses in contracts in some parts of the world also provide for automatic tariff adjustments. If the tariffs are not sufficiently high to provide an operating profit, the local authority must compensate the company for any losses.

Sometimes municipalities have to take an unreasonable degree of responsibility. The World Bank encouraged private-sector involvement in Colombia, and Aguas de Barcelona was able to bank increasing profits, at least in 1999. Yet the municipality had to take responsibility for pension obligations to retired staff. Furthermore, all personnel were made redundant and had to reapply for their jobs in the new company. In this way jobs were cut from 510 to 262. According to the company, 90 per cent of the population of Cartagena had water coverage in 1999. Yet according to the World Bank nearly a third remained without water and sanitation. The difference is explained by the fact that the company ignored people who resided outside the legally defined urban area.

David Hall says he came to believe that the World Bank had changed its attitude and had become more balanced. But he was mistaken: 'Now I see that the World Bank still insists on regarding privatisation as the best remedy without evidence that this remedy is greatly superior to any other. It will continue to be a feature of loan conditions.' In December 2001, the World Bank published the *Strategy for Private Sector Development*. 'It hints that there may be occasions when public solutions are preferable to private ones. This varies from case to case, but in general it is a strategy which gives direct support to the private sector', Hall observes.

As a consequence, the government may actually adapt its policies to the requirements of the lender. In practice, this undermines democracy. In Uganda, for example, the International Development Association, part of the World Bank, advised the government to privatise electricity. At the same time another part of the World Bank, the International Finance Corporation, was helping the multinational American company AES to finance the electricity project in Uganda without exposing it to any competition.

Another disadvantage is the high transaction costs involved when the private sector takes over operations. Countries must even borrow money from development banks to undertake technical, legal and financial studies to prepare the bid. For example, the World Bank gave Paraguay a loan of $12 million in 2000 to prepare for privatisation of the state water company, Corposana, and tele-communications. The Bank's money was also spent on a campaign to tell the public about the advantages of the privatisation.

Hall has published a report together with research fellow Robin de la Motte. It shows that aid agencies and development banks still force developing countries to adopt privatisation policies in public services. The pressures to privatise have been strengthened, instead of ensuring that local democratic processes determine policymaking in developing countries. Formerly, aid was given on condition that it was spent on purchasing goods and services from companies based in the donor country. Now aid is increasingly channelled by international institutions requiring the sectors to be opened to the international business community.

At the core of this policy, as usual, are the World Bank and IMF. Now they have begun to coordinate their actions with the EU and other donors. One is the Public–Private Infrastructure Advisory Facility (PPIAF); others are multi-donor technical assistance facilities. PPIAF's aim is to help developing countries to improve the quality of their infrastructure through private-sector involvement. It has funded meetings in India to convince businessmen and politicians that the privatisation of India's water resources is the only way forward.

Tactical withdrawal

The most striking trend, however, is that companies are withdrawing. International Water, the well-known company driven away from Cochabamba, is set to end its water activities. Its owners, American Bechtel and Italian Edison, have been trying to sell the company. It has already sold its stake in Estonia, Bulgaria and Poland to the European Bank for Reconstruction and Development, which will take an equity stake of up to 50 per cent in its European subsidiary.

Management of the private Thames Water, for its part, has clearly stated that World Bank plans for private water sector activity up to 2007 are unrealistic. In the companies' business plans there are no calculations that resemble those of the World Bank. In January 2003, Suez decided to restructure its business to reduce its debts. Among other things, the company is reducing its investments in developing countries, especially in water and sanitation services. 'The strategy of the companies is based on lobbying multilateral organisations and governments. The private sector depends on public solutions', David Hall maintains. This situation has occurred before. 'Multinational companies have always had a high degree of dependence on development banks paying for their activities.'

The private international sector in fact provides less than 10 per cent of capital investments worldwide. The public sector is responsible for much of the rest, with 17 per cent made up by foreign aid. Private-sector investment has declined from a peak of $128 billion in 1997 to $58 billion in 2002, according to the Camdessus Panel. The panel advocates the use of more aid and money from international financing institutions to provide guarantees for private companies against political risks, to finance private-sector tendering costs, and to reduce currency risks through use of public-sector funds. Hall says that the economic strategies to find ways to finance a growing private sector advocated by the World Bank, the Camdessus Panel itself, and the EU Water Initiative, are strange, as the companies are in fact withdrawing. 'Suez has tried to leave Manila in the Philippines. This led to the World Bank and the other development banks looking for ways to induce Suez to stay', he says, with a bemused air. He obviously thinks that the situation is absurd. Hall draws the conclusion that companies are no longer concerned with 'business as usual'. When they do invest, they make enormous demands for further aid grants and guarantees.

David Hall is not at all convinced that private companies will invest in developing countries, irrespective of the inducements they are offered. The unstable political situation in some countries may make private enterprise doubtful about the wisdom of establishing a presence there. There may be a political shift or some other event that renders the guarantees worthless – witness what happened in Argentina. 'It's not clear that it's all that easy in the USA either. There consumer organisations are very cost conscious', he says. He is sure that development is pointing in a new direction. The largest multinationals acknowledge that they cannot make money by supplying the poor with water. Thus the strategy of the Camdessus Panel will not work. On the other hand, Hall believes that Suez stands on firmer ground when it comes to contracts with industry – for example, working with companies like Esso Exploration and Production Norway AB, a subsidiary of ExxonMobil.

Nevertheless Hall is a realist. He knows that private companies will continue running water systems in some parts of the world. Yet he insists that the one demand that should be met is that if water and sanitation services must at all cost be put out to tender, then the local utility, generally the municipality, must have the opportunity to make a bid of its own. 'To simply ignore public utilities means that there is no major competitor at all to the large private companies. Sometimes they have already decided to submit a joint bid.'

The myth of badly run utilities

What Hall finds most depressing is that many well-run public utilities have already been sold. One such was the water utility Emos in Santiago, Chile. The city sold Emos simply to boost its budget; the utility ran the water and sanitation services well. Even the World Bank regarded Emos as a model public utility. Just as in Cochabamba, the company – with the new name Aguas Andinas – was guaranteed a certain profit margin. For a period, Emos's profits were as high as 33 per cent. 'It is thus not plausible to constantly claim that the private sector is needed because public companies are so inefficient', Hall emphasises. Today he knows many municipalities and towns all over the world that give the lie to the myth that public water systems are badly run or that they are not capable of modernisation and reform.

Japan and USA, for example, have well-run water utilities with lower water charges and fewer staff, in relative terms, than private companies in France. David Hall is convinced that the role of the public sector is growing. Contracts and control of the water service are being taken back by municipalities – for example, in Atlanta in the USA, in Ho Chi Minh City in Vietnam, and in Paraná in Brazil. Furthermore, there have been important decisions not to privatise – for example, in Bratislava, the capital of Slovakia.

Hall believes that it is incumbent on the World Bank and other donors to develop positive strategies for supporting the public sector, if the Millennium Development Goals are to be achieved. He considers it vital to study those places where the public sector is successful, rather than be misled by those who label the public sector inefficient and a failure. 'Very little effort has been made to analyse good examples of public services', he says. He gives some examples of the public sector reforming its own companies and improving them.

In São Paulo, Brazil, a public utility succeeded both in upgrading water and sanitation services and in reducing operational costs through restructuring and modernising its infrastructure. At the same time, the utility is taking part in an environmental programme to clean up a river. During 1995 alone, the percentage of people with access to clean water increased from 84 to 91 per cent.

In Honduras, the state-owned SANAA has helped to build up capacity to develop a water system in the rural areas. The majority of the population have a more or less constant supply of water to their homes. SANAA has improved both its efficiency and management, among other ways through cooperation with the trade unions. The unions have even accepted a reduction in the workforce.

One of the best-run water companies in Latin America is the cooperative Saguapac, in Santa Cruz in Bolivia. Some 96 per cent of users pay their bills. The water utility reaches 80 per cent of households, despite a growing population. Consumers are supplied with water twenty-four hours a day without fail. When the World Bank compared projects in Santa Cruz, Cochabamba and La Paz (where water and sanitation services are privately run), Santa Cruz did remarkably well. Between 1988 and 1999 the number of connections was increased from 70 to 94 per cent in Santa Cruz, and in La Paz from 75 to 92 per cent. According to the World Bank, an efficient and transparent administration in Santa Cruz has to all intents and purposes eliminated corruption. The Bank has granted loans to the city, which has completed its projects and investments in the allotted time.

In Botswana the public Water Utilities Corporation increased water connections more than tenfold, from 30,000 to 330,000, between 1970 and 1998. A water plant in Phoenix, Arizona, is another successful example of cooperation between management and trade unions.

In Poland, Veolia was preparing to take over water and sanitation services in Lodz, but then the municipality and trade unions realised that the business plan drawn up by the municipality was better. It duly obtained a 20-year loan from the European Investment Bank (EIB), to finance improvements in water and wastewater networks, and has negotiated further funding from the Instrument for Structural Policies for Pre-Accession (ISPA). The Polish city of Poznan has similarly decided to turn its back on privatised water and sanitation services. The municipal water company has improved its efficiency so much that it is no longer necessary to involve any private interests. An ISPA grant had previously allocated €60 million on condition that Poznan privatised. Many companies had already shown interest, including Bechtel, Veolia, RWE and Suez.

According to David Hall, financing water does not necessarily require international capital. Poor communities may be capable of mobilising the necessary resources to construct domestic extensions even if the government, municipal and water authorities fail to deliver. Public water services can be made affordable for the poor through a combination of taxation, tariffs, efficient collection methods, and cross-subsidy, which implies that the rich pay more and the poor less.

For example, in Ahmedabad in India the municipality organised a more efficient tax collection system, employed tax collectors and stamped out corruption. The money collected increased by 60 per cent. A capital investment programme for water and sewerage was drawn up, financed by the revenues, loans and a municipal bond. The municipality succeeded in delivering water to 60 per cent of the population.

Investment finance can be raised through loans or bonds issued within a country itself, if the basic requirements for capital markets exist. National as well as local governments are themselves capable of accessing international capital, if necessary without the intervention of private companies. Corporatised public water utilities can also borrow money themselves, if they have a good international credit rating. 'Development banks should have a role to play', is David Hall's opinion, 'but that depends on whether it is possible to avoid the damaging effects of forced privatisation'.

Hall lists the advantages of having water in public ownership:

- There can be no secret business deals.
- There is no threat of bankruptcy.
- An egalitarian service is virtually guaranteed, so that water and sanitation services supply both urban and rural areas.

- The expense of preparing for the bidding process, possibly employing consultants and procuring service, is avoided.
- Public solutions foster citizen participation. In the Netherlands, for instance, employees sit on the board of the regulatory authority that supervises water companies and take part in the setting of charges.

The multinational companies have in some cases tried to solve the problem of the poor being unable to pay, by charging the wealthier more. In Buenos Aires, for example, Suez introduced a solidarity fee, but the middle classes protested.

'It is easier if the public community introduces such charges', David Hall believes, and gives an example. In one area in South Africa, local groups, trade unions and the state run the water and sanitation services together. Conditions for the population are difficult. If consumers do not pay, their water is turned off. Yet they know this is in the interests of the general welfare: it is the condition for the scheme working. This is quite different from Suez saying 'We will cut off your water if you do not pay your bills, because then we cannot make a profit.'

Times change. Both Thames Water and Suez are showing interest in working together with NGOs in various parts of the world. I ask David Hall whether this may perhaps be a good way to achieve a better understanding of how the distribution of water should be solved in the world, a model for the future? His response is consistent with the case he has made, at length and in detail, during our meeting: 'Private companies just use this strategy in order to reduce their risks. In the final analysis, all they are concerned with is profitability.'

Hall turns to his computer and begins a search. He then prints out a report, which he gives to me. It deals with Porto Alegre, the most renowned and prominent example of good public solutions.

20

Public–public partnerships:
a new global model

Participatory decision-making in Porto Alegre

The city of Porto Alegre in Brazil has shown that it is possible to
run a publicly operated water company well and at the same time
enable users to participate. By 1961, the water utility was operating as an autonomous and financially independent municipally
owned company. It takes its own decisions on investment. It is
not subsidised and all earnings are reinvested in the system.

In 2001, there was a struggle to prevent privatisation of the
water company. Trade unions and civic organisations led the
protests. The city retained the water utility as a municipal asset.

The water company, DMAE, wanted to build a sewage treatment
plant costing $150 million and applied to the Inter-American
Development Bank, for a loan. Their interest rate is lower than
that of domestic banks. The IADB was interested but stipulated
as a condition that a private company should be engaged. DMAE
refused and explained that the utility's financial profile was sufficiently good and that it was a competent company. Despite
initial reluctance, DMAE was granted the loan.

DMAE has a Deliberative Council, equivalent to a board of directors, with the power to approve all major decisions. It consists of representatives who reflect different views and interests: engineers, trade unions, lawyers, neighbourhood associations, and other organisations. Members of the council serve for three years. Each year a third are replaced. The council approves work plans, contracts, tariffs and financial operations.

Citizens take part in the budget process in a form of direct democracy and thereby participate and exert an influence on investment priorities. DMAE then analyses this input and draws up an investment plan, which has to be approved by the Participatory Budget Council. All activities are public; there are no commercial secrets.

DMAE has a staff education programme. Employees who were illiterate or partially literate have been educated. Technical, operational and computer training is also offered. There is a special office at DMAE where workers can complain, criticise, ask questions, and make suggestions.

An impressive 99.5 per cent of residents have direct access to water; DMAE supplies the rest from tankers. Some 84 per cent of households are connected to sewerage. Water tariffs are among the lowest in Brazil. Furthermore, there has been a campaign among the residents to build awareness and not to waste water. There is a free phoneline for customer queries and complaints. Problems are usually solved within a day. Of the work subcontracted to the private sector, 95 per cent goes to Brazilian companies and the rest to Ondeo, a part of Suez.

Porto Alegre City has one of the lowest rates of infant mortality in the country, due to excellent water supplies and sanitation. Hans Engelberts, general secretary of the trade-union federation PSI, suggests that DMAE's success should serve as a benchmark for the World Bank and national governments as they seek to reform public sector enterprises. Benefits accrue, since DMAE does not have to pay dividends to any shareholders and can thus use all its earnings for the public good.

A new spirit of cooperation

An increasing number of public–public partnerships are taking shape, involving close cooperation between publicly owned water and sanitation services. An example of a successful partnership is the northern city of Recife in Brazil, where citizens campaigned successfully against the privatisation of the state water company. The company had been in bad shape. A new entity, the Recife Municipal Department of Water and Sanitation, was set up to improve water delivery in partnership with the state company. The results have been very good, similar to those in Porto Alegre.

Efficient public companies are ready to share their knowledge and competence with other public companies/utilities, especially those which are not so effectively run. This, in 2002, four public service water provider organisations came together at the World Summit on Sustainable Development (WSSD) in Johannesburg. They signed up to a declaration committing them to a public–public collaboration. In their founding statement they assert that 'access to potable water is a human right, as is the right to live in a healthy environment – which includes adequate sanitation services. It is a government obligation to provide basic water and sanitation services to everyone in the nation. The social value of water must be recognised and strengthened. Water is a common property, a public good, to be used for providing water security for people, local production needs and ecosystems.' They noted the many public-sector service providers that are efficient, possess good management expertise, have access to capital, and are less expensive than the private sector. In Johannesburg, the managers of these water organisations took the first step towards creating national and international public–public partnerships to strengthen and develop the capacity of public water and sanitation services. The partners will explore international assistance programmes to support and strengthen those public water service providers that wish to improve their efficiency and capacity. They acknowledge that from time to time it may become necessary to enter into contracts with private-sector companies on a short-term basis. In this case, contracts will be awarded on a public tender basis; they will be short-term only; ultimate control and ownership will remain in public hands, and a strong component of public participation will be built in. A system of independent monitoring and regulation should ensure that such operations are independent of both government and service providers.

The declaration raised hopes that similar initiatives would be undertaken elsewhere in the world. A follow-up summit for all public institutions in the developing world is envisaged. Those who signed this declaration are executives/managers of Rand Water and Umgeni Water in South Africa, DMAE in Porto Alegre, and the public Water and Sanitation Department of Recife Municipality in Brazil.

Antonio da Costa Miranda Neto, a manager from Recife, is one of the signatories. In the autumn of 2003 Neto has come to Europe to visit and learn from the experience of the Swedish public water company, Stockholm Water. Keith Naicker from Johannesburg is also present; he is marketing manager for the public Rand Water company, which supplies bulk water to the surrounding municipalities.

During their visit to a water treatment plant in a Stockholm suburb they ask a seemingly endless number of questions. 'Stockholm Water uses a biological treatment that is very interesting for us', they say, totally absorbed in every element of the process, from the chemicals used in the cleaning process to the treatment of sludge. They are also in Stockholm to lobby for the public–public concept among directors of water utilities all over the world. The intention is to learn from each other. What sorts of things can they learn? Keith Naicker, a calm, well-organised man, explains: 'From Brazil I can learn more about their experiences of privatisation and how they have handled it. We now have legislation in South Africa that says that municipalities can choose from where to get their water and sanitation. Several large municipalities are very seriously considering a private sector option. I must position myself so that the municipalities get the best deal at the end of day from my company.' He likes the concept of people's participation in Brazil – that consumers are directly involved in the decisions. 'We also have participation, but not at the level of Recife.' Naicker would also like to know more about integrated planning.

In Recife they plan the houses, water supply, roads and schools in an integrated way. Antonio Miranda says that 70,000 inhabitants in Recife discussed the budget last year. So what can he learn from Keith Naicker? Miranda, a lively and energetic person, says: 'Keith is working in a very efficiently run company, Rand Water. I am very impressed by how well organised they are as a public company. I would like to know more about Rand Water as an enterprise and how it operates with municipalities. It can be an example for us.' He is also interested in how Rand Water works in the poor areas.

During the apartheid regime, not enough capital was spent on maintaining the infrastructure. Half of the water that goes in to Soweto is lost, for example. Naicker is sure that if the leaks are repaired it will be possible to save water. People might then get as much as 10,000 litres per month free per household. 'Must water have a price?' I ask him. 'It should have a price', Naicker answers. He explains that everybody must realize the value of water, and should receive information about saving water and how to help ensure the sewerage network remains fully functional. Water has an economic value, yes, but if you are too poor you cannot pay. 'Do not confuse people who do not want to pay with those who cannot pay. The discussion is about willingness and ability. We have to force those who can pay to really pay. To reduce their consumption, the big consumers of water have to pay much more.'

At this point, the two men get involved in a lively discussion about the billing system. Before I leave them, Keith Naicker tells me that Rand Water has actually developed a public–public partnership with the municipality of Harrismith. Through this collaboration, the municipality has gained access to the experts and experience of Rand Water. Harrismith has thereby been able to strengthen its own municipal water system without losing control over it. Keith Naicker refers me to a report written by Laila Smith and Ebrahim Fakir at the Centre for Policy Studies in Johannesburg.

I later read in Smith and Fakir's report that the water company in Harrismith is an autonomous business unit, Amanziwethu Water Services (AWS). A three-year contract between Rand Water and AWS has already produced good results. Staff, seconded by Rand Water, manage the business; the workforce, seconded by the council, operate AWS. Rand Water carries the commercial risk. To avoid increases in the water price, no more than 5 per cent of the revenue is returned to Rand Water, through management fees. Unaccounted-for water has been reduced from 30 to 12 per cent. In the first sixteen months the company generated a surplus of 1.6 million rand and in the following year 2 million. It was all reinvested in the company. With regard to labour and service users, extensive consultation throughout the negotiation process has led to general support for the partnership.

The AWS's earnings are ploughed back into the operations. The local authority is guaranteed 5 per cent of the sector's revenues to pay for non-profitable services such as community centres and libraries. Those who use between 30 and 50 kilolitres per day in the higher income brackets have borne the greatest tariff increases. A 2 per cent increase has also been levied on major consumers and industries. This levy provides a fund for local economic development. The municipality is also trying to create jobs, which in the long run will lead to the currently unemployed being able to afford to pay their bills. Rand Water was careful to adopt the principle of full cost recovery, to sift out those who cannot pay because they are poor and to punish those who can afford to pay but don't bother – for example, by cutting off first their electricity and later their water.

There are three key industrial complexes in the municipality, among them Nestlé. In practice, they used to be subsidised by the poor as they paid low water tariffs. AWS began early on to negotiate price rises of 60–70 per cent for the factories. The income received from industry goes to pay for the 6,000 litre quota of free water per family per month that the government introduced in 2002.

AWS employees have retained their conditions of employment. The report notes that: 'Support by the trade union SAMWU at national and local levels has created an environment conducive to improvements in the performative culture of the workplace; there has been an absence of strikes, decline in absenteeism and a general increase in worker productivity.'

Municipal officials still have limited knowledge of contract details, and that leads to them agreeing with the technical experts instead of questioning them. They must become better at control-ling the company. Another problem is that there are many poor households with large families, and they obviously need a greater volume of free water – 6,000 litres does not suffice for a household of six or eight people. In the case of those who cannot pay for water, tricklers are installed: once the 6,000 litre quota has been used access to water is drastically reduced.

It is not a popular system. One resident offers this opinion: 'The tricklers are inhuman. Water is a necessity. Really we try to save water and use as little as possible. But with seven people in the house, it's not easy to cope with what we get. We often run short. And this thing plays havoc with the sewerage. It takes so long for the toilet to fill up. So, if someone uses the toilet, you will have to wait for a very long time before it can be used again. What is the sense of having infrastructure when you can't use it when you need it? How must you relieve yourself?'

Households earning less than 1,100 rand a month are encouraged to register, so that they are at least guaranteed 6,000 litres a month. The intention of the water company is not to subsidise the poor, but to ensure that the national fund allocated to poor households is appropriately channelled.

There has been a comprehensive information campaign on the radio, in newspapers and at meetings, as well as consultation with NGOs. How the information is received varies. The well-educated with high incomes naturally find it easier to absorb information than the poor. In the conclusion to their research, Smith and Fakir observe that 'AWS has demonstrated more flexibility, with regard to people who are too poor to pay, than the private companies.'

They express surprise that so little attention is being paid to public–public partnerships, not least given the difficulties experienced with private companies in South Africa. Such partnerships are also to be found in other places in the world, of course. One of the most developed models is in northern Europe.

Success in the Baltic

I am in Stockholm, aboard the ferry to Riga, the capital of the Baltic state of Latvia. The shabby ferry glides slowly out of the harbour into the Baltic Sea. It's a polluted sea. The release of poorly treated sewage water is a serious problem in the Baltic, not least in its threat to the sensitive marine environment and fish stocks.

Fifteen hours later the ferry sails into Riga bay, past the cranes and the rows of timber products lining the quayside waiting to be loaded for export. Latvia shares a border with Russia. The occupation museum in Riga depicts the unhappiness of the Latvians when the country was forced to join the Soviet Union in 1940. In 1991 Latvia became independent again. Today Latvian flags flutter from poles on a modernised hotel and from old wooden buildings, their green and brown paint now faded. In the city centre, the renovated facades are in the graceful Art Nouveau style.

In the Soviet era, just 24 per cent of the city's sewage was treated. The rest was simply pumped directly into the river and the Bay of Riga. It ended up in the Baltic Sea. In 1992, less than half of Riga's population were connected to the sewerage system; the old town in the city centre was particularly poorly provided for. In consequence, fish were disappearing from the polluted bay. It was in 1992 that the countries around the Baltic Sea signed a new convention to protect the marine environment.

Not far from Riga is the Daugavgriva Sewage Treatment Plant. It is part of Riga Water, nowadays an independent municipal shareholding company. The plant is huge and self-important, resembling a colossal, ugly factory site. The pumps and rusty pipes are of the Soviet era. In one section of a huge building, four bright blue automated air compressors have replaced old mechanical equipment. A sludge centrifuge comes from the Swedish public company, Stockholm Water.

In 1997, Riga Water and Stockholm Water began an environmental project, a twinning arrangement – a public–public partnership. The collaboration had begun several years earlier when Stockholm Water received economic support from the Swedish Environmental Ministry. Riga Water later received contributions from the Swedish, Finnish and Swiss governments, development cooperation funds from the Swedish assistance agency Sida, loans from the European Investment Bank, and the European Bank for

Reconstruction and Development. The objective was to copy the Nordic model of water supply and sewerage. During 1998/99, the plant was reconstructed. Among major investment projects were an aeration system and sludge treatment facilities. As a result of this project involving Stockholm Water, the environmental load on the Gulf of Riga and the Baltic Sea has been greatly reduced. Some species of fish have even returned to the Daugava river.

The sewage treatment plant and the Daugava water treatment utility were apparently constructed in part by prisoners. Aivars Zants, now project manager at Riga Water, has worked at the plant since 1977. He remembers buses driving prisoners onto the site, and the police and dogs guarding them. 'Had the old waterworks been built today it would have been three times smaller', Zants says. In the Soviet era, there was an abundance of land; electricity and heating were cheap. 'No one thought of the cost, everything belonged to the state. In addition, everything should be as monumental as possible to show how powerful the Soviet Union was', he remarks. Yet there were failings. The water pressure was so low that water only reached the third floor of tall buildings. The water quality was not the best.

So, with the assistance of staff from Stockholm Water, the water treatment plant, sludge removal facilities and the purified collection system were upgraded and filters reconstructed, to mention just a few of the changes. Valves and pumps were also replaced. Stockholm Water shared its experience and expertise, from scientific and technological know-how to managing a company effectively and economically. Advisers came from Stockholm Water and remained for up to three years. Management reorganisation took place over several years, supported by an experienced counterpart with the necessary knowledge and skills.

Aivars Zants considers it a valuable experience having cooperated with Stockholm Water. Even the process of arranging a loan with a bank was quite new. He paid study visits to both Helsinki and Stockholm to see first-hand how Western water and sewage treatment plants were built and run. 'We had thought of building a network of new pipes, but our Swedish advisers wondered why we wanted to build with steel pipes which rusted. During Soviet times stainless steel was only used for military purposes, and our minds were still running along the old lines', he tells me.

Riga Water has in turn met representatives from various towns in Russia to share its experiences with them. Even banks have shown interest in developing this type of partnership. 'At the same time we are currently absorbed in continuing to develop our water and sewerage system', says Zants. Riga Water is still overstaffed. Formerly the pump stations were manned; the pumps are now fully automated. 'Natural wastage' is one way to reduce personnel – not employing new staff in place of those who retire. Yet many people over 65 still work for the company. 'Since the standard of living is so low, they simply cannot afford to retire', says Zants.

There are other problems, such as the meters. Politicians took the decision to install them in every dwelling, yet the meter readings in apartments tend not to correspond with the master meter. 'To some extent people cheat. There are ways of changing the meter readings', says Aivars Zants. Meters allow residents to see how much water they are consuming. Consumption has fallen. Today the average is 130 litres per household per day. During Soviet times, the figure could be as high as 400 litres per day. The system also had considerably more leaks then, adding to the wastage.

Charges for water and sanitation are low. Janis Karpovics, chairman of the Communal and Apartment Issues of Riga Council, does not want to increase water tariffs, even though raising them would allow the company to cover its costs. 'The average income is quite low, so it is not a good option. There are, for example, 150,000 pensioners and they only get $90 a month. 1 cubic metre (1,000 litres) costs 75 cents.'

Karpovics tells me that some areas of Riga still do not have a water supply. People have no option but to fetch their water from wells contaminated by heavy metals. Some 70,000 people live like that. It is an area where the Russian military forces used to live; the people now occupy their houses. Thus the second phase of the project is to supply these people with water and sewerage. He says that support from Stockholm Water and the EU is good: 'There was a French water company here that wanted to manage the water supply as a concession. We rejected the proposal. We are responsible to the inhabitants of Riga.'

Karpovics is worried, but for a quite different reason. Notwithstanding the investment and other major inputs, a Finnish company now wants to build a huge pulp factory, which might well pollute the Daugava river again. He explains that if the factory is built, the municipality will have to seek another site for water intake. 'We are not a very rich municipality and the costs will be enormous.' Later I meet an engine man (mechanic) at the sewage treatment plant. Life is not easy: he has about $180 per month to live on after tax. The trade union Lakrs seeks better conditions for employees. However, trade unions are not popular, as they used to be in league with the old Communist regime. They must be built up anew and earn a new identity.

Juris Kalnins, president of Lakrs, expresses his concern when I visit his office. He fears that the company, once restructured, could be sold to a private multinational company. 'In Tallinn in Estonia the company was sold and the charges have increased', he says. The possible sale of the company is not, however, the immediate issue. Riga Water is so well run that in 2000 the EBRD decided to grant the company a €39 million loan. It was the first Latvian utility to receive a direct corporate loan from an international financial institution. Furthermore, it was granted without any financial guarantees from the city council as Riga Water was now a modern, self-financing public company.

Sten Bjergaard, a project leader from Sweden, confirms that the two water companies work together on the basis of full trust and mutual understanding. This obviously opens up communication, thereby maximising the chances of success. Stockholm Water has not only supported Riga but also other towns in Lithuania, Poland, and Russia. There is a similar partnership in the town of Kaunas in Lithuania. In that country's capital, Vilnius City Council has also decided to keep its water and sanitation services under municipal control, instead of privatising it. Suez had earlier been lobbying for a concession.

Sven-Erik Skogsfors, formerly executive director of Stockholm Water, was very engaged in the public–public partnership in Lithuania and Latvia. He is now a consultant to the International Water Association (IWA), which connects the broad community of water professionals around the world. He says that there is a fear in the Baltic States that foreign capital will buy up natural resources like water. 'They would like to have foreign capital but want to retain a strong influence over their natural resources', he says.

Due to their suspicion, it took time to convince the Baltic States that Stockholm Water was not trying to buy up their water facilities. Stockholm Water wanted to help them to develop their own water company and at the same time make them aware of the common interest in cleaning up the Baltic Sea. It took time to convince the population that if they wanted to have clean water and a healthy marine environment, they must pay for water, and that this must take priority over television sets and other material possessions.

To collaborate on this basis was a positive experience for the Baltic countries. 'We did not make any profit. If we earned any extra money, it was sunk into the project', says Skogsfors. Subsequently, Stockholm Water participated in forming a new organisation, Swedish Water Development (SWD), which is jointly owned with two other towns, Gothenburg and Malmö, and with Swedish Water, a non-profitmaking business association.

In St Petersburg in Russia, SWD cooperated with Helsinki Water of Finland to build a sewage treatment plant. To qualify, SWD had to take part in competitive bidding, a demand put by Sida, the Swedish development cooperation agency, and others. This made it necessary to collaborate with a company that could take the business risks. In this case, it was Severn Trent from the UK. (Swedish law does not permit a municipal water company to use income from water and sanitation fees for anything other than operations within its core business.)

Another project was started in South Africa. 'There, as elsewhere in Africa, the government is worried that existing opportunities to supply water may be exploited to create profits for foreign private water companies, not least companies from the former colonial powers', says Skogsfors. SWD's task was to create functioning public-sector organisations that are able to supply the population's demand for water and sewerage and also succeed in getting them to pay their bills. Banks give loans more readily if there is a guaranteed income. 'To make use of our support to raise competence may be an important first step. Afterwards it should be possible to evaluate what one can do oneself and what should perhaps be done by others', he says.

SWD has already participated in other projects in Africa. These projects have set out to improve the whole operation: management, financial planning, and the operations themselves. With funds from Sida, together with UN–Habitat, SWD is running classes at water and sewage treatment plants in six African countries. By learning the techniques of testing water and through study, young people learn to conserve water, protect the environment, care for water assets and, in the long run, preserve their health. Networks are evolving between schools and in different towns. There are plans to set up exchanges with Swedish schoolchildren.

SWD may also become a sounding board for countries considering whether to contract out their water services, so that they can gain a better understanding of what is involved, hear of reasonable agreements and receive good advice. In the case of those planning to end a contract, they must be sure of having the knowledge to continue to run operations on their own. 'One should not enter any contract before one has a well-functioning organisation', says Skogsfors.

In the meantime, however, SWD is having a tough time at home in Sweden. Formerly it was possible to discuss projects with Sida and later submit proposals and calculations of costs. Today that is no longer possible. Instead SWD must nearly always submit a bid in competition with foreign, private companies for donor funding, according to the EU's procurement rules. If SWD does not win, costs must still be paid – these are termed so-called 'to no avail' projects.

Skogsfors stresses the need to differentiate between SWD's competence and that of consultant companies. 'We work with the knowledge that we have directly from our practical operations. Consultants may be good at theories about how one should manage and develop a company, but lack practical experience of daily operations. Cooperation with consultants instead of competition ought thus to be the model', he says.

Skogsfors participated in the Third World Water Forum in Kyoto. He says that the private sector dominated and that issues were kept at too high a level of abstraction. 'The major international organisations formulate problems in big important documents on what has to be done in poor countries. Too little is said about how to break down the problems at a global level and what can be done in practice. This may involve finding the best technical solutions in the poorest areas round cities, smaller towns and in rural areas.' He has noticed that the large companies keep to those parts of the cities where residents have capital resources. He sees a clear risk that they may export their expensive solutions to developing countries, solutions which they have developed themselves and which suit industrialised countries. He maintains that it is not possible simply to transfer Western technology to other parts of the world. To be useful, inputs must be adapted to recipients' knowledge, culture and religion, and not least to their ability to pay. 'The World Bank has regarded privatisation as the safest way of getting a return on loans it has made, in addition to seeing good results. Thus it has been hard for us to get World Bank support, even if we have won some projects.'

On the horizon, Skogsfors perceives a new dawn. He believes that even the World Bank has begun to understand the value of utilising the knowledge that public companies have. It understands that in many cases the results achieved by the projects of large private companies can hardly be called successful. In the best-case scenario, this may entail increased opportunities for public water and sewage treatment plants, and even the chance of working together with the private sector.

As executive director of Stockholm Water, Skogsfors came across French companies in the Baltic States. The French companies, in contrast to Stockholm Water and Riga Water, had difficulty in perceiving any advantages to cleaning the Baltic Sea. Their interest was simply in making a profit from the operations. Skogsfors also learnt how a private company loves politicians and officials and how it influences public opinion. It was hard for Stockholm Water and SWD, with their open philosophy and their limited resources, to stay afloat in this competition. 'The French companies were extremely good at lobbying. They knew exactly which politicians and influential people to cultivate. We, in turn, asked our Swedish politicians for help in convincing the Baltic States about our line', he says.

Stockholm Water functions less like a monopoly than do the French companies. For example, it buys pipes, chemicals and other services from various private firms in a competitive market. The large private water companies usually buy what they need from their own subsidiaries and transport materials over entire continents. 'We can command a lower price, since we buy material and services on a competitive basis', Skogsfors says.

Skogsfors has noticed an interest among personnel in local authorities in Sweden in doing international work. If finance was forthcoming and with adequate planning, there would be willing staff. 'To become involved in giving people clean water and a better standard of living is meaningful, if one can develop operations where need is greatest', he believes. Many people in public water utilities in the Nordic countries have international experience, not least of Africa.

SWD is now being wound up. It has not been able to survive in competition against the large multinational companies. Sven-Erik Skogsfors is convinced that the idea of SWD was correct. The problem was the necessity of participation in the competitive procurement process with an insufficient capital base. This required economic support from public authorities. Thus, what is required is a reasonable reserve of working capital, along with will to give financial support to public water operations. It must be done this way because water operations in Sweden may not be run for profit, and their earnings cannot be used to assist developing countries. Skogsfors remains hopeful: 'With economic support, public water utilities can assist developing countries in one of the key sectors to achieving a safer and more secure world, namely clean water and sufficient water for health and sustenance.' He believes it is possible to develop meaningful collaboration, for example between the Nordic donor agencies, which would make it feasible for the municipal water sector with its competence to work together with public water utilities in developing countries. Such collaboration should include a resource fund of knowledgeable water and sanitation personnel. Consultants, contractors and manufacturing industry should also participate. Together it ought to be possible to develop research and environmental technology that can be adapted to local conditions in developing countries, both in smaller and larger towns and in the slums of the big cities.

David Hall, head of PSIRU's London database, later remarked that contributory factors to the successful operation of public water utilities in the Baltic States was, one, they could combine loans from local and international commercial banks, and, two, the support of Swedish, Finnish and Danish aid agencies and others. They also received contributions from the EU and loans from EBRD. Hall indicates two reasons why the EU is investing in the states around the Baltic: environmental gains and greater influence over the former Communist countries.

Other voices and opinions

Must the solution be either private or public water – despite the criticism, private companies have, after all, successfully supplied a lot of people with water. The arguments for and against go round and round in my head. I decide to make contact with Robin Simpson at Consumers International in London. This organisation supports and represents consumers all over the world and is campaigning for policies that respect consumers' concerns.

Robin Simpson, it turns out, has just finished a course and is on his way to a dinner with the participants. However, he can't resist the opportunity to chat about water, so he parks his bicycle outside my hotel in Bloomsbury and we spend some time in the bar, discussing his work. He has travelled the world studying the effects of water privatisation, especially on consumers. He says that the debate about privatisation has been oversimplified, not least because in some countries the state has run water disastrously. He rejects the notion that water supply is straightforwardly either a commodity or a human right. Access to water is the basis for eco-nomic development: to install water and sanitation in an apartment increases its value. He considers it an insult to the poor to refuse to enter into discussion about the financial value of water.

The municipal water company DMAE in Porto Alegre is for Simpson the exemplar of good public operation. The company has reached almost the entire population. 'A wonderful example', he says. However, he then mentions a large number of public sector schemes where only the elite is served and the poor are ignored.

Simpson is not prepared to defend the standpoint that under no circumstances should one allow variations, and that there should be no private involvement at all, although he concedes that the private sector has overseen some spectacular disasters. 'What if the network just covers 20 per cent? And people have to buy from vendors because of failing public systems? Pointing a finger and saying that you are a bigger failure than I am is not getting us very far.'

Simpson is much more interested in discussing what he sees as the key issue: the pricing of water and the level of cost recovery. Cost recovery is when people pay the water price without being subsidised and the revenue from the consumers is reinvested in water distribution.

'You cannot cover the whole population and expect it not to cost money. If you charge far below the cost of water, the obstacles to getting proper coverage are immense', he says. At the same time, he warns that cost recovery, as it is currently being promoted by the World Bank, among others, is becoming an excuse for letting the private sector charge higher prices just in order to make a profit. He has discovered during his travels that, with a few exceptions, like Porto Alegre, low prices either mean immense non-coverage, as in many parts of Africa, or a deteriorating technical system, as in Russia. Porto Alegre works because it operates cost recovery. 'Raising the tariff is the progressive thing to do because how else how are you going to extend the network. In Cochabamba very few told the story of those who were not connected. Only 50 per cent were connected, and since the failure of the scheme only a few more have been connected. The real losers are not the company or the government but the people who are not connected.'

The traditional pattern has been for domestic consumers to be subsidised through preferential tariffs, or through the system running at a loss. 'But if the poor are excluded from the service and the better-off are connected, is this subsidy justified? It could even be that the poor are subsidising the better-off.' What he has seen during his travels is that the poor will then have to buy into the system through excessive connection charges, bribery or theft. Illegal connections are often done with considerable technical skill and ingenuity. Such are the levels of theft that up to 50 per cent of the water supply of major Latin American cities is said to be 'missing'. These losses cannot be sustained in the long term without very serious consequences. Latin America is not alone in having to face these problems. They are also to be found in several EU accession states in eastern and central Europe, and in particular in the former Soviet Union. 'Families need to have water, so what can they do?'

Simpson is sure that one of the greatest challenges facing the water industry, public or private, is to structure incentives so that companies do not have to incur losses by extending the network. This could, for example, involve an element of cross-subsidy by way of a levy on existing consumers. Solidarity taxes are another possible solution. Existing customers pay an additional sum and that money goes to extending the network. Part of the solution, of course, is to reduce the numbers who do not pay. And this means not only domestic consumers but also business and industry – and even the local authorities themselves. 'All must be motivated to pay and the best way to achieve that goal is to convince people that it is in their own interests to do so. This has been achieved in some very poor locations such as West Africa and countries in the ex-Soviet Union.'

Simpson believes that a combination of self-interest and social solidarity, achieved through local self-management, can greatly increase payment rates. Of crucial importance also is that every citizen has access to information on price setting, relevant to the costs of the industry, and that the accounts of the company should be in the public domain. This is the case in the US and in Canada, where all price increases have to be justified at 'rate hearings', in public tribunals. There the companies and the advocates of consumer groups contest the arguments in the presence of the state regulator. Tough regulatory terms with strict price limits will reduce the sale price; conversely, generous terms for the companies will increase it. 'Since transparency in private companies is zero, people suspect that private companies make huge profits on them.' This changes if consumers can follow what is happening. Simpson mentions Lima, where some residents started a cooperative. Since the consumers themselves took charge of the finances, they knew what the water costs were and agreed to tariff increases.

Simpson has seen many cases where the regulators have been badly prepared for negotiations with the companies bidding for the concessions. In some cases the companies have even been invited to design the concession contracts! In some major Western European cities, for example Berlin, water contracts have never been published. Simpson is not uncritical of the private sector. For example, he does not like it that companies so often renegotiate contracts, although they may well have received too little information from the local government when negotiating.

Simpson is sure that the day of mega-contracts is over. There will have to be much greater self-discipline in municipalities, running services by themselves without subsidies from the government. He has noticed that the World Bank is becoming more interested in cooperatives and well-run municipal utilities. 'There are fanatics in the World Bank who do think everything has to be run privately. You do hear fanatical positions at conferences at a higher level, but I have met staff and consultants who are really quite pragmatic', he says. He is also sure that there is much more agreement than is apparent. And only two countries have overseen the complete sale of the industry: Great Britain and Chile.

Robin Simpson flings out his arms and wonders why his friends keep studying failures. Why, he wonders, is no one talking about Costa Rica. Costa Rica has high levels of coverage, while tariffs seem to be reasonable. There is very strong consumer influence. Water there is operated within the public sector. 'We should study successes wherever they come from, mixed, public, private or whatever', he concludes. He says goodbye and jumps onto his bicycle again to risk life and limb in the London traffic. His words ring in my ears: 'The right position is to be unsure, not to have all the answers.'

The acceptable face of private water?

Rumour has it that Thames Water, owned by the German company RWE, has begun to adopt a quite different strategy to make itself attractive to the market. It is striving to present itself as a caring multinational company. The new image is premised on the assumption that it is the responsibility of central and local government to decide whether or not they wish to open up their water and sanitation services to private competition. Thames Water says it is opposed in principle to both coercion in this regard, and to the inclusion of water and sanitation services in trade agreements.

I want to learn more about Thames Water so I travel to Reading, a half-hour train ride from London. It's raining when I arrive. The rain is good, though, because it fills the River Thames with water, says Richard Aylard, a director of Thames Water. Outside his office the Thames flows languidly by. London's drinking water comes from the Thames and is purified largely by Thames Water. When the polite small talk is over, Aylard says straight out that the private sector does not have all the answers. Future developments will differ from those of recent years. 'There has been a push led by one or two multinational corporations, not Thames Water, and the international financial institutions to present the private sector as being the solution to all problems in the developing world.' We are now moving away from a situation in which the private sector was expected to make major long-term investments in infrastructure in the developing world, he observes. Instead, the private sector will play a role in partnership with other sectors of society in providing water and sanitation. The model for the future is the public and private sectors and civil society working in partnership. A lesson that Thames Water has learnt is that no single model can be applied to the range of situations that exist across the world. 'We have to accept that water needs to be under public control and the public sector then decides what role the private sector might play in service delivery. We want to know first of all: will the company be welcome?'

Aylard does not want Thames Water to establish itself in a country as a result of pressure from the World Bank or other development banks, or due to conditional loans, or on the basis of ideology. The company also needs to be quite sure, of course, that its involvement is sustainable in economic, social and environmental terms. The right systems have to be in place: primarily strong regulation and good finances. 'Without regulation we do not get the right framework in which to operate.'

He insists that, regardless of whether the private sector is involved or not, a robust regulated regime is crucial. The future may see Thames Water involved in a whole range of different models, from short-term consultancy projects that last only a few months to contracts that last years. A key problem in any long-term engagement is the significant risk involved. 'I do not think any of the major water companies will be making large financial investments in the developing world in the near future, partly because of the experiences of the big companies during the last two or three years', Aylard says. He mentions Buenos Aires, where exchange rate fluctuations undermined an otherwise viable company. That was a lesson for everyone; Argentina was thought to be a stable, relatively developed country. 'Even there', he remarks. 'If it can go wrong in Argentina it can go wrong anywhere. The financial market and the shareholders would not consider any projects that involve very large long-term financial investments.' That is also one of the reasons Thames Water is looking at ways in which the company can make a contribution in partnership with others.

Thames Water has grown very rapidly, from 17 million customers in 1999 to 70 million in 2003. The company's immediate future plans involve expanding business in the three main markets where the company is already strong: the United States, Britain and Germany. This is more important than expanding operations to new markets.

Aylard avoids discussions about ideology, believing that the defending of entrenched positions and intemperate exchange will not help to advance matters. He thinks one of the problems is with terminology. 'As soon as you start talking about privatisation, people have the idea that our aim is to come in, take total control of the water and set our own prices, an operator's monopoly with a minimum of regulation.' He says that nothing is further from the truth: they don't want to own the water, set tariffs or operate without regulation. He recognises that some groups oppose the private sector from an anti-capitalist standpoint, but knows also that there is no common ground for discussion. 'We simply have to demonstrate that we do have a role.'

Thames Water is in discussion with major international NGOs and funding institutions about the development of a new model of partnership. Thames has the track record of managing large projects, including construction and maintenance of infrastructure; the NGOs, for their part, are able to mobilise their skills, advocacy and capacity at the local level. In Aylard's words, 'They think small and we think big. They have the capacity to build trust within local community-based organisations. You can combine this with the municipal authority to improve service.' That Thames Water has started looking for a new model has a simple explanation: by working in partnership the company need not stake large amounts of capital and avoids the risks involved in bill collection. 'The reason why we are working on this project is to find ways of lowering the risks so we can lower the accepted rate of return. The money from bill collection may be recycled back to improving the system. If Thames Water is involved in billing collection, there is always the perception that the world's poorest people are paying for water to one of the world's richest companies', Aylard says.

I later ask David Boys of PSI whether this new model offered by Thames Water will find acceptance among critics. 'It's doubtful', he replies. 'The important thing for the company is still to make a profit on something as basic as water and that is what we object to.'

WaterAid

The next day I visit the office of charity organisation WaterAid, in a high-rise block on the other side of the Thames, almost opposite the Houses of Parliament. Here I meet Belinda U. Calaguas, the advocacy manager. She contributes a further perspective on the proposed new model of cooperation: 'What you should appreciate concerning the invitation from Thames Water to work with NGOs is that it was a former public utility before it was sold. It still has quite a strong public service ethos among the employees. The employees say that "I work for Thames Water because water is a basic service and it is about public health." Some of the old employees are still there.' She accepts that some of the managers in the company are trying to think creatively: how they can actively be part of the solution. 'Obviously there is also a profit agenda. If they position themselves well, if they understand how to work in poor countries and what kinds of services poor countries need, they can use that information in the future if that country decides to privatise. Then they are best placed.'

This is a principle that applies equally to other companies. She had been talking to the managing director of Veolia about a contract the company had won to improve the billing system of the water utility in Mumbai, India. She had asked 'where the profit motive came in'. The manager had answered her frankly, saying that if the public authority, or the city or council, decided to engage the private sector, then Veolia was best placed to win the bid, as the company has already assisted the authority.

'The long game is always focused on the profit motive. You cannot turn them into something else', Calaguas says. At the same time she thinks that the debate is oversimplified if it concentrates solely on the large, multinational companies as soon as the private sector is evoked. There are many other types of private enterprise: domestic, medium-scale and large-scale businesses, as well as small-scale operators. One must look at the whole picture. Small-scale operators include, for example, water vendors, artisans, masons, plumbers and small drilling companies. 'Informal water vendors are probably the biggest element in provision, especially to poor communities and to a growing extent to middle income communities. This is because of the inability of public service utilities to supply water and sanitation to the growing numbers in the population.' Water vendors range from those pushing carts to men with big tankers, to a neighbour who has a connection and sells water, to community-managed systems or water co-operatives. There are the construction companies and, of course, the big international water operators. 'The large ones, like the French multinationals, get a lot of attention in the press and from activists, but in reality there are also Chinese and South African companies and water consultants. They are not so big. There are Chinese drilling companies in South Africa and South African consulting firms working abroad.'

Calaguas thinks it is understandable, however, that activists have focused on the large multinational companies, not least because of the GATS debate. 'The European Commission has been pushing for water to be included under environmental services, which will benefit these big multinational water companies. Some of the companies bring criticism upon themselves. They have, for example, been involved in corruption. But we need to look at the totality. Otherwise we are not being honest.' She emphasises this since multinational companies provide only 5 per cent of the water supplied to people who are connected to a network. Very few people in the developing world are connected.

'What is the reason that so many governments fail at providing their citizens with water?' I ask. She responds: 'No doubt some of the reasons have to do with the structural adjustment policies of the World Bank and IMF and the debt burden.' Calaguas believes that part of the reason is that the governments do not bother to provide services to the poor. 'In Europe a public service is a public service, but in many countries in Africa and Asia the public sector is a tool for the elite.'

One of the fears WaterAid had was that private companies would raise charges, which indeed they have done. She does question, however, whether the former tariff was sufficient for the old utility to function. 'Maybe the price was not adequate at all in the first place, maybe a price increase was needed but could not be implemented for various reasons.' Private companies charge the poor a lot for new connections. 'Who can pay?' she wonders. 'Is there any way that a government can subsidise poor customers or cross-subsidise between richer and poorer communities? That assumes there is a rich community, but if it is does not exist, you have to look to consumer charges or taxes.'

Calaguas and others in WaterAid often ask the anti-privatisation movement, 'What is the solution to get the urban poor connected, because protest is about the poor getting access.' It is a tough question. She is sure that to persuade various actors, politicians, water authorities and citizens to respond to the needs of the poor requires a lot of advocacy of poor people's needs and rights. WaterAid is working with some poor urban communities to persuade them to map out what services they get and where. Sometimes the government is unaware that some households lack connections. 'You have to raise the knowledge of politicians and confront them with facts, and ask them how they are going to solve the problem. It is a political issue.'

Calaguas seems critical that the anti-privatisation movement has used so much energy in objecting and resisting the privatisation agenda. It has only recently started to seek the answers. Nevertheless she considers that the protests were generally a positive thing. 'It raised the whole issue about why more than a billion people are without access to these most basic services.' The activists took the privatisation angle, but for WaterAid the important point is that the matter has been raised and that everybody realises its importance. Calaguas rejects the idea, as do the activists, of imposing privatisation as the key element of urban water sector reform. This one-size-fits-all model is still part of the World Bank's (and to some extent also the IMF's) assistance strategy. 'We support any movement resisting that.'

WaterAid has noticed that the big multinational companies no longer look for contracts as they did before. Formerly the private sector was seen as a kind of magic bullet. But then it came up against all kinds of difficulties, which have caused many companies to retreat. The solution, for WaterAid, lies in increasing the capacities of the public sector, civil society and the champions of the poor to advocate better water services; to direct the intellectual energy of the people and self-help movements. WaterAid does not think that international finance will play a big role. The solution will lie with local financing, household investments, the ways governments use taxation and grant aid. It will be important to use what is available within a given society, be it, say, a small-scale domestic private sector or cooperatives. 'Nobody really knows the value of community and household financing for water supply and sanitation and improvements. Our sense is that household investment of time, effort, and money is far bigger than investment by someone else. So governments should do more enabling of more community financing.'

Calaguas is optimistic about achieving the Millennium Goals, providing low-cost technology is used and the focus is on the system's sustainability. One very important subject, often forgotten, is the treatment of wastewater, in terms of both environmental impact and sustainability. Such facilities are very expensive to build and operate. It is therefore essential to develop lower-cost options. The final point is that it is not enough to achieve targets. At the same time the water and sanitation systems must be maintained to a consistently high standard. To all these ends, WaterAid is working in partnership with local organisations in fifteen countries in Africa and Asia.

UN–Habitat

UN secretary-general Kofi Annan has stated that he is sceptical of the claim that the private sector is capable of solving the world's water problems, given its apparent caution and the recent slow-down in investment. However, some blame Annan for reaching this conclusion too late and for overindulging a flawed private sector. It is surprising, furthermore, that he has appointed to the

Advisory Board on water and sanitation representatives of the old guard, with links to the World Bank, IMF and Suez, who have been working for private solutions all the time.

UN–Habitat's report *Water and Sanitation in the World's Cities* concludes unequivocally that 'Privatisation is not going to resolve the problems of inadequate water and sanitation provision found in most urban centres in Africa, Asia and Latin America.' UN–Habitat observes that many of the problems encountered with privatisation can equally arise with public utilities, while the many strengths of private-sector participation can be matched by reforming public-sector utilities. Of course, some obstacles – such as housing problems and corruption – are beyond the power of either public or private companies to clear. The strengths of the private sector can also be built by the public sector. The urban centres and neighbourhoods most in need of improvement tend to be those that are the least attractive to private investors and operators, the report states. The stress should be on getting the best out of public, private and community organisations.

Connection charges to the water supply are often too expensive for low-income households. In Lima, Peru, for example, contracts for privatisation were prepared, but it turned out that the connection charge would be set so high that most of those targeted would not be able to afford it. The price of water, too, would be prohibitive for many – water costs would rise to 16 per cent of the average income, even more expensive than buying water from vendors. So privatisation did not take place.

Privatisation, according to the report, seems to have been driven by the financial rewards it can bring to elites and the improved provision it gives to those who are already connected to the system. Private companies have been known to refuse to supply water to inhabitants of informal settlements, as it was far from clear that the opportunity existed for the company to make a profit. Where there is a rapid shift to privatisation, little time is built in for consultation or to involve different stakeholders. Smaller urban centres are unlikely to be attractive unless they house a high-income population. Sewerage provision is the least attractive to the private companies, as it is more complex to install than water supply.

The UN–Habitat report confirms that most finance for investment in water and sewerage in the cities of low- and middle-income countries continues to come from development loans, equity finance and the public sector; comparatively little comes from international corporations. Investment statistics do not distinguish between the different sources of finance, and can even give the false impression that all investments are privately financed. In some cases governments receive development loans, which they use to pay the private companies. The governments assume the risk for such loans. In sub-Saharan Africa virtually all investments still come via the public sector, through development loans, with governments bearing the risk.

The report stresses that it is unrealistic to set a standard of water and sanitation provision that matches the standards in high-income nations. Better provision for everyone is preferable to excellent provision for a few. In practical terms, this might mean providing a tap within 50 metres of every home rather than piping water directly to only the richest 20 per cent of households.

Why is it that inhabitants in some countries have not been supplied with water and sanitation? There are many reasons. One is that colonial governments made it a very low priority to develop local government structures. Others include a lack of existing infrastructure, economic recession, debt burden, political conflict, rapid population growth. Another factor is that households simply cannot afford to pay. In Bangladesh, for example, water was not reaching the poor in the cities of Dhaka and Chittagong. The poorest had monthly incomes below US$10. If they were to pay a water fee they would have to reduce their food consumption.

There are solutions other than the private ones. Although Chile already had good coverage before privatisation, the country's water was nevertheless privatised in the late 1990s. The UN–Habitat report suggests that if more had been known about the water cooperatives in Santa Cruz de la Sierra in Bolivia or in Cordoba in Argentina in the 1980s, or about the community-built sewers in Karachi, or of the many local NGO-supported programmes for standpipes and public toilets, then the World Bank and other agencies might perhaps have put less energy into promoting conventional large-scale privatisations involving international corporations.

There are examples of innovations introduced by certain international agencies, national governments, local governments, NGOs, and community-based organisations in different cities that have significantly improved water and sanitation provision. For example, the town of Ilo in Peru, with its population of 60,000, managed to increase the proportion of its population with a drinking water connection from 40 to 85 per cent between 1981 and 1998, and to enhance the regularity of supply. During this period the local government followed a consistent policy of supporting projects undertaken by community-level management committees.

Another good example is the partnership between local authorities, utilities and community organisations established in Faisalabad, Pakistan, a city of close to 2 million inhabitants. A local welfare organisation has shown that it is possible for a community to build and finance piped water supplies and sewers in informal settlements. Yet it was not easy at the start: the local authorities showed little interest, one official demanded a bribe, and a local politician tried to undermine the initiative. But when the authorities began to see that families were willing to pay the cost of piped water, they became interested. The leader of the organisation was subsequently offered state funds to extend the activities to other settlements.

Another innovative project is in Pune, India, a city of over 3.5 million inhabitants. Pune's municipal commissioner invited NGOs to bid for the construction of toilets. The NGO chosen, SPARC, was in partnership with two people's organisations, one of them a network of slum and pavement women's savings and credit groups. The partnership constructed more than 2,000 adult and 500 children's toilets. The city provided the capital.

Yet another example is the NGO Orangi Pilot Project in Pakistan, a partnership between communities and local government. Its success proves that low-income households can afford and will pay for good-quality sewers if the costs are kept down. Local public water and sanitation utilities can concentrate on providing the trunk sewers and drains, to which each community-developed neighbourhood system can then connect. The sanitation system that was installed kept the cost to less than a quarter of what a private contractor would have charged. Such a model is not always easy to implement, however. Local government officials may dislike it, as it deprives them of the informal payments they receive from private contractors. Regardless of such petty corruption, the model has proved its worth. Thanks to the Orangi Pilot Project, hundreds of thousands of people in low-income areas in Karachi and other cities in Pakistan now enjoy good quality sanitation.

PART III

Water privatisation in Europe

22

Europe:
a growing market?

Europe has seen the introduction of various forms of private water and sewerage service. There is a strong likelihood that the sector will continue to expand. In its 2003 annual report, for example, Suez declares as its priority targeted, profitable growth in Europe. Germany and Italy are considered to be two of the most interesting markets in terms of development prospects. Suez believes that the stringent environmental standards stipulated in EU directives and governmental budgetary pressure will serve to encourage partnerships with the private sector. Municipalities need to invest in the replacement and upgrading of existing facilities to conform to requirements. There is thus significant potential for long-term growth, according to Suez, as only four old EU countries currently comply fully with environmental standards.

Furthermore, new EU proposals are on the way. Water is identified as next in line to be opened up to market forces. The EU Commission has published several papers on the issue. In its *Internal Market Strategy Priorities, 2003–2006*, for instance, the European Commission writes that the internal market does not function particularly well and now is the time to eliminate the remaining weaknesses. The EU makes demands on water quality and requires environmental directives to be followed. The EU is pledged to supply the water industry with an effective legal framework that simultaneously does not hinder competition. The EU claims it is neutral on the question of who should own water resources. Nevertheless, the Commission maintains that in those countries that joined the EU in 2004 the massive investments required need the private sector, which will finance and modernise water supply. In the former Communist countries, in particular, a great deal needs to be done.

The European Commission has also published its *Guide to Successful Public–Private Partnership*, PPP. According to David Hall of PSIRU, the guide is intended to push through PPP and in the process collect grants from the Instrument for Structural Policies for Pre-Accession. This is the Commission's instrument for funding the investment needs of those accession countries recently accepted into the EU and those countries still negotiating for acceptance, such as Romania and Bulgaria. Hall tells me that the European Bank for Reconstruction and Development also helped speed up privatisation in eastern and central Europe.

One fervent advocate of private solutions is former EU commissioner Fritz Bolkestein. He has criticised the Netherlands for not following the liberalisation trend; indeed, he says, 'worse still, some people want to have nothing whatsoever to do with it'. He warms to his theme: 'I make no apology for the Commission's intention to review the situation in the water sector, as we announced in the Strategy. Water is the only one of the "network industries" which remains largely fragmented and shielded from competition. There may be substantial gains to be made from modernisation in this important sector.' Bolkestein equally has no time for those who criticise market solutions in the UK water sector, which he sees as quite different from that in the rest of Europe. 'In 1989 Britain started to privatise the water companies but not to liberalise the market. That was putting the cart before the horse. One should begin by opening up the market and giving the consumers a choice, only then letting government and companies decide on the structure that they wish to adopt for operating on this market.' He foresees the introduction of competition between networks, and indeed of a form of competition based on concessions along French lines. 'The private concession-holder has access to capital markets and may form partnerships. The World Bank vigorously promotes the concession model', he asserts.

Notwithstanding such aggressive advocacy, the EU parliament has for now, albeit with a tiny majority, opposed liberalisation of the European water market on the grounds that specific regional characteristics and local responsibility for supplying drinking water should be respected. With the EU, then, water is seen by many as unsuited to the logic of the market. Yet it is a different story when it comes to the EU exporting private water solutions to developing countries. The EU Water Initiative and the EU Water Fund aim to create positive conditions for the private sector in non-EU countries. The first was launched in 2002 at the World Summit on Sustainable Development (WSSD), in Johannesburg.

In 2001, the EU spent over €220 million on water supplies in developing countries, especially in Africa, according to David Hall at PSIRU. Three-quarters of this money was spent on administrative changes and preparing the ground for private solutions. The Water Initiative makes no attempt to invest in improving capacity in the public sector, even though the private companies themselves are becoming increasingly doubtful about the viability of extending services to the poor.

The EU Commission, however, is keen to liberalise the public sector in Europe, as is made clear in the Green Paper on Services of General Interest. This deals with the public sector's role in Europe in the future. The two important issues of concern are: (1) Has the public sector as much priority as the principles of competition in the EU's internal market? (2) Can the EU's laws take over and complement national and local decisions concerning the public sector?

The public-sector trade unions have been particularly critical of this Green Paper, including David Hall of PSIRU. He says it fails to deal with the two vital issues, and indicates that the Commission wishes to extend the liberalisation of the internal market further into public services, and that it is willing to use both the internal market and competition rules of the EU and the GATS negotiations of the WTO in order to do so, even where these cause conflicts with states' preferred policies on public services.

The proposed EU constitution also devotes insufficient space to the public sector. This, in the view of the European Federation of Public Services Unions (EPSU), is alarming. The Federation represents 8 million employees in the public sector, in 189 trade unions across Europe. EPSU, whose offices are in Brussels, says that the EU is increasingly taking the road of competition and liberalisation, and that this has repercussions on public interest services. Thus, in alliance with municipalities and water activist groups, EPSU has mobilised against the Internal Market Strategy, Jan Willem Goudriaan, deputy general secretary of EPSU, tells me. He refers me to a number of European Commission papers. A closer look at the EU services directive indicates that whereas water distribution services are excluded from the Market Strategy, this is not the case with wastewater treatment. Thus it may become easier for private companies to establish themselves in this area in various European countries. Indeed, it is one of Veolia's and Suez's strategies to operate in all utility sectors: water, electricity and waste management. And the question arises, if electricity and waste management are already privatised, why not include water? After all, the companies can offer all the services.

Goudriaan is adamant that certain basic rights should never be subservient to market rules – for example, access to water and health care. 'Electricity blackouts and disruptions of the railway systems in a number of EU countries demonstrate the need for public control', he says. EPSU's own analysis shows that some 300,000 jobs have so far been lost as a result of liberalisation in Europe. For EPSU it is 'essential to lay the ground for a framework directive to secure a decent future for public services; to exempt water, education, health and social services from competition rules; to leave local authorities free to decide on the running of public services; to put an end to the dogma that public service users are best served by private interests.'

Bengt Hedenström works for European Centre of Enterprises with Public Participation and of Enterprises of General Economic Interest (CEEP), which represents employers' organisations. He has written a study on water and sanitation services in Europe. He has seen little to suggest that the EU has any concerns about the practices of the private water monopolies. 'There are obviously different opinions within the EU, those who think that water is a public matter and those who do not think so. But market thinking is very strong', he says.

The CEEP insists that water supply is above all about environmental protection in the interests of all citizens; it is wrong to view it primarily as the marketing of a product. Protecting both consumer health and the environment are objectives of the highest importance at the European level. This principle is written into the EU Charter of Fundamental Rights, and as such has the status of a common value within the EU. It follows that the encouragement of stronger competition for single supply areas through the awarding of concessions, by way of time-bound contracts, is not beneficial to the consumer. Due to the high fixed costs of the supply network (approximately 80 per cent of the total), there is scarcely any scope for achieving savings through efficiency increases, which might otherwise be reflected in lower water rates. According to many economists, there can be little financial benefit for the consumer in the long run in the liberalisation of the water sector. There is a real danger that the water supply will remain in the hands of the big companies, and hence the intended benefits of market competition will not be achieved.

The CEEP rejects the term 'liberalisation', preferring the value-free notion of 'modernisation'. This can include respect for the freedom of choice of a public authority to provide water services by itself or through local enterprises, or to tender them out to third parties, although here transparency must be guaranteed and infrastructure retained as a public-sector asset.

Western Europe

Many of the problems developing countries struggle with today were experienced in past centuries in the countries of Western Europe. Consider the cholera epidemics that periodically raged across the continent. Sewage flowed in open drains in the street, and often polluted drinking water. Rubbish, too, was simply thrown into the street, where it would attract vermin and aid the spread of disease.

The mid-nineteenth century saw the first modern sewerage systems built in Europe and in the USA. Leeds began the construction of its sewerage system in 1850; New York's system was operating by 1855. In Great Britain a doctor, John Snow, proved that cholera was a waterborne disease. To get rid of disease the Water Act of 1852 in Great Britain required the water companies to filter their water. Nowadays the water is filtered to remove fish and coarse objects such as leaves and aquatic plants. Thereafter the water undergoes chemical treatment, during which a precipitant is added. The impurities form flocks and sink to the bottom. The chemically purified water then passes through a so-called 'rapid filter' which traps the remaining flocks. Finally, the water is treated biologically. Before the purified water leaves the waterworks small amounts of chlorine and lime are added to guarantee the quality while it is transported to customers.

Today, 70 per cent of Europe's population receives its drinking water piped from municipal/public plants. There is thus an enormous potential market waiting for the private companies to enter. Only England and Wales have gone so far as to sell off all their water assets. Water has historically been regarded generally as a common good in Europe: it belongs to the community and access to water is seen as a human right; organisation of supply is public and local (local authorities, in most cases municipalities, have generally had the right to decide how to operate the service). Aqualibrium, an EU research project, has undertaken a study focusing on the privatisation debate in fourteen European countries. It looked at the different structures, legal frameworks, consumption patterns, and a number of other important issues. The research showed that:

- most countries need to invest heavily in water infrastructure;
- consumers demand quality at a reasonable price;
- due to new pollutants, the quality of raw water tends to deteriorate, which may favour private operators as they are doing considerable research to develop new technology;
- many countries have created autonomous water companies under municipal control, though management methods are similar to those of private companies;
- private participation is growing in most countries, but a broad majority of services remain publicly operated;
- private participation exists in the old EU member states, except in Luxembourg and the Netherlands.

Luxembourg believes there is no need to privatise: their water is of good quality; consumption is subsidised. In the Netherlands, the law forbids the use of the private sector to provide drinking water to the public. The trend is to focus on improving the performance of publicly owned utilities. The Ministry of Economic Affairs is developing a tool for competition within the public utility sector. In Sweden, the law similarly forbids profit-making on water. As in Finland, a few private companies have nevertheless emerged. Thus, for example, in 2002 the small town of Norrtälje engaged Veolia Water for ten years with the option of a two-year renewal of the contract. In 2001 another town, Norrköping, sold its entire infrastructure to Sydkraft, a subsidiary of E.ON. A commission of the environment department has proposed a new law which states that the infrastructure cannot be sold at all. Thus in January 2005 Sydkraft sold the water company back to the municipality.

According to Aqualibrium, there is broad consensus among politicians, municipal water professionals and trade unions in Sweden that the water sector is operated most beneficially under public ownership and control. One trend in Sweden is to cooperate at local or regional level to provide a more efficient service. There are already municipalities that have formed joint companies. This reduces costs and makes it easier to recruit competent staff. In one water company, Roslagsvatten, the staff say that working in such a company have given them more influence over their work.

In the case of Finland, the debate in recent years has become more active and aggressive. Both Finland and Sweden outsource construction, sludge transportation and certain other specialised services on short-term competitive contracts; tendering takes place between private firms at local and national levels.

In France, the big, well-known companies have operated water services for over 150 years; at the last count, 77 per cent of the water supply was privately operated. Veolia, Suez and, to some extent, Saur thus hold very strong positions in the water market.

Between them they serve 98 per cent of all consumers in France supplied by the private sector. Local authorities have responsibility for water supplies; it is they that contract out to the private sector. It is their job to monitor provision and ensure that operations run smoothly. Their record in this last regard is patchy. The small municipalities tend simply to rely on the private company running their services. Furthermore, traditionally concessions were frequently renewed without competitive tendering. The company got in touch with the mayor, which sufficed to sign a contract, without consultation with local politicians or the inconvenience of a bidding process. In 1993 a law put an end to this lack of accountability. A number of cases came to light of illegal practices involving private companies. Water companies paid 'entrance' fees for the right to the contract: these monies could be used for other purposes such as ice rinks, swimming pools and even election campaigns. Consumers ultimately carried the costs. What is more, the price of water also began to rise. This created mistrust of the private operators; their reputation was dented.

The heat has now gone from the issue. Municipalities and local executives have learnt their lessons. There is now a higher degree of control being exercised over private operators' activities and increased consumer awareness. A few major politicians and unions, mainly on the left, have called for a national water service. Some local groups have tried withholding payment of water bills, but have been unable to circumvent the legal recovery process. Yet, according to Aqualibrium, the private sector is not facing serious challenge. Nevertheless, in some municipalities, water supply has been a major electoral issue. More and more local authorities are engaging consultants to assist them. Some even employ full-time staff to keep a watchful eye on the water companies.

In France, a local authority has the option to break a contract. However, just as in developing countries, this can be an expensive move, for the company will demand compensation for loss of income. Currently a local authority must engage in a tendering process. A contract will generally run for a maximum of twenty years. Formerly contracts could run for thirty, or in a few cases forty, years. Once a private company has been awarded a contract in a municipality, it is unusual for water and sanitation services to be returned to the local authority. It follows that the professional competence possessed by a local authority, in terms of experienced staff, will inevitably disappear in time. One investigation, from 2000, shows that in only 6 of 336 cases studied was a contract taken back by the local authority. In those cases where the local authority did take the work back, the most notable factor was that the water tariffs dropped. Water is on average 16 per cent cheaper when services are taken back into the public sector.

Germany, for its part, takes the view that the waste-disposal, energy and water services belong together. As refuse collection and energy are to an increasing degree being privatised throughout Europe, one future development may be to follow the German lead and commit to the model of multi-utilities, to combine the energy and water sectors. It is unthinkable that Germany could adopt the English model of private ownership. Any further participation by the private sector is rejected by trade unions, the environmental lobby and consumer organisations. Nevertheless moves seem to be afoot to increase private-sector involvement, according to Aqualibrium.

In Austria, on the other hand, the move towards privatisation has begun. Here it is the mayors who decide to what extent private operators are to be involved and who determine the scale of outsourcing projects. As in other countries, the municipalities tend to need legal assistance in drawing up contracts with private companies due to their lack experience. In Austria, interestingly, there is discussion about the possible export of water.

Spain has relied on the private sector since the nineteenth century. The 1980s saw the beginning of a period of expansion.

The incentive for local authorities to privatise service management is the lack of economic resources. Private operation removes the need for subsidies. The country's largest private company is Aguas de Barcelona, 25 per cent of which is owned by Suez.

In Italy, private-sector participation is also growing, though it is not yet significant. Rome's partly privatised ACEA has undergone rapid expansion.

The Aqualibrium report concludes that in the fourteen EU countries 'More and more actors seem to consider that a general set of rules ought to apply to all the countries. There is a general opinion in favour of specific legal frameworks applying to private operators, in order to ensure full satisfaction of consumers' interest and equity of actors in the competition to enter the market, whether they are public or private (in the case of oligopoly).' Those in favour of liberalisation of water say it leads to monetary savings, competition, decreasing prices, increasing customer services, and more efficiency. Those against say it would cause private monopolies, decreasing quality, less interest in sustainable development, loss of competence within the public sector and a reduction in the workforce.

Eastern and central Europe

In eastern and central Europe the main players are Veolia, Suez, RWE–Thames Water and Berlin Wasser (as we have seen, partly owned by Veolia and RWE–Thames Water), which are operating with the support of the European Bank for Reconstruction and Development, and the World Bank. These companies hold many contracts for water and sanitation services, reaching from Croatia, Albania and Romania to the Czech Republic. Veolia has interests in Kazakhstan. In some cases, the banks have granted loans to municipalities, for example in Serbia and Russia.

It is estimated that 65 per cent of water and sanitation services in the Czech Republic involve a private operator. In Hungary, the proportion is 30 per cent. In both countries Suez and Veolia have the biggest stake. Saur, RWE and International Water also hold contracts. PSIRU says that Veolia has pushed strongly for expansion in the Czech Republic, often using middlemen, and has encouraged municipalities to avoid public tender. Poland, by contrast, is continuing to restructure the public sector.

Meanwhile the World Bank continues its privatisation efforts in the region, through its support of concessions in a number of countries – for example, Macedonia, Albania, and even Uzbekistan and Tajikistan.

Tallinn and the EBRD

In Tallinn in Estonia the water utility was sold when the city required an injection of funds. Initially International Water and United Utilities owned between them 50.4 per cent of the new company, Tallinna Vesi. (International Water, we recall, became notorious as the part-owner of the company that led to so much chaos in Cochabamba in Bolivia.) International Water later sold its shares to the European Bank for Reconstruction and Development, which now has a 50 per cent stake in the company. In 2001 Tallinna Vesi paid 182 million Estonian krooni (€10 million) in dividends to its shareholders out of last year's profit and previous years' retained profit. 'The Supervisory Council of Tallinna Vesi also agreed the last year's financial report, according to which the company earned 24 million krooni (€1.3 million). The reason for the payment of such a large sum in dividends was the obvious overcapitalization of the Tallinna Vesi balance sheet and the large amount on idle money on the bank account', according to Emanuele Lobina of PSIRU.

The following year the company's income was considerably higher. It distributed nearly 80 per cent of its profit as dividends. This left only 37 million krooni for investment. (This sum would in fact have been only 22 million krooni if the municipality had not intervened.) In all, by the end of 2002 the private companies had received a total of 636 million krooni in dividends from Tallinna Vesi.

As Tallinna Vesi divested itself of its own capital, so it borrowed money from the EBRD. That is, the Bank is financing investment instead of Tallinna Vesi.

Tariffs are expected to double by 2010.

Private or public?

Is there, at the end of the day, any difference between a privately run and a municipally operated water company? Robin Simpson of Consumers International and David Hall of PSIRU have both studied developments in Hungary.

In 1994 in Szeged a partnership was set up between Générale des Eaux (now Veolia) and the municipality. There was no tendering procedure. The management fee was criticised for being excessive. Potential company losses were underwritten by the municipality. The contract has been renegotiated several times since the socialists came to power. In 1999 the council decided to terminate the concession and take back the operation of the water company, having finally had had enough of the steady rise in operating and maintenance costs.

The council and the company finally reached an agreement in 2001. The terms were more favourable than under the earlier agreement. Under the agreement the company will remain for a further fifteen years. However, a number of changes have been made to the operation. Before Veolia had a majority on the board of directors. Now representatives of the municipal council hold the majority, as they do also on the supervisory board. The municipality has the final say on tariff levels. If the company does not earn enough to cover costs, additional charges will not be imposed on the customers. Instead, development and reconstruction work will be cut back to make up the shortfall.

The council has decided to build a new sewage treatment plant, a sludge treatment plant and extend the pipeline network. If the council had dismissed the company, it could have instituted a process of competitive local tenders for these operations. Instead it had no choice but to give Veolia the work. For, under the agreement, a special company had been formed, of which Veolia owns 70 per cent. This company has exclusive rights to works contracts, according to David Hall. Robin Simpson has a more positive take, though. He says that prices remain low, and that increases are moderate, in line with inflation.

The town of Debrecen chose not to privatise. The council concluded that it was able to run water and sanitation services itself, even though Veolia and Euro Wasser had been in the frame. Cashflow remained healthy due to the good payment record of its customers. In 1994, when the socialists came to power, as they had done in Szeged, the company was transformed into a corporate entity separate from the municipality. With the support of the trade union, the management drew up a business plan. The cost of the necessary investments has proved to be 40 per cent lower under public provision than had been estimated in the Euro Wasser bid, partly due to the use of local suppliers of equipment, such as meters and pipes. Significantly, 300 more people are employed compared with the scale of the workforce planned by Euro Wasser.

The water company has been able to raise loans from one of the largest commercial banks in Hungary in order to finance investments, as it is regarded as financially secure. It also has loans from EBRD. There has been a moderate increase in water and sanitation charges. Profit levels have risen to 8–9 per cent annually compared to 3 per cent previously. Profits have also increased due to adjustments to sewerage charges, which had run in deficit in the past. It thus proved possible to operate water services within the local authority, without the need for privatisation. Public debate and exposure could well have been factors beneficial to both workforce and the consumers.

In Budapest the water service concession was awarded to the company that bid the highest. The winning consortium was Suez/RWE, which received 25 per cent of the shares. The consortium paid 3 billion forints more than the nearest bid, although its charges were higher for water. The city also had to compensate the losses of the water company – which it did at the rate of 3.5 billion forints per year. Job losses were higher than other estimates. In addition, the management fee had to be renegotiated.

Robin Simpson says of these cases in Hungary, 'If there is a message to draw from the contrasting examples it is that the greater degree of public scrutiny of the Szeged and Debrecen agreements led eventually to better outcomes than the more secretive Budapest agreement.'

The **European Bank for Reconstruction and Development** was founded on the initiative of President François Mitterrand. It opened for business in 1991, after the fall of the Berlin Wall. According to the Bank's homepage, it uses investments and influence to foster the transition of former centrally planned economies to open markets and democracies. Notwithstanding its public-sector shareholders, it invests mainly in private enterprises, usually together with commercial partners. The EBRD's president is Jean Lemierre. The former president, Horst Köhler, subsequently became managing director of the IMF. He is now the president of Germany.

23

England and Wales revisited

In 1996, the North of England experienced the worst drought in living memory. Leaking pipes, water shortages and the high salaries of directors at the privatised Yorkshire Water dominated the headlines (as we have seen). The company had to fetch water from Northumbria, and transport it by river to York, where it was diverted into a pipe system to Leeds. From Leeds it was transported by tanker to Yorkshire, which did not have an integrated grid system. Environmentalists were upset when cold water was transferred from a reservoir to a river, thereby changing its ecological balance.

Things would not be done this way today, as a grid system has been constructed, according to John Kidd, the regional branch secretary of the trade union Unison. Kidd, who lives in Bradford, tells me the story of what has happened since privatisation in 1989. The public water utility was sold very cheaply, for £324 million. Two years later it was worth billions. The company wanted changes to the workers' terms of employment, which would reduce holiday entitlement and introduce performance-related pay. To this end, individual contracts were sent to employees offering them financial inducement if they agreed to the new terms. The union was preparing to take industrial action. However, following negotiations the majority accepted the new pay system. The number of employees in the core business has since fallen from 7,000 to only 2,800. 'At first the company went too far with the staff cutbacks and had to start to recruit employees again. The trade union would not accept any more redundancies', says Kidd.

In addition, the company outsourced virtually everything it could, Kidd says. Although the union lobbied against this, nothing could be done to prevent the company putting the work out. 'The company had an onion strategy, that is to peel off every layer until you are left with the core business, the managing director and a few people', says Kidd. When the company tried to outsource sewage treatment, however, the union lobbied Members of Parliament, who declared that sewage treatment was a core business function and could not be outsourced, so the company changed its mind.

John Kidd believes that Yorkshire Water is now questioning the value of having outside companies provide part of its service. Indeed, one company has already been transferred back. He says that many problems arise with outsourcing in general, as there must be constant monitoring to ensure that the companies involved are doing their job. 'After privatisation in 1989 there was a honeymoon period when Yorkshire Water expanded in to many different areas outside the water industry. They were busy involving themselves in unregulated businesses, like property and laboratories. During one period the company probably had forty to fifty businesses.'

Yorkshire Water is now itself a subsidiary, of the British company Kelda. Although Kelda is like a small breeze in comparison with the giant French corporations, it nevertheless aspires to be a player on the international stage. To this end it has bought five water companies in North America, where it trades under the name Aquarion. Kelda's subsidaries have secured various other contracts. For example, it manages facilities for the UK blood transfusion service and for the Welsh Tourist Board, and organises revenue collection for local authorities. Kelda has also set up a waste recycling company which both organises rubbish landfill and is the biggest incinerator of clinical waste in the UK. John Kidd shows me a large Kelda incinerator in Bradford.

Relations between Yorkshire Water and the union have changed for the better over the years. The company has begun to involve the union in policy decision-making. The staff are happier, according to John Kidd. 'From having been the most hated water company in the United Kingdom, we have become the most respected', he says. The quality of the water has also improved, as a result of massive injection of finances. There had been no real investment in water and sanitation since the Second World War. Kidd does not find it surprising that water quality has improved: 'The company has financed investments by raising water bills, so why should we not have the best water? However, all this could have been achieved by the service remaining in the public sector, but the government was restrictive on borrowing within the public sector.'

Despite the general improvement in water quality, Yorkshire Water was fined £250,000 in 2000, after prosecution by the Drinking Water Inspectorate. More than 15,000 residents had complained of a liquid resembling flat cola coming out of their taps in 1997 and 1998. In summing up the case, Judge Norman Jones observed that water is 'the blood of life' and people have a special feeling for water: when they see black sludge oozing from the tap, they have a strong emotional response.

All water and sanitation services in England and Wales are privatised. Nevertheless, operating conditions have now become tougher for companies. Ofwat, the Office of Water Services, the regulator for the water and sewerage industry, is no longer so complaisant. Ofwat has clearly taken the line that Yorkshire

Water's egregious failure to maintain the water supply during conditions of severe drought, combined with its apparent inability or unwillingness to set about reducing the scale of leakage in the system, stemmed directly from the company's policy of putting profit before investment in infrastructure.

In 2000, another storm broke in Yorkshire. Kelda proposed converting Yorkshire Water, complete with properties and the entire infrastructure, into a not-for-profit company, a mutual entity with bond financing. Consumers would pay £2.5 billion to form a company and take over the company's debts of £1.4 billion. Kelda's shareholders would earn £1.5 billion on the transaction. The cost of water and sanitation would be lower, as repayment of the loans would be cheaper than paying dividends to shareholders. John Kidd was quoted in the press as saying: 'The time has clearly come when the pigs have guzzled at the trough and there is nothing left. The company is teetering on the edge of ruin and now wants to ditch its commitments.' Ofwat, however, rejected the proposed deal. Kelda, it said, had not succeeded in showing how water and sanitation clients would benefit by the change of ownership. There were others, though, who did sell their water interests.

Welsh Water: a hybrid model

In 2001, Welsh Water was purchased from its American owner, Western Power, by a non-profitmaking entity, Glas Cymru, in a deal that involved it taking over debts of £1.8 billion. Income from water and sanitation tariffs and bonds finance the company's operations. There is no shareholder interest. Forty-six individuals drawn from across Wales have been appointed as members of Glas Cymru and will carry out the ordinary corporate governance. Their only function is to ensure that Glas Cymru delivers good water and sewerage services to customers at the lowest price. Members receive no dividends and have no financial interest in the company. They meet regularly and follow up on operational decisions. Current members include a stockbroker, a retired wholesale butcher, company directors, a civil servant, a water-sector consultant, a farmer, a former teacher and a retired chief constable of the North Wales Police. The company may only engage in water and sanitation services and may not invest in quite different sectors.

Welsh Water employs only 142 people directly, however, though in its contractual relationships it indirectly employs the services of approximately 4,000 people across Wales. Staff were transferred to the different private companies that now have day-to-day operational responsibility. Almost immediately 185 job losses were announced by United Utilities. United Utilities is responsible for asset operation and meter installation; Thames Water bills customers; Severn Trent has responsibility for laboratory work. A further seven different companies look after the sewerage sector.

Steve Bloomfield, senior national officer of Unison, has mixed feelings about this model. 'We thought that to some extent we had been proved right, the private sector had shown that they could not succeed in running water as a private business, but we were concerned about the fragmentation following all the work being contracted out in this way. It is more difficult for the trade union to keep an eye on a lot of different employers. Some people lost their jobs and were forced to change their work routines. Hitherto it has however generally been good and now at least water and sanitation services are run by a not-for-profit company. Moreover this model received strong support from the Welsh Assembly where the Labour Party has a strong base.'

The return of regulation

The water companies in England are in a tight corner. Having started out free of debt, they have since taken out huge loans, which has made them less creditworthy. The companies maintain that one reason debts have increased is because they are no longer legally permitted to cut off water supplies. Another is that most have been forced to write off large sums as a result of high-risk ventures. It has been very common for companies, in a drive to increase profits, to invest in other areas of economic activity, where they are free from regulatory controls. Many have diversified widely, from hotels to recreational resort businesses. 'Very few of these ventures have been successful. Recently most water companies have started to shed subsidaries that do not involve water and are focusing on what they are best at', Steve Bloomfield tells me.

Anglian Water is an example of a company retreating to its core functions by selling its non-water portfolio abroad and then outsourcing as many internal operations as possible. 'I believe that the company is trying to differentiate between ownership and providing service. Other companies can operate the services. In that way, they have better control over their costs. If subcontractors are not performing well, they can break the contract, fine them or turn to someone else. Thus they do not bear the entire risk themselves', observes Bloomfield.

Ofwat is making greater demands of all water companies, not least by means of comparative performance data. Companies are no longer permitted to move money over from the profitable water business to another part that is making a loss. It is thus no longer possible to make speculative investments in fields other than water and sanitation services and then allow these core operations to pay for them. In addition to such controls, the government in 1997 levied a one-off windfall tax based on the profits made by the privatised utility companies.

Water consumers meanwhile have an organisation of their own, Water Voice. Its main current concern is that the water industry does not invest enough on maintenance of water and renewal of sanitation pipes in the face of evident deterioration. Other voices demand that Ofwat should be replaced by a stricter regulatory agency, on the grounds that the body is not sufficiently hard on the companies. As soon as Ofwat signals price reductions, the water industry reacts by threatening job cuts, postponing repairs and replacement of pipes. They claim that their work in the aftermath of floods and the programme of reducing leaks will inevitably be compromised by the reduction in cashflow. Yet Ofwat doesn't always heed such complaints. In 2000, for example, Ofwat reduced water charges nationally by 12 per cent, which led to a drop in accumulated pre-tax profits for the companies of at least £50 billion. Consequently some companies signalled their desire to convert into non-profit organisations, where the risk can be spread via debts repayable by consumers. 'We are not against a non-profit form of ownership, but object to consumers having to take the risks exactly at the time that the opportunistic industry becomes less profitable', Bloomfield tells me.

Ofwat receives advance notice of each company's five-year expenditure plans and sets the charges for that period. During the 1990s the companies systematically overestimated their expenditure and of course it was in their interest to do so, because it meant that Ofwat allowed them to charge a higher price. (Conversely, as we have seen, if it is in their interests to underestimate costs in order to get a contract, they will do so.) Companies must offer a special tariff for vulnerable metered customers – that is, those in financial hardship. This they do by charging normal customers a slightly higher rate, rather than allocating resources from their profits. Currently Ofwat permits companies to increase charges only if they have a justifiable reason. On the environmental side, they have to improve water quality and invest more money, not least in response to EU directives. The message, therefore, is: reduce leakage and improve the environment, but don't increase tariffs.

Steve Bloomfield tends to refer to the actions of Ofwat in personalised terms, as if the agency were an individual. For instance, Bloomfield remarks on how generous 'he' was towards companies in the beginning. I realise that he is in fact referring to the director-general of Ofwat, who, until the 2004 Water Act takes effect, is the appointed regulator, albeit supported by a team of experts. The director-general has been important in the process of price-setting. In the future authority will be invested in a board, to which the director is accountable. There are two other such regulators in the UK, the Environment Agency and the Drinking Water Inspectorate. Such control stands in contrast to the position in certain developing countries, where very often there is no functioning regulatory agency to control the activities of private water companies.

A very positive aspect of this control is that rivers have become cleaner; their water quality has steadily improved over the years. England and Wales have some of the best water test values in the world – better than in Scotland, where water supplies have remained in public control. 'But consumers have paid too much', Steve Bloomfield thinks. 'Tariffs that businesses have to pay have decreased, while they've risen for ordinary consumers. Previously it was the opposite, that in practice industries subsidised households.' What has changed is that some water companies have gained foreign owners. For example, Veolia now operates in the UK, as does Suez; a Malaysian company owns Wessex Water. And indeed business has been good for the foreign firms: they have made higher profits in the UK water business than elsewhere in Europe.

Interestingly, one perceived advantage is that trade unions have found it easier to deal with the French companies than with their British representatives and counterparts. Alan Roberts from Hastings has participated in Vivendi Universal's European Works Council. He says that although Vivendi was prepared to respect the fundamental rights of those in the labour market, in practice this line was not always followed, since the managers in England were less enlightened than the central management in Paris. 'One can come up with fancy programmes in Paris but no shareholder will stand and knock on the door of a subsidiary in England and ask whether they are following the rules', he remarks. Nevertheless, even if it is the case that some companies in England, when they take over public utilities, recruit staff on less advantageous terms, trade unions are today accepted where once they were sidelined.

One matter is quite clear: the private companies are here to stay for the foreseeable future. Initial contracts were to run water and sanitation services for twenty-five years. Government was required to give ten years' notice of a contract's termination. This has now changed: government must give twenty-five years' notice. This means in practice that the companies can, without interruption or interference, control the country's water and sanitation at least until 2027, and probably much longer.

PART IV

People and corporations

24

Why should we care?

Why should an auxiliary nurse in Sheffield bother about whether a poor woman and her family in India have access to water? Certain countries suffer from a shortage of water. There is no apparent reason to save water in northern Europe because there are shortages of water elsewhere. There are nevertheless other reasons to exercise care and to value the water we use. For instance, taking a shorter shower or stopping a tap dripping unnecessarily will help reduce the strain on watercourses. This means that less wastewater has to be purified, which in turn saves energy. Similarly, we should avoid polluting water with foreign substances that sewage treatment works cannot deal with. Nor should we pour solvents and other chemicals down the drain. Every time that we do, the system must work harder.

Yet perhaps an auxiliary nurse precisely should bother. I put the issue to Ylva Thörn, president of the Swedish Municipal Workers' Union and also of the global trade-union federation PSI, who has long been urging that water management is a social responsibility and should never be run for profit. Her answer is that 'We are all affected by the global economy. Thus we must become internationally involved with how people in the rest of the world are living.'

My interview with Thörn requires that I simply sit beside her on a flight to a PSI board meeting in Geneva. In the air, there are no mobile phones or other distractions. We range across the issues that occupy her busy professional life. 'When we talk about human rights we often think about the UN Charter. The PSI has an addition to the list of human rights and that is the right to water', says Thörn. To her it is obvious that access to water must never become a privilege for those who can afford to pay most. In this debate the PSI must speak up clearly. She also mentions the ruthless exploitation of the environment that is under way in many countries, such as the mines in Ghana. Such exploitation pollutes watercourses. 'Water takes no notice of national boundaries. Nor does the effluent that pollutes it. Hence we must work together and cooperate.'

Thörn suggests several ways to be involved in this work. First, one can learn more about conditions in the world around us and use this knowledge to exert an influence over our surroundings and affect politicians and decision-makers at all levels. 'Water is not simply a question of life and death', she emphasises. 'To a great degree it also affects equality. For who goes to fetch the water? Why, women and young girls.' She wishes that these girls and women who now carry water could instead set the heavy pots down, and instead attend school and take part in building up their communities. Water is one of the key developmental factors. She is scathing about the sluggish progress made towards getting a women's perspective onto the international agenda. At a seminar on gender roles and water at the World Water Forum in Kyoto, only one of the five keynote addresses made reference to women's vulnerability and to the existence of a clear gender perspective – and that was given by the one woman speaker. The men preferred to talk of the need for more conferences, for more research and, last but not least, for capital. The UN has declared the years 2005–15 'the international decade for action for water for life'. The goal is a greater focus on water-related issues, emphasising women in leading positions. 'It is to be hoped that it becomes reality. If any development is to occur for women, they need access to water at their homes so they can do things other than just carry water', says Thörn.

Ylva Thörn returns to the question of access to drinking water. People should not have to rely on a company that asks first whether it is profitable or not to distribute drinking water. Such corporate self-interest stands in contrast to what is usually proclaimed: 'We want to bring water to the poor.'

'Water is a human right and belongs to all. Clearly, those who distribute and purify water should be paid for this service, but it should never become an ordinary commodity!' A private company will often withdraw when it is not profitable to run water supplies. Thörn thinks it is time for donors to shift focus and concentrate on the main players: municipalities, governments and public water utilities. They should concentrate on public–public partnerships. 'It is imperative that people influence their governments, representatives in the World Bank, the International Monetary Fund, donor agencies, and other organisations, to find ways of financing local public-sector providers.'

PSI wants a society where economic, social and ecological goals are in harmony; one in which all people's internal resources are used in the best possible way and carefully husbanded. 'International streams of capital play different countries and employees against one another. Their short-sighted perspective takes neither the environment nor social circumstances into account', remarks Ylva Thörn. To the question, 'What advantages exist in keeping water and wastewater services in public control?' Thörn summarises:

• Contracts are not secret. This creates space for a democratic process.

- Competence remains within in a municipality.
- Earnings are reinvested in the municipal water and sanitation systems.
- Responsibility for operations and strategies is not divided between municipal and private actors. No conflicts can arise between social interests and the private-sector need for profit, or regarding interpretation of the contract.

I ask, 'What is required to facilitate achievement of the Millennium Goals, and also to develop and improve public water supplies?' Again, Thörn summarises:

- Governments, donor agencies and international development banks must invest in and reinforce the public water sector.
- Those responsible for water utilities must ensure that they deliver a high quality service.
- Corruption must be combated.
- Development banks must stop insisting that a country must engage the private sector as a condition for granting a loan.
- Trade unions and ordinary citizens must be able to influence the planning and control of water and sewage treatment.
- To support the poor, the tariff system must be structured differentially so that the rich pay more for their water.

Ylva Thörn has watched developments in Europe with increasing concern. When municipalities are under strain economically and are looking to make cuts, it is easy to opt for the quick fix, such as selling off the public water company or farming out responsibility for water and sewage treatment, she says. She is adamant: 'We must conserve our well-run public water plants. One solution is instead to cooperate with other municipalities. This creates better resources to raise competence and recruit good staff.' Nevertheless, Thörn says that it would be mistaken to rule out private-sector involvement totally. There may, for instance, be a private company that manufactures pumps and other material for water plants. Yet she insists that, as the supply of water is a natural monopoly, it should be managed by the public sector. And this indeed is the policy of the Swedish Municipal Workers' Union.

Many of the trade unions PSI organises have members employed in water and purifying plants. 'The right to water is also linked to strong unions. Then employers cannot treat their employees just as they please', declares Thörn, before returning to the issue of union demands to participate in decision-making processes.

The World Bank, in its *World Development Report 2004*, criticises public servants for not even turning up for work in some countries, so I ask her: 'Is there a problem with work-shy employees?' She offers this considered reply: 'While it is necessary to democratise societies, employees must get quite different conditions of employment, then they will have greater motivation to go to work.' That is, employees must feel they are participating, to be consulted on a particular problem to be solved, or how their jobs should be developed. At the same time, they must earn an income that can support them and their families. It is then likely that they will show interest in their work. Employees' work patterns and routines must be well-organised; they must feel secure in their jobs; there must be scope for incorporation of their innovations and ideas.

Municipalities, in some cases, must become better employers. When Veolia took over the water contract in the town of Norrtälje in Sweden, employees indicated that they felt more appreciated by their new employer than by the municipality. 'This shows that municipalities have something to learn about taking care of their personnel in a different way', says Ylva Thörn. Her own organisation, the Swedish Municipal Workers' Union, has had success in running on-the-job development projects. The starting point is for the employer to enable employees to analyse the company's current situation. On that basis, employees are encouraged to make proposals for operational change and improvement. Many such proposals have been implemented, thereby raising the quality of the services provided. Municipalities have in turn become more efficient and reduced costs as a result. When employees exert influence, they gain a greater understanding of the changes that may be needed in work practices. Stockholm Water is a company that ran such a project with its employees.

Trade unions in the Nordic countries organise employees at all levels: blue-collar, clerical and academic. In Sweden, over 80 per cent of all employees are union members. This contrasts with the USA, which has a total membership of only 14 per cent. In certain countries public-sector employees are suppressed for trying to form free trade unions – for example, in Belarus and in China. Many trade-union leaders have been victims of violence – for instance, in Turkey, Colombia and Uganda.

'Surely it is overoptimistic to believe that trade unions can achieve anything? I say, playing devil's advocate. Ylva Thörn remains an optimist. She maintains that even though conditions vary greatly in different countries, unions have the same basic tasks: they negotiate agreements and organise new members. 'The PSI has 20 million members. We must be present everywhere where decisions are taken, not least when it comes to access to clean water.' She adds that one advantage of globalisation is that it brings people closer. Trade unions can make rapid contact over the Internet, whether they are in Johannesburg, Buenos Aires or Paris. Union networks are developing across the world.

25

Private or public water?
A stakeholder review

My task appeared to be so simple at the beginning: to travel to Cochabamba and talk to people about their troubled water supply. By the end of my travels, I knew better: the politics of water supply is a very murky business.

Some people argue that the public-versus-private debate should end, so that the focus can be on those who have no water. It is not just a question of supply: 4 billion people may be facing real water shortages by 2025. 'There has been a lot of conflicting information. Policymakers, decision-makers, consumers, and all the others in the water sector are at a loss. They don't know who is telling the truth, or from whom to learn. There is a need to take the picture on the ground and put it on the table, so that everyone can see it.' These words, from a consumer organisation representative in Africa, are to be found at the end of the report: *Global Water Scoping Process: Is There a Case for a Multistakeholder Review of Private Sector Participation in Water and Sanitation?* Let us look at the process that gave rise to this report.

At the 2001 Bonn Freshwater Conference, the German minister for economic cooperation and development welcomed the notion of a stakeholder dialogue as it might lead to a better understanding of the successes and failures linked with privatisation. A working group was subsequently formed to explore the case for a multi-stakeholder review. The group includes several people whom I had interviewed in my travels: Robin Simpson of Consumers International; David Boys of PSI; Richard Aylard of RWE–Thames Water; Antonio Miranda of the Brazilian Association of Municipal Water and Sanitation Public Operators, ASSEMAE; and Belinda Calaguas of WaterAid. Another member is Liane Greeff of the Environmental Monitoring Group in South Africa. The report was written by two moderators: Penny Urquhart, a livelihood and sustainability consultant from South Africa; and Deborah Moore, an environmental consultant from the United States.

The group's brief was to examine and try to defuse the controversy surrounding private-sector participation in the water industry. A total of 234 individuals were interviewed and 82 responded to an email survey questionnaire; 137 organisations participated, including public utilities, private water providers, large multinational companies, government regulators and agencies, service delivery NGOs and other consumers, trade unions, development and environment NGOs, academics, researchers, UN agencies and multilateral and bilateral donors.

The great majority of those consulted expressed their support for multi-stakeholder review on the grounds that it would act as a safeguard against the repetition of mistakes and help guide future decisions. Many stakeholders agreed that the main underlying reasons for lack of access to water supply and sanitation services are poor performance, lack of political will and finance, and the political powerlessness of the poor. Many believe that private-sector participation has failed to address these. One advocacy NGO from Africa, for example, observed that 'the present PSP is predicated on an untested presumption that it is only the private sector that can help us deliver – and the focus is on multinational companies. A review is necessary to look at what the areas are where the private sector could play a role, to assign them less sensitive, less controversial areas.'

The stakeholders raised five themes in all, which represent priority areas for any future review. There follows a very brief presentation of some of the issues.

Theme 1: financing water and sanitation services

Efficient funding The private sector and donors find that private-sector participation has increased investment to the water sector, for example in Casablanca. NGOs, on the whole, take the opposite view. Most stakeholders agree that high risks are associated with financing in foreign currency and say that lessons have been learned from the expensive mistakes in Argentina and the Philippines. Many agree that existing funds and investments can be used more efficiently and that alternative sources of financing exist. The focus might be on mobilising domestic capital markets and reducing currency risks, or on funding for smaller-scale projects. NGOs and researchers say that the allocation of funds and the type of project funded privilege large-scale, conventional technologies and approaches, with most aid flowing to a limited number of middle-income countries.

Tariffs Most donors, professional associations, researchers and think-tanks consider the setting and collecting of tariffs to be the main priority in the water sector, whether public or private. Their view is that private-sector participation tends to produce tariffs that more realistically reflect service provision.

However, in some countries a range of stakeholders – government regulators, NGOs, private small-scale providers, the labour force – have found that tariffs increased without a commensurate improvement in service under PSP. Examples are the Philippines and Indonesia. On the other hand, some stakeholders, including private companies, feel that tariffs have been reduced as a result of private-sector participation; it was more expensive to buy water from informal vendors.

Some poor communities are levied lower tariffs when connected to the formal network. However, NGO and public utility stakeholders claim that the private sector is in general not sensitive enough to the realities of poverty in developing countries. Most stakeholders agree that social tariffs and cross-subsidies (the poor pay less, the rich more) are needed to ensure access and fairness.

Profits Private providers feel justified in making a reasonable profit. NGOs, labour organisations, consumer organisations and many public utility stakeholders consider it inappropriate to make a profit from water, adding costs to a service that governments are striving to make affordable, especially as profits are often excessive and are taken out of the country to France. Many also note that profits are neither reinvested in water nor used to lower tariffs.

Conditionality Many stakeholders, especially NGOs, perceive that donor conditionality and tied aid form the crux of decision-making regarding delivery of a water service in developing countries. Forced privatisation contributes to poor performance and underinvestment in many public utilities. This in turn serves to stiffen the resolve of advocates of private-sector participation, and further encourages the international financial institutions.

Theme 2: meeting the Millennium Development Goals

Impact on poor communities Some stakeholders feel that private-sector participation has been extremely positive; others have a wholly negative view. This is the major faultline in the debate. A number of donors and the private sector point to success stories like La Paz/El Alto in Bolivia. There is also positive feedback from the poor themselves, research institutes and NGOs. Other stakeholders consider such large-scale projects to have failed in their impact. NGOs, labour organisations, public utilities and regulatory bodies note that not all promises made by the private sector have been kept and that, crucially, affordable services have not been extended to poor people – indeed, some have even lost their access to water. A wide range of stakeholders indicated that while full cost recovery has been strongly promoted by some donors, targeted subsidies are needed to ensure that the poor are served.

Servicing rural areas   Many stakeholders agree that rural areas have been neglected under both public and private systems of water delivery. A number note that local and national private operators play an increasing role, as they are more responsive to the needs of the poor.

Sanitation and sewerage   Sanitation and sewerage have been ne-glected by both public and private systems of delivery. In Kenya, where the public toilets in city centres have been taken over by the private sector, the poor cannot afford to use them. NGOs urge the re-examination of national policy, which is often based on donor policies that see private-sector participation as a panacea. This emphasis serves to block exploration of alternatives to what often turn out to be inappropriate technologies. Water coopera-tives and research organisations stress that people must be given the freedom to select appropriate options.

Technology choice and innovation   Alternatives to privatisation are water cooperatives, small-scale providers, low-cost technologies like rainwater harvesting, a variety of public-sector options, and a range of community–government collaborative efforts. Participation in decision-making and access to better information are important factors for stakeholders. In some cases, private companies lack information on the status of existing water systems; this can lead to unrealistic contracts.

Theme 3: achieving good governance and accountability

Responsibility According to stakeholders ranging from labour organisations, NGOs and public-sector agencies to both large- and small-scale private companies, private-sector participation has led to the abdication of state responsibility concerning provision of services to the poor. NGOs and government agencies have also noted an erosion of democracy. Both the private sector and NGOs have noted that political interference – for instance, promises of free water during election campaigns – has hampered the successful implementation of private-sector participation.

Shared decision-making Organisations on both sides of the debate agree that shared decision-making has been neglected and should be instituted. There is agreement that social legitimacy is fundamental if private-sector participation is to be successful.

Regulation and monitoring There is general agreement among stakeholders that governments have failed to regulate water providers. Consumers lack protection. The regulatory system is usually neither independent nor developed, with those charged with the responsibility unable to look after the interests of consumers, especially the poor. There is a lack of will or capacity to manage and regulate private-sector partners.

Contracts A range of stakeholders agree that contracts are a problem. A weakness might involve, say, bad contract design, the setting of a price that promotes underbidding, or a lack of community participation. There may be grey areas in the agreement, unclear targets, inadequate sanctions, or scope for constant renegotiation.

Theme 4: managing efficiently

Performance   All the private water providers and donors note that large-scale private water providers have improved coverage and quality. Others say that positive impacts include technical capacity, flexibility, research and development, and management culture. Many stakeholders raised the negative impact of private-sector participation on management effectiveness and the non-performance of the private sector. Many maintain that the private sector has not kept its promises. Donors, government agencies, regulators and NGOs all held that, in principle, the private sector is not inherently better than the public sector.

Corruption   Corruption has always been present to some degree in the public sector. Private-sector participation has not eliminated the problem. Many NGOs state that large long-term secret monopoly concession contracts, often funded by IFIs or bilateral donors, tend to encourage corruption.

Labour   Some stakeholders note that private-sector participation has in some cases had a positive impact on labour. Staff receive more training, enjoy better terms and conditions, and a more positive management culture exists, resulting in a more motivated and productive workforce. In other cases, however, the opposite is apparent: job discrimination, bias towards expatriate workers, long-term loss of local technical capacity due to reliance on foreign experts. In addition, workers' rights to collective bargaining are undermined in such regimes. One labour representative notes that reducing expenditure on maintenance can increase occupational health and safety risks.

Theme 5: safeguarding public interests

Public health   Donors, private water providers, and other stake-holders highlight the improvements in public health. On the other hand, most note that improving public health depends on expanding sanitation and sewerage services, and that neither public nor private service providers are adequately addressing these needs.

Environmental protection   A few water providers expressed the view that private-sector participation has had a positive impact; it focuses on resource conservation. In contrast, researchers and environmental NGOs note that there are no incentives for the private sector to focus on water conservation, river and watershed protection, and water quality.

Social and cultural values   A range of stakeholders mention that the private sector has been insensitive to social and cultural values in developing countries, and has made no effort to understand local realities, especially in regions where strong cultural traditions place moral value on the free sharing of water with neighbours and strangers.

Trade agreements   Strong concerns are expressed by NGOs in northern hemisphere countries about the implication of the WTO and GATS, regional and bilateral trade agreements, and ISO (International Organization of Standardization) standards. They could undermine national sovereignty over a resource as fundamental as water.

How to continue?

Can the different stakeholders with their disparate interests come together to agree on common goals? It's not impossible. The private sector has conceded, for example, that it has not managed the social side of its commitments adequately. And some stakeholders totally opposed to privatisation have indicated that they do see a role for the private sector, albeit subject to strict limits and regulations.

The working group proposes in its report a balanced, independent review of private-sector participation. This could reduce polarisation, dispel myths about both private and public sectors, and provide the arena for the various interests to meet and their voices to be heard, which would give all the opportunity to hear directly from poor communities. Such a review would represent real progress towards the meeting of the Millennium Development Goals, and, in particular, the commitment to 'reduce by half the proportion of people without access to safe drinking water and sanitation facilities' by 2015.

26

The politics of water:
is the tide finally turning?

Water provokes strong commitment, heated debate, and on occasion confrontation. The issues are pressing, complex and touch on a host of interests and ethical issues. Let us consider some of the points of contact in order to gain a fuller sense of the politics of water being played out in the world.

Pollution, pesticides and people

Water is becoming an increasingly important issue for the International Union of Food, Agriculture, Hotel, Restaurant, Catering, Tobacco and Allied Workers' Association (IUF). All over the world, employers are falling far short of the ILO convention that requires agricultural workers to be supplied with potable water and good sanitation facilities. Although all employers are legally obliged to conform, many simply do not care. They give fresh water to the animals but none to their employees. There have been cases where employers reacted negatively to union demands for separate toilets for women.

IUF-affiliated unions around the Nile basin are coordinating work to reduce pollution in the river. A clear link exists between water pollution and pesticides. Many workers handle pesticides; the IUF is accordingly working to build up the capacity of its affiliates to negotiate with employers about pesticide reduction within the workplace and also to urge support for organic production. Andrew Addoguaye Tagoe, an official of the General Agricultural Workers Union in Ghana (GAWU), tells me that small farmers in Ghana have no piped water, and what they do get can be contaminated by pesticides. The farmers' clothes are exposed to pesticides. They irritate the skin, and can cause blindness if the eyes are exposed. People need to be educated about the hazards of pesticides. It is common to use pesticide-contaminated containers to fetch or store water. Ghana does not produce these chemicals — but the American multinational Monsanto does.

Unfortunately the use of pesticides is likely to increase as the World Bank promotes export-oriented agriculture, including flowers and horticultural products whose cultivation is pesticide- and water-intensive. This runs counter to everything the IUF is advocating. Its priority is to encourage domestic production of nutritious food without dependence on external markets or distant distributors, and to ensure that food is produced in a way that does not harm the soil and compromise water resources.

Women and water

IUF is also encouraging its affiliated union, the Self-Employed Women's Association (SEWA) in India. It comprises approximately 600,000 women workers who earn a living from their own labour and from small businesses. They started a water campaign. Village women were taught how to repair hand pumps and to construct rainwater harvesting tanks. SEWA is represented on water-related boards and committees and in water management at state level, especially in Gujarat. Yet SEWA's members, women farmers, nevertheless have difficulty in obtaining access to water for irrigation and the household.

Bottling our water resources

While SEWA women and poor people all over the world lack access to water, others are making a great deal of money out of it. The growing commercialisation of water resources is a matter of great concern. In 2001 almost 90 billion litres of bottled water were sold around the world, mostly in non-recyclable plastic bottles. Danone, Nestlé, Coca-Cola and Pepsi are all big players in this market.

Before Coca-Cola set up business the village of Plachimada in Kerala, India, the area was rich in both surface and ground water. The farmers' water sources have now dried up. Women must walk long distances to fetch water. In 2003 the Kerala High Court gave Hindustan Coca-Cola Beverages one month to close down its wells and find an alternative source of water. The Court observed that groundwater is a natural resource that belongs to the whole of society. Even the government had previously ordered Coca-Cola to stop drawing groundwater from the plant premises until the monsoon rains began.

Water has become to an increasing degree an international commodity. Companies exist that build and operate enormous pipelines and supertankers to transport water long distances, in exactly the same way as oil is transported.

Numerous issues linked to water inspire people throughout the world to protest and to attend conferences to discuss solutions. Consider the large dams and canals that reduce the amount of water that finally reaches the oceans, with negative effects on the ecosystem along the watercourses. Think of rivers like the Ganges and the Colorado, which at certain times of the year no longer run all the way to the sea. The ecological consequence are devastating, not least for fish stocks. The disruption to community life can be profound. For instance, nearly 2 million people will be forced to make way for China's new Three Gorges Dam project.

Travelling home

'It is the local authority that is master over water.' These words, spoken in Paris by Veolia's director, Charles-Louis de Maud'huy, have remained with me. Were this the case, I reflect, the politics of water would not be the battleground it is. Ideally, yes, it is the people who should decide, through the authority of their elected representatives, how to manage water distribution. The corporations should be at their service, if they need them. Instead, however, people are in the hands of the corporations. It is not the authority that is master over water.

I am sitting thinking thus, about the power of water and the power of words, as I stare at the turning propeller of the Fokker 50 plane that is preparing to take me on the two-hour flight from Stockholm to Vilhelmina in northern Sweden. When I was young, it took fifteen hours by bus, railcar and overnight train to travel home from Stockholm, as there was no airport in Vilhelmina.

I am on the way back to my home town. The plane settles above the clouds. The airline is new, an unknown quantity. The ticket was cheap – the consequence of competition. That is the way of the world today: freedom of choice and the survival of the fittest. A while ago I wasted hours in choosing the cheapest energy provider for my needs; otherwise the power bills were set to ruin me. I did not ask for this – the market steals my valuable time. Three large energy companies dominate the energy sector in Sweden; they are making a killing. This is happening in all areas of life, or rather all sectors of the market.

I have met industrious small business people, doctors and nurses among them, who once worked in private care of the elderly in Malmö in southern Sweden. There were once sixteen such private companies in the city; now only four large companies remain.

In many other fields, public-sector work has been contracted out or operations have been sold. This is the case in cleaning, catering, public transport, energy, rubbish disposal, laundering, health and elderly care, and, not least, water. All the fine talk about choice is based on an idealised model, not on reality. For example, Danish ISS cleans buildings around the world; French Sodexho and British Compass prepare food; Britain's Davis Service Group is taking over laundries; Connex now runs buses and trains in several countries. The list goes on; the pattern is clear.

I sit in the plane wondering why this has happened, how municipal work has simply disappeared in certain sectors. No one any longer considers the possibility that local authorities could make their own bids. I increasingly hear the refrain: 'It must be cost effective! We have raised productivity, which brings a good rate of return; shareholders will not accept anything less.' Business interests and market-based preferences follow the resolutions of neoliberal ideology, which believes that only defence and justice should remain in public control.

Many employees working in water and sewage treatment plants have lost their jobs due to privatisation. It is not good when people see work simply as their livelihood, with no involvement and interest. Yet nor is it good when the pendulum swings too far in the other direction, and creates an environment wherein 'efficiency' and 'higher productivity' become mantras. At the end of the day it is employees who pay the price of increasing work tempo, perhaps with repetitive strain injuries to the shoulder or back, or, worse still, forced out into an insecure existence among the growing army of the unemployed.

There are however signs that the debate is, finally, changing. Before flying north I attended the World Water Week in Stockholm and met William J. Cosgrove, former president of the World Water Council, the think-tank that has so zealously backed private management of the water sector. Cosgrove admitted that the public–public partnership is a sound one. He accepts that most of the world's water will remain in the public sector. I also met there Antonio Miranda from Recife; he has been busy promoting public–public partnership in cooperation with South Africa's Rand Water. Miranda told me that although this form of cooperation has not been actively pursued, its guiding principles have been kept alive. An International Association of Public Water Operators is being formed. It has a draft constitution and meetings are already taking place between a dozen or so of the most representative public operators. These are in Sweden, Brazil, South Africa, Uganda, Tunisia, Indonesia, North America, France and Spain. A strong team from the public utilities has been contacting other potential members. The association requires financial backing to get off the ground, but subsequently progressive fees from the public operators themselves will finance it. The poor utilities will pay less than the larger ones with greater means.

Antonio Miranda is now a member of the UN Advisory Board. He has been witness to a more positive attitude evolving at the World Bank with regard to public–public partnerships. Even those supportive of water privatisation will find it hard to come out against this initiative. Given that some 95 per cent of water utilities are run by the public sector, even if, as seems unlikely, privatisation were to make big advances, the capacity of the public sector must be built up and improved on if we are to achieve the Millennium Goals, Miranda observes.

There have also been suggestions that the World Bank is finally recognising that its privatisation programme for public utilities has been motivated more by ideology than by reality. In

Reforming Infrastructure, the Bank declares that privatisation offers potential benefits but should not be pursued blindly. Although the Bank continues to search for ways to make privatisation work, it concedes that there is no universal model.

It seems likely that most of the world's water supplies will continue to be run by the public sector in the future. It seems all the more remarkable, then, that the major financial institutions, donor agencies and think-tanks appear unable to come up with genuinely new and viable solutions. The private sector will have a role. After all, it is able to supply a diverse range of water facilities and services, from construction and pipelines to specialist know-how. The great challenge is, however, for the public sector to reform itself through advice and support from other public water utilities around the world: that is, to advance through public–public partnerships. In this way, competence will be gained and spread to others. This future should arouse interest and support, not be viewed as in any was a threat. I fail to understand the reluctance to attempt to roll out this model on a much more ambitions scale. This may be the step needed to settle once and for all the issue of whether water is a human right or simply another commodity.

As I sit wrapped up in my thoughts, the plane begins to descend. Soon it lands gently on the runway at Vilhelmina airport. The pilot brakes hard – the runway is short, surrounded by pine forests, beech trees and marshland.

My rented car turns onto the road to the village of Dikanäs. I drive past a few houses, where the occasional car is parked, but mostly I pass endless forest and the odd abandoned farm. In Dikanäs, the white church and the school are still in use; yet where the dairy once produced quantities of milk, there is now a block of serviced flats for the elderly. In the early twentieth century Sweden had 1,700 dairies; today only 10 remain. The smaller dairies were swallowed up in the competition to become as large as the multinational Arla Foods, which exports powdered milk to the Dominican Republic.

I drive on until I come to a small track, where I turn left. The road is narrow and climbs steeply up the mountain slope. My eyes comb the left side of the track. Suddenly I spot it: the spring with its ice-cold fresh water. The water trickles from a small pipe covered by moss. I stop the car, step out, bend down and cup my hand, fill it with water and drink. My childhood memory does not let me down. The water is still wonderfully fresh and pure-tasting. If I chose, I could stand here all night and drink as I wished. The summer nights are light in the north. Best of all, though, the water is free. It does not cost a penny – at least not here.

References

Chapter 1

Natural Resources Defence Council (NRDC), www.nrdc.org.
Pure Vilamina Natural Spring Water, hem.passagen.se/tore4/products2.html.

Chapter 2

Interview with John Kidd, Unison, in Yorkshire, 2003.

Bakker Karen J., 'Paying for Water: Pricing and Equity in England and Wales', University of Oxford, 2000.

Brendan, Martin, *In the Public Interest*, Zed Books, London, 1993.

Gustafsson, Jan-Erik, *Vägen till privatisering: vattenförvaltning i England och Wales* (The Road to Privatisation: Water Management in England and Wales), Royal Institute of Technology, Stockholm, 2001.

Lobina, Emanuele, *UK Water Privatisation – A Briefing*, PSIRU, London, 2001.

Ofwat, www.ofwat.gov.uk.

Simpson, Robert, *The Consumer Perspective on Water Privatisation in the UK*, April 2001.

Sjölander, Ann-Christin, 'When Water is Privatized', *Kommunalarbetaren* 12, 1996.

UN–Habitat, *Water and Sanitation in the World's Cities*, UN–Habitat, Nairobi, 2003.

Chapter 3

'$5 Million Bonus for Vivendi Chief', CNN, 5 June 2002.

Halimi, Serge, 'Vivendi, une leçon de choses, Les fous de roi', *Le Monde diplomatique*, May 2002.

Hall, David, *The Water Multinationals: Financial and Other Problems*, PSIRU, London, 2002.
PSI, www.world-psi.org.
Shultz, Jim, 'Bolivia's War over Water', February 2000, www.democracyctr.org.
Saur, www.saur.com.
Suez, *Annual Report*, 2001, 2002, 2003; press release, 31 January 2003, www.suez.com.
www.thames-water.com.
Veolia, *Annual Report*, various years, www.veolia-environnement.com.

Chapter 4

Interviews in Cochabamba with Oscar Oliviera, Carlos Crespo, Edwin Oquando Oranda, Ricardo Ayala Antezana, Jorge Cortez and coca-leaf farmers, October 2002.
Antezana, Raquel Yaksic, *Social and Environmental Concern Actions Assessment: A Case Study of Water Supply Management in Cochabamba, Bolivia*, Royal Institute of Technology, Stockholm, January 2004.
Crespo Carlo, *The Water War and the Capacity of the State to Manage the Conflict*, Centro de Estudios Superiores Universitarias, Cochabamba, 2002.
Lobina, Emanuele, *Water War in Cochabamba, Boliva*, PSIRU, London, 2002.
Lobina, Emanuele, and David Hall, *Water Privatization in Latin America*, PSIRU, London, 2002.
Nickson, Andrew, and Claudia Vargas, Superintendencia de Aguas, La Paz, Bolivia, 'The Limitations of Water Regulation: The Failure of the Cochabamba Concession in Bolivia', University of Birmingham, November 2001.
World Bank Operation Evaluation Department, 'Bolivia Water Management: A Tale of Three Cities', Precis 222, Spring 2002.
Schultz, Jim, www.democracyctr.org/bechtel.
Swedish International Development Cooperation Agency, *Half Year Annual Report about Bolivia*, Sida, October 2001–March 2002.

Chapter 5

Interviews in Tucumán with Lorenzo Santiago Marcos, Scania workers, Maria de Valle, Oscar Adolfo Torres and Benito Garzon, October 2002.
Lobina, Emanuele, and David Hall, *Water Privatization in Latin America*, PSIRU, London, 2002.
Some of the text was first published in *Kommunalarbetaren* 22, 2002; and 8, 2003, www.kommunalarbetaren.com.

Chapter 6

Interviews in Rosario, Santa Fe, and in Buenos Aires, Argentina, with Maria Jordán, Alberto Munoz, Olga Rossi, Gloria Fumagelli and Alexandre Brailowsky, October 2002.

Lobina, Emanuele, and David Hall, *Water Privatization in Latin America*, London, PSIRU, 2002.

WaterAid, Tearfund, Case Study Argentina. *Everyday Water Struggles in Buenos Aires: The Problem of Land Tenure in the Expansion of Potable Water and Sanitation Service to Informal Settlements*, 2003.

UN–Habitat, *Water and Sanitation in the World's Cities*, UN–Habitat, Nairobi, 2003.

Chapter 7

Interviews with Jean Bernard Lemire, Carlos Riez, Alexandre Brailowsky and Julio Godio, Buenos Aires, October 2002.

Alcázar, Lorena, Manuel A. Abdala and Mary Shirley, *The Buenos Aires Water Concession*, Washington DC, World Bank, 2000.

Ente Regulador del Aguas (ETOSS), *Multas*, 1999, 2000, 2001, 2004, www.etoss.org.ar.

Lobina, Emanuele, *Water and Privatization in Latin America*, PSIRU, London, 1999.

Llorito David, 'Maynilad Has Left Gaps in the Privatisation Picture', *Manila Times*, 27 March 2003.

Shofani, Endah, *Reconstruction of Indonesia's Drinking Water Utilities – Assessment and Stakeholders' Perspective of Private Sector Participation in the Capital Province of Jakarta*, Royal Institute of Technology, Stockholm, 2003.

Suez, *Annual Report*, 2003, www.suez.com/finance/english/rapport-annuel/.

International Consortium of Investigative Journalists (ICIJ), *The Water Barons*, Center for Public Integrity, March 2003.

Yergin, Daniel, and Stanislaw, Joseph, *The Commanding Heights: The Battle for the World Economy*, Simon & Schuster, Hemel Hempstead, 1998.

Chapter 8

Bailiss, Kate, *Privatisation and Poverty: The Distributional Impact of Utility Privatisation*, PSIRU, London, February 2002.

Jubasi, M., 'Arrested for Stealing Water', *Sunday Times*, 20 January 2002.

Kasrils, Ronnie, 'A Decade of Delivery: The Water Sector in South Africa', speech, Minister of Water Affairs and Forestry, London 2003.

McDonald, David, and John Pape, *Cost Recovery and Crisis of Service Deliveries in South Africa*, HSRC, Pretoria, 2003.

Mdleleni, Mayor of Nkonkobe, 'Executive summary to the Minister of Local Government', National Government and the Republic of South Africa, September 2001.

Muller, Mike, *Water 2003: What Should Be Done? Lessons from Johannesburg and Pointers for the Future*, Department of Water Affairs and Forestry, South Africa, November 2002.

Smith, Laila, Shauna Mother, and Fiona White, *Testing the Limits of Market Based Solutions of the Delivery of Essential Services: The Nelspruit Water Concession*, Centre for Policy Statistics SA, Survey on Employment and Earnings, March 2004.

War on Want and Unison, *Water for Sale: Workers Examine the Effects of Privatisation of South Africa*, February 2002.

International Consortium of Investigative Journalists (ICIJ), *The Water Barons*, Center for Public Integrity, March 2003.

UN–Habitat, *Water and Sanitation in the World's Cities*, UN–Habitat, Nairobi, 2003.

Chapter 9

Hall, David, *Water in Public Hands: Public Sector Water Management, a Necessary Option*, PSIRU, London, July 2001.

Hall, David, and Emanuele Lobina, *Private to Public: Lessons of Water Remunicipalisation in Grenoble, France*, PSIRU, London, 2001.

International Consortium of Investigative Journalists (ICIJ), *The Water Barons*, Center for Public Integrity, March 2003.

Drew, Kirsty, 'Whistle Blowing and Corruption, An Initial and Comparative Review', Unicorn, January 2003, www.psiru.org.

OECD, *Corruption*, www.oecd.org.

Chapter 10

Telephone interview with Mats Karlsson, World Bank, Ghana.

Nancy, Alexander, *The World Bank Group's Facilitation of the Trade Agenda Undermines the Bargaining Power of Developing Countries*, Citizens' Network on Essential Services, 7 January 2003.

World Bank, *The New World Bank Water Resources Strategy*, 2003, www.worldbank.org.

Chapter 11

Interviews with Mats Karlsson, World Bank, and Jan-Erik Gustafsson, Royal Institute of Technology, Stockholm, 2002.

Amenga-Etego, Rudolf, *Water Privatisation in Ghana: Still-born or Born Deformed?* ISODEC, July 2003, www.ghanaweb.com.

Bayliss, Kate, *Water Privatisation in SSA: Progress, Problems and Policy Implications*, PSIRU, London, November 2002.

Bayliss Kate, *Water Privatisation in Africa: Lessons from Three Case Studies*, PSIRU, London, May 2001.

'Keep the water public!', *Fokus* 2, 2002, www.world-psi.org.

Ghana Statistical Service, *Ghana Living Standards Survey Report*, October, 2000.

Christian Aid, *Master Or Servant? How Global Trade Can Work to the Benefit of Poor People*, November 2001, www.christian-aid.org.uk.

Hansson, Stina, and Iman Aman, *A Study of the Privatisation of the National Water Utility Company in Niger*, Stockholm School of Economics, 2003.

Menard, Claude, and George Clarke, *Transitory Regime Water Supply in Conakry, Guinea*, World Bank, 2000, www.worldbank.org.

Report of the International Fact-finding Mission of Water Sector Reform in Ghana, August 2002, www.ghana.co.uk.

Chapter 12

Interviews with Jacinta Njoroge-Lahti and Julius F. Mwandembom.

Björkman, Pia, and Elisabeth Wikström, *Är vatten en bristvara, Miljöekonomins grunder* (Is Water a Scarce Commodity? The Basics of Eco-economy), Åbo Akademi, Åbo, 1999.

Jägerskog, Anders, 'Vattnet i Mellanöstern – en källa till konflikt eller samarbete' (Water in the Middle-East – a source of conflict or cooperation?), *Världspolitikens dagsfrågor* 4, 2000.

Kessides, Ionnis N., *Reforming Infrastructure Privatisation, Regulation and Competition: A World Bank Policy Research Report*, Oxford University Press, Oxford, 2004.

Nordström, Anders, *Jordens vattenresurser*, Vattenvärnet, 2000.

www.worldwaterforum.org, 2003.

Chapter 13

Global Water Partnership, www.gwpforum.org,

Camdessus, Michel, *Financing Water for All: The World Panel on Financing Water Infrastructure*, World Water Council, 2003, www.worldwatercouncil.org/publications.shtml.

World Water Council, 'Finacing Water Infrastructure', www.worldwatercouncil.org/financing_water_infra.shtml.

World Water Vision, Commission Report, *A Water Secure World: Vision for Water, Life and the Environment*, World Water Vision, World Water Council, London, 2002.

International Consortium of Investigative Journalists (ICIJ), *The Water Barons*, Center for Public Integrity, Washington DC, March 2003.

USAID, www.usaid.gov.

Chapter 14

Interviews with Jean-Luc Trancart, Alain Mathys and Charles-Louis de Maud'huy in Paris, March–April 2003.
Hall, David, *Water Multinationals: No Longer Business as Usual*, PSIRU, London, 2003.

Chapter 15

Cupe (Canada), www.cupe.ca.
Kessides, Joannis N., *Reforming Infrastructure Privatization, Regulation, and Competition: A World Bank Research Report*, Oxford University Press, Oxford, 2004.
International Consortium of Investigative Jouranlists (ICIJ), *The Water Barons*, Center for Public Integrity, Washington DC, March 2003.
PSI, www.world-psi.org.
SAMWU, www.cosatu.org.
Water-For-All-Campaign, www.citizen.org/cmep/water/.

Chapter 16

Hall, David, Kate Baylis and Emanuele Lobina, *Water in the Middle East and North Africa: Trends in Investment and Privatisation*, PSIRU, London, October 2002.
Suleiman, Rebhieh, *Privatisation of Jordan's Capital Water Utility: Assessment and Evaluation of Water Supply and Wastewater Services of Amman Governorate*, Royal Institute of Technology, Stockholm, 2002.
Llorito, David L., Meryl Mae and S. Marcon, 'Maynilad: A Model in Water Privatization Springs Leaks', *Manila Times*, 26 March 2003.
WaterAid and Tearfund, *New Rules, New Roles: Does PSP Benefit the Poor?*, London, 2003, www.tearfund.org.

Chapter 17

Interview with David Boys in Geneva, March 2003.

Chapter 18

Interview with Mike Waghorne in Genvea, March 2003.
GATS – General Agreement on Trade in Services, Kommerskollegium, National Board of Trade, www.kommers.se.
Attac, www.attac.nu.
World Development Movement, 'A Preliminary Analysis of the EU's Leaked GATS Requests to 109 WTO Member States', 25 February 2003.

GATSwatch, www.gatswatch.org.

Polaris Institute, www.polarisinstiute.org.

Reply from P. Lamy to PSI/PRSU on GATS, April 2003, www.europa.eu.

Chapter 19

Interview with David Hall, 2003.

Byliss, Kay and David Hall, *PSIRU Response to the World Bank's Private Sector Development Strategy – Issues and Options*, PSIRU, London, 2001.

Hall, David, *The Water Multinationals: Financial and Other Problems*, PSIRU, London, 2002.

Hall, David, and Robin De la Motte, *Dogmatic Development: Privatisation and Conditionalities in Six Countries*, PSIRU, London, 2004.

Hall, David, Emanuele Lobina, Maria Odete Viero and Hélio Maltz, *Water in Porto Alegre, Brazil: Accountable, Effective, Sustainable and Democratic*, PSIRU, London, 2002.

World Bank Operation Evaluation Department, Precis 222, Spring 2002.

Chapter 20

Interviews with Antonio Miranda, Keith Naicker, Aivars Zants, Janis Karpovics, Juris Kalnins and Sven-Erik Skogsfors, 2004.

Hall, David, Emanuele Lobina, Maria Odete Viero and Hélio Maltz, *Water in Porto Alegre, Brazil: Accountable, Effective, Sustainable and Democratic*, PSIRU, London, 2002.

DMAE, www.portoalegre.rs.gov.

Riga Water, *Annual Report*, 2003, www.daugavpils.udens.lv.

Utzig, José Eudardo, 'Participitory Budgeting of Porto Alegre: A Discussion in the Light of the Principle of Democratic Legitimacy and of the Criterion of Governance Performance', paper.

Smith, Laila, and Ebrahim Fakir, *Social Policy Studies, The Struggle to Deliver Water Services to the Indigent: A Case Study of the Public–Public Partnership in Harrismith, Johannesburg*, Centre for Policy Studies, Johannesburg, 2003.

South African–Brazilian Public–Public Partnership for Implementing the Right to Water Services for All, Johannesburg, 2002.

Chapter 21

Interviews with Robin Simpson, Consumers International, Richard Aylard, Thames Water and Belinda U. Calaguas, February 2004.

Brown, Paul, and Sam Jones, 'Storms Kill 10,000 Fish in Thames', *Guardian*, 5 August 2004.

UN–Habitat, *Water and Sanitation in the World's Cities*, 2003.

Chapter 22

Aqualibrium, The EU Research Project, *European Water Management between Regulation and Competition*, European Commission, 2004.

European Centre of Enterprises with Public Participation (CEEP) and Enterprises of General Economic Interest, 'On the Future of the EU Water Policy', *Environment*, 2003/Avis 18.

De la Motte, Robin, and David Hall, *The European Commission's Guide to Successful Public Private Partnerships: A Critique*, PSIRU, London, May 2003.

EU Commission, Communication from the Commission to the Council, the European Parliament, the European Economic and Social Committee of the Regions, *Internal Market Strategy Priorities 2003–2006*.

Glas Cymru, www.glascymru.com

Hall, David, and Emanuele Lobina, *Public–Public Partnership in Northeast Europe*, PSIRU, London, 2003.

Hall, David, and Emanuele Lobina, *International Solidarity in Water: Public–Public Partnership in North-east Europe*, PSIRU, London, March 2003.

Hall, David: *EC Internal Market Strategy: Implications for Water and Other Services*, PSIRU, London, May 2003.

Hall, David, *The Bureaucracy of Privatisation: A Critique of the EU Water Initiative Papers*, PSIRU, London, 2002.

Hedenström, Bengt, *Om Va-frågor i Europa* (On Water and Wastewater Service Issues in Europe), Brussels, September 2001.

Lobina, Emanuele, *Water Privatisation and Restructuring in Central and Eastern Europe*, PSIRU, London, 2001.

Chapter 23

Interviews with John Kidd and Steve Bloomfield, March 2003.

Gow, David, '500 Jobs Go at Yorkshire Water', *Guardian*, 8 December 1999.

Lobina, Emanuele, *UK Water Privatisation*, PSIRU, London, 2001.

Ofwat, www.ofwat.gov.uk.

Wainwright, Martin, '£250,000 Fine for "Black Coffee Water"', *Guardian*, 9 December 2000.

Chapter 24

Interview with Ylva Thörn, June 2004.

Chapter 25

Moore, Deborah and Penny Urquhart, *Global Water Scoping Process: Is There a Case for a Multistakeholder Review of Private Sector Privatisation in Water and Sanitation: A Scoping Review*, 2004.

Chapter 26

Kessides, Ioannis, N., *Reforming Infrastructure Privatisation, Regulation and Competition, A World Bank Policy Research Report*, Oxford University Press, 2004.

Sreedevi, Jakob, 'Coke Enters Decisive Phase', January 2004, www.indiatogether. org.

The Water Campaign, www.sewa.org.

Upadhuay, Videh, *Beyond the Cola Wars*, September 2003, www.iwmi.cglar. org/iwmi-tata.

Websites

Cosatu, www.cosatu.org (South Africa)
Cupe, www.cupe.ca (Canada)
PSI, www.world-psi.org
PSIRU, www.psiru.org
EU och GATS, http//gats-info-info.eu.int/gats-info/guide
IMF, www.imf.org
IUF, www.iuf.org
Polaris Institute, www.polarisinstitute.org
Public citizen, www.citizen.org
Sewa, www.sewa.org
World Bank, www.worldbank.org
Suez, www.suez.org
Veolia, www.veoliaenvironment.com
WaterAid, www.wateraid.org.uk

Index

About this series

'Communities in the South are facing great difficulties in coping with global trends. I hope this brave new series will throw much needed light on the issues ahead and help us choose the right options.'

MARTIN KHOR, *Director,*
Third World Network, Penang

'There is no more important campaign than our struggle to bring the global economy under democratic control. But the issues are fearsomely complex. This Global Issues series is a valuable resource for the committed campaigner and the educated citizen.'

BARRY COATES, *Director,*
World Development Movement (WDM)

'Zed Books has long provided an inspiring list about the issues that touch and change people's lives. The Global Issues series is another dimension of Zed's fine record, allowing access to a range of subjects and authors that, to my knowledge, very few publishers have tried. I strongly recommend these new, powerful titles and this exciting series.'

JOHN PILGER, *author*

'We are all part of a generation that actually has the means to eliminate extreme poverty world-wide. Our task is to harness the forces of globalization for the benefit of working people, their families and their communities – that is our collective duty. The Global Issues series makes a powerful contribution to the global campaign for justice, sustainable and equitable development, and peaceful progress.'

GLENYS KINNOCK, *MEP*

The Global Issues series

Already available

In preparation

Julian Burger, *First Peoples: What Future?*

Koen de Feyter, *A Thousand and One Rights: How Globalization Challenges Human Rights*

Susan Hawley and Morris Szeftel, *Corruption: Privatization, Transnational Corporations and the Export of Bribery*

Roger Moody, *Digging the Dirt: The Modern World of Global Mining*

Edgar Pieterse, *City Futures: Confronting the Crisis of Urban Development*

Vivien Stern, *Crime and Punishment: Globalization and the New Agenda*

Nedd Willard, *The Drugs War: Is This the Solution?*

For full details of this list and Zed's other subject and general catalogues, please write to: The Marketing Department, Zed Books, 7 Cynthia Street, London NI 9JF, UK or email Sales@zedbooks.demon.co.uk

Visit our website at: www.zedbooks.co.uk

Participating organizations

Both ENDS A service and advocacy organization which collaborates with environment and indigenous organizations, both in the South and in the North, with the aim of helping to create and sustain a vigilant and effective environmental movement.

Nieuwe Keizersgracht 45, 1018 VC Amsterdam, The Netherlands
Phone: +31 20 623 0823   Fax: +31 20 620 8049
Email: info@bothends.org   Website: www.bothends.org

Catholic Institute for International Relations (CIIR) CIIR aims to contribute to the eradication of poverty through a programme that combines advocacy at national and international level with community-based development.

Unit 3, Canonbury Yard, 190a New North Road, London N1 7BJ, UK
Phone +44 (0)20 7354 0883   Fax +44 (0)20 7359 0017
Email: ciir@ciir.org   Website: www.ciir.org

Corner House The Corner House is a UK-based research and solidarity group working on social and environmental justice issues in North and South.

PO Box 3137, Station Road, Sturminster Newton, Dorset DT10 1YJ, UK
Tel.: +44 (0)1258 473795   Fax: +44 (0)1258 473748
Email: cornerhouse@gn.apc.org Website: www.cornerhouse.icaap.org

Council on International and Public Affairs (CIPA) CIPA is a human rights research, education and advocacy group, with a particular focus on economic and social rights in the USA and elsewhere around the world. Emphasis in recent years has been given to resistance to corporate domination.

777 United Nations Plaza, Suite 3C, New York, NY 10017, USA
Tel. +1 212 972 9877   Fax +1 212 972 9878
Email: cipany@igc.org   Website: www.cipa-apex.org

Dag Hammarskjöld Foundation The Dag Hammarskjöld Foundation, established 1962, organises seminars and workshops on social, economic and cultural issues facing developing countries with a particular focus on alternative and innovative solutions. Results are published in its journal *Develpment Dialogue*.

Övre Slottsgatan 2, 753 10 Uppsala, Sweden.
Tel.: +46 18 102772   Fax: +46 18 122072
Email: secretariat@dhf.uu.se   Website: www.dhf.uu.se

Development GAP The Development Group for Alternative Policies is a Non-Profit Development Resource Organization working with popular organizations in the South and their Northern partners in support of a development that is truly sustainable and that advances social justice.

927 15th Street NW, 4th Floor, Washington, DC, 20005, USA
Tel.: +1 202 898 1566   Fax: +1 202 898 1612
E-mail: dgap@igc.org   Website: www.developmentgap.org

Focus on the Global South Focus is dedicated to regional and global policy analysis and advocacy work. It works to strengthen the capacity of organizations of the poor and marginalized people of the South and to better analyse and understand the impacts of the globalization process on their daily lives.

C/o CUSRI, Chulalongkorn University, Bangkok 10330, Thailand
Tel.: +66 2 218 7363 Fax: +66 2 255 9976
Email: Admin@focusweb.org   Website: www.focusweb.org

IBON IBON Foundation is a research, education and information institution that provides publications and services on socio-economic issues as support to advocacy in the Philippines and abroad. Through its research and databank, formal and non-formal education programmes, media work and international networking, IBON aims to build the capacity of both Philippine and international organizations.

Room 303 SCC Bldg, 4427 Int. Old Sta. Mesa, Manila 1008, Philippines
Phone +632 7132729   Fax +632 7160108
Email: editors@ibon.org   Website: www.ibon.org

Inter Pares Inter Pares, a Canadian social justice organization, has been active since 1975 in building relationships with Third World development groups and providing support for community-based development programmes. Inter Pares is also involved in education and advocacy in Canada, promoting understanding about the causes, effects and solutions to poverty.

221 Laurier Avenue East, Ottawa, Ontario, KIN 6PI Canada
Phone +1 613 563 4801   Fax +1 613 594 4704
Email: info@interpares.ca   Website: www.interpares.ca

Public Interest Research Centre PIRC is a research and campaigning group based in Delhi which seeks to serve the information needs of activists and organizations working on macro-economic issues concerning finance, trade and development.

142 Maitri Apartments, Plot No. 28, Patparganj, Delhi 110092, India
Phone: +91 11 2221081/2432054   Fax: +91 11 2224233
Email: kaval@nde.vsnl.net.in

Third World Network   TWN is an international network of groups and individuals involved in efforts to bring about a greater articulation of the needs and rights of peoples in the Third World; a fair distribution of the world's resources; and forms of development which are ecologically sustainable and fulfil human needs. Its international secretariat is based in Penang, Malaysia.

121-S Jalan Utama, 10450 Penang, Malaysia
Tel.: +60 4 226 6159   Fax: +60 4 226 4505
Email: twnet@po.jaring.my   Website: www.twnside.org.sg

Third World Network–Africa   TWN–Africa is engaged in research and advocacy on economic, environmental and gender issues. In relation to its current particular interest in globalization and Africa, its work focuses on trade and investment, the extractive sectors and gender and economic reform.

2 Ollenu Street, East Legon, PO Box AN19452, Accra-North, Ghana.
Tel.: +233 21 511189/503669/500419   Fax: +233 21 511188
Email: twnafrica@ghana.com

World Development Movement (WDM)   The World Development Movement campaigns to tackle the causes of poverty and injustice. It is a democratic membership movement that works with partners in the South to cancel unpayable debt and break the ties of IMF conditionality, for fairer trade and investment rules, and for strong international rules on multinationals.

25 Beehive Place, London SW9 7QR, UK
Tel.: +44 (0)20 7737 6215   Fax: +44 (0)20 7274 8232
Email: wdm@wdm.org.uk   Website: www.wdm.org.uk

This book is also available in the following countries

CARIBBEAN

Arawak Publications
17 Kensington Crescent
Apt 5
Kingston 5, Jamaica
Tel: 876 960 7538
Fax: 876 960 9219

EGYPT

MERIC
(Middle East Readers'
Information Center)
2 Bahgat Ali Street,
Tower D/Apt. 24
Zamalek, Cairo
Tel: 20 2 735 3818/3824
Fax: 20 2 736 9355

FIJI

University Book Centre,
University of South Pacific
Suva
Tel: 679 313 900
Fax: 679 303 265

GHANA

Readwide Books Ltd
12 Ablade Road
Kanda Estates, Kanda
Accra, Ghana
Tel: 233 244 630 805
Tel: 233 208 180 310

GUYANA

Austin's Book Services
190 Church St
Cummingsburg
Georgetown
Tel: 592 227 7395
Fax: 592 227 7396

IRAN

Book City
743 North Hafez Avenue

15977 Tehran
Tel: 98 21 889 7875
Fax: 98 21 889 7785
bookcity@neda.net

MAURITIUS

Editions Le Printemps
4 Club Rd, Vacoas

MOZAMBIQUE

Sul Sensações
PO Box 2242, Maputo
Tel: 258 1 421974
Fax: 258 1 423414

NAMIBIA

Book Den
PO Box 3469
Shop 4
Frans Indongo Gardens
Windhoek
Tel: 264 61 239976
Fax: 264 61 234248

NEPAL

Everest Media Services,
GPO Box 5443
Dillibazar
Putalisadak Chowk
Kathmandu
Tel: 977 1 416026
Fax: 977 1 250176

NIGERIA

Mosuro Publishers
52 Magazine Road
Jericho
Ibadan
Tel: 234 2 241 3375
Fax: 234 2 241 3374

PAKISTAN

Vanguard Books
45 The Mall, Lahore

Tel: 92 42 735 5079
Fax: 92 42 735 5197

PAPUA NEW GUINEA

Unisearch PNG Pty Ltd
Box 320, University
National Capital District
Tel: 675 326 0130
Fax: 675 326 0127

RWANDA

Librairie Ikirezi
PO Box 443
Kigali
Tel/Fax: 250 71314

SUDAN

The Nile Bookshop
New Extension Street 41
PO Box 8036
Khartoum
Tel: 249 11 463 749

UGANDA

Aristoc Booklex Ltd
PO Box 5130,
Kampala Road
Diamond Trust Building
Kampala
Tel/Fax: 256 41 254867

ZAMBIA

UNZA Press
PO Box 32379
Lusaka
Tel: 260 1 290409
Fax: 260 1 253952

ZIMBABWE

Weaver Press
PO Box A1922
Avondale, Harare
Tel: 263 4 308330
Fax: 263 4 339645